D0164302

# CURRENT CONCEPTIONS OF SEX ROLES AND SEX TYPING

WITHDRAWN

# CURRENT CONCEPTIONS
# OF
# SEX ROLES
# AND
# SEX TYPING

## Theory and Research

*Edited by*

# D. Bruce Carter

# PRAEGER

New York
Westport, Connecticut
London

377250  Tennessee Tech. Library
Cookeville. Tenn.

**Library of Congress Cataloging-in-Publication Data**

Current conceptions of sex roles and sex typing.

Bibliography: p.
1. Sex role.  2. Sex differences (Psychology)
3. Stereotype (Psychology)  I. Carter, D. Bruce.
HQ1075.C87  1987        305.3        87–13157
ISBN 0–275–92430–0 (alk. paper)

Copyright © 1987 by Praeger Publishers

All rights reserved. No portion of this book may
be reproduced, by any process or technique, without
the express written consent of the publisher.

Library of Congress Catalog Card Number: 87–13157
ISBN: 0–275–92430–0

First published in 1987

Praeger Publishers, One Madison Avenue, New York, NY 10010
A division of Greenwood Press, Inc.

Printed in the United States of America

The paper used in this book complies with the
Permanent Paper Standard issued by the National
Information Standards Organization (Z39.48–1984).

10 9 8 7 6 5 4 3 2 1

# Contents

# CURRENT CONCEPTIONS
## OF
## SEX ROLES
## AND
## SEX TYPING

# 1
# Overview
## D. Bruce Carter

The study of gender and its influence on the behavior and personality of children and adults has a long history in the field of psychology—stretching back beyond the time of Sigmund Freud. Indeed, sex differences (both biological and psychological), sex roles, and sex typing form the central core of a number of influential theories of socialization and social behavior. Moreover, gender appears to be of central importance in a number of nontheoretical realms, for example, the cultural, the political, the experiential, and so forth. As a result of the importance attributed to gender and gender-related concepts, a large amount of research in psychology and a number of related fields (sociology, anthropology, sociobiology, etc.) has been undertaken to examine and explicate relationships between gender, sex roles, and sex typing in cognition and behavior. This importance is exemplified by the fact that a large percentage of research articles, an entire interdisciplinary journal (*Sex Roles*), and large numbers of book chapters (e.g., Huston, 1983) are devoted to this particular topic.

Despite the importance of sex roles and the obvious interest in this topic, no single integrative volume has been devoted to examining the concomitants of sex typing since Maccoby's (1966) edited volume. This volume proved to have an enormous impact on the field of sex role socialization research and is one of the most heavily cited references in the field despite the fact that it is nearly two decades old. In the years since publication of Maccoby's book, however, conceptions of sex typing and sex roles have undergone dramatic changes. For example, the concepts of psychological androgyny and gender schemas (unheard of in 1966) have proven to be important sources of research and theoretical speculation in the past decade. Moreover, several factors that had central importance in Maccoby's volume (e.g., acquisition of stereotype knowledge, gender constancy, sex differences in dependency, etc.) apparently have outworn their theoretical and empirical usefulness and have been replaced by concepts emerging from advances in social psychology, biopsychology, personality psychology, and cognitive psychology. In essence, the field of sex roles and sex typing has undergone dramatic changes in the last two decades—changes that are reflected in the conceptions underlying current research.

The present volume is designed to offer the reader an integrative picture of current thinking and research in the areas of sex roles and sex typing. To the best of my knowledge, the material contained in this book represents the first integrative treatment of the area of sex roles since the publication of Maccoby's (1966) edited book. Unfortunately, today the field of sex roles and sex typing is so disparate, complete coverage of the area would be impossible in anything less than a multi-volume work. Thus, while I attempted, in organizing this volume, to encompass as much of the field as possible, some topics may have received less attention than their advocates might feel would be warranted. The emphasis of this volume is on the psychological antecedents and consequences of sex roles and sex typing, although chapters on the biological (Chapter 4) and sociological (Chapters 11 and 12) ramifications of gender have been included since these topics seemed directly relevant to the field.

This volume is organized in four major parts. Part I reviews the major theoretical treatments of gender (Chapter 2) and the ways in which gender-related concepts have been measured (Chapter 3). In both chapters, special attention is given to the benefits and shortcomings of our ways of thinking about and measuring gender-related issues. Part II focuses on lifespan development in the area of sex roles and sex typing. This section begins with an integrative view of the influence of biological, social, and psychological factors on sex role socialization, and this is followed by chapters on specific issues arising in the course of sex role development. This section concludes with an integrative approach to the ways in which gender operates in adulthood and aging. Part III focuses on behavioral and psychological implications of sex roles and sex typing. Included are chapters on the roles of gender in the labor force (Chapter 11), on the psychological impact on families of two working parents (Chapter 12), and the influence of sex-typing factors on adjustment (Chapter 13). Finally, Part IV offers alternative views of the ways in which sex role research may best be directed in the future. Eccles (Chapter 14) focuses on an integrative approach to the influences of cognitive and sociocultural changes on the development of gender-role transcendence during adolescence; my chapter (Chapter 15) offers an historical perspective on the field and identifies directions that I feel would prove profitable for future research.

The material included in this volume represents conceptions and research that are on the forefront of endeavors in this area. Moreover, from my perspective, the authors of the various chapters are among the most productive and theoretically compelling individuals within their respective areas of research. I am grateful to each of them for their willingness to participate and for the careful and thought-provoking way with which each approached his/her particular topic.

I hope that you, the readers of this volume, will find the chapters included as valuable to your own thinking about this topic as I have.

## REFERENCES

Huston, A. C. (1983). Sex typing. In P. M. Mussen & E. M. Hetherington (Eds.), *Handbook of Child Psychology* (Vol. 4). *Socialization, personality, and social development.* (pp. 387–467). New York: Wiley.

Maccoby, E. E. (1966). *The development of sex differences.* Stanford, CA: Stanford University Press.

# PART 1
# THEORY AND MEASUREMENT
# ISSUES IN SEX ROLE
# RESEARCH

# 2
# Current Theoretical Issues in Sex Roles and Sex Typing
## Jaipaul L. Roopnarine
## Nina S. Mounts

I am a girl because I have long hair.

4–year-old girl

My brother is a boy because he has a penis.

4–year-old girl

Within the last century, several theoretical notions or perspectives have been postulated regarding sex role development (see Lamb & Urberg, 1978). Despite the extraordinary scientific interest in sex role development, researchers and theoreticians differ in their explanations as to how we come to display the sex-stereotyped behaviors and attitudes that we do. Nonetheless, there is some uniformity in the theoretical propositions. For example, a number of theorists believe that parental influences are important in early sex role socialization, while others believe that cognition might be the salient factor in understanding the acquisition of sex-typed behaviors. We will see, however, that the acquisition of sex-typed behaviors is as multifaceted and complex as it is intriguing.

In this chapter, we will attempt to examine various theoretical perspectives on sex role development and sex typing. We will focus on contemporary theories of sex role development and sex typing, including a discussion of self-schema and gender-schema theories, the neo-Freudian, feminist, cognitive social learning, and neo-Kohlbergian theories of development. A discussion of contrasting theories of androgyny and their development will also be included in this chapter.

A grant from the Senate Research Committee at Syracuse University facilitated the preparation of this manuscript.

Finally, the implications and limitations of current theoretical thinking will be discussed, and directions for further research in this area will be offered.

## ORGANIZATION

For purposes of convenience, organization, and to achieve some sense of chronology of theory development, we will begin with a discussion of the traditional theories of sex role development (See Table 2.1). Furthermore, in order to discuss modifications and extensions of more traditional theories that have generally been under-represented in terms of research substantiation, we will need to discuss the original tenets of these theories. A discussion of a sense of origin for any theory in any school of thought is absolutely necessary since modern day advancements in thinking in any given theory owe much to these initial conceptions. However nearsighted or myopic they may appear, they served as the foundations for more contemporary ideas. Finally, our discussion of theories or perspectives on sex role development drew heavily on other reviews of the literature (e.g., Brooks-Gunn & Matthews, 1979; Huston, 1983; Lamb & Urberg, 1978; Sutton-Smith & Rosenberg, 1972).

## THE PSYCHOANALYTIC PERSPECTIVE

### Freud's Theory

Perhaps the earliest and one of the least substantiated theories of how individuals acquire sex-typed behaviors was postulated by Sigmund Freud (1905/ 1962). The Freudian perspective, rooted in biology, proposed a sequence of stages that all individuals supposedly pass through toward appropriate sex role identity. The developmental stages—oral, anal, phallic-urethral, genital, and latency—are marked by their specific reference to particular erogenous zones of the body. During the first two stages (the oral and the anal), children form attachments to and identify primarily with their mothers. The mother is perceived as the primary love object and the source of warmth and nurturance. This conception also prevailed in other theories of identification (see Parsons & Bales, 1955). As we will see later, this narrow conception may have embodied one of the major drawbacks in theory construction in developmental psychology.

During the third stage (phallic-urethral), identification with the same-sex parent is motivated by fear; fear of the loss of love in girls and fear of retaliation in boys. Anaclitic and defensive identification, as they are more formally termed, are presumably triggered by the anatomical differences that exist between boys and girls. According to psychoanalytic theory, when boys discover that girls do not have penises, they reason that girls once possessed them but that they were cut off. Boys interpret this as proof of what might happen to them. Since the boy's primary love object is the mother, he perceives the father as a competitor for the mother's love and fears that the father might castrate him. Realizing that

**Table 2.1**
**Issues Regarding the Theoretical Approaches to Sex Role Development**

| Theories | Strengths | Limitations | Implications | How well does the theory explain sex role development |
|---|---|---|---|---|
| Psychoanalytic Freud, S. | Recognizes parental influences; biological basis | Largely nonempirical; sexist | "Anatomy is destiny" | Poorly—served as a stimulus for the development of other conceptions |
| Cognitive social learning | Intermeshing of cognitive and socialization factors | Role of cognition appears cursory to the mechanistic school of thought | Formation of internal conceptions of models and their behaviors | Fairly well—needs to delineate role of cognition further |
| Information-Processing Self-schema | Emphasis on the development of schemas of appropriate and inappropriate sex role behaviors | Lack of treatment of the emergence and differentiation of gender schemas | Role of cognition in understanding and displaying gender roles; gender constancy not necessary for early sex typing | Fairly well—needs to trace the covariation between cognitive development and sex role conceptions |
| Gender-schema | Stresses the importance of the construction of internal schemas of sex-typed roles and behaviors | Lack of clarity on dichotomous sorting and information processing | Sex typing is so salient in society that it forms the basis for most decisions regarding social functions | Fairly well—needs to explore further why gender is such a salient schema |
| Kohlberg perspective | Sex role development occurs within the realm of cognition | Gender constancy is a necessary prerequisite for appropriate sex-typed behavior | Children do not display strong sex-typed preferences until they have achieved gender constancy | Fairly well—however children may have an understanding of sex-typed preferences far sooner than Kohlberg predicts |

**Table 2.1**—*continued*

| Theories | Strengths | Limitations | Implications | How well does the theory explain sex role development |
|---|---|---|---|---|
| Approaches to androgyny (collectively) | Egalitarian relationships are far better than more sex-delineated ones | The lack of consensus on the definition and measurement of psychological androgyny | Decision making with respect to social roles will be non-gender based | Very well |
| Feminism | More egalitarian relationships in all aspects of life would be far more beneficial to individuals and society | Continued flogging of Freud's Oedipal complex conception | Equal access and participation in child-rearing, political, social, intellectual, and economic pursuits | Fairly well |

*Source:* Compiled by the authors.

he cannot conquer the father to win the mother, however, the young boy represses his sexual desires for his mother and identifies with the strength and authority of the father. Through identification with the father, the aggressive parent, the boy acquires masculine behaviors.

The odyssey appears more traumatic for girls. In effect, when the little girl discovers that boys have penises and she does not, she feels cheated and disappointed. Consequently, she turns away from the mother, blaming her for the lack of a penis. Since the mother is the one responsible for sending her ill-equipped into the world, the young girl transfers her love to the father. Despite such renouncement, she realizes that her desires for the father cannot be fulfilled and once again identifies with the mother whose love she cannot afford to lose (Freud, 1905/1962). The wish for a penis is replaced by the desire to have children.

Between five and ten years of age, having resolved the Oedipus and Electra complexes, boys and girls become immersed in other activities, such as school, peers, and appropriate sex-typed play. The ego assumes a central role in the development of cognition and personality attributes. Movement away from infantile sexual interests leads to the continued growth of the ego and superego through the internalization of societal values and mores.

The onset of adolescence marks a reintroduction of conflicts. Libidinal energy is now concentrated in the genital areas. The transition to heterosexuality brings new problems (Freud, 1924). Thus the homeostasis between the id and ego is once again in disharmony, and the adolescent uses the peer group to modulate his/her genital impulses that would be directed toward parents. To some degree, Oedipal fantasies are aroused again. However, new attachments act as substitutes for these unrealistic fantasies, but the attachments are invariably abandoned as unfulfilling.

## The Neo-Freudians

The term neo-Freudian is perhaps a misnomer for some of Freud's contemporaries. Traditional psychoanalytic formulations, in terms of sex role development, may have had one of the strongest impacts on feminist psychology. Indeed, a number of feminists have questioned the original tenets of psychoanalytic thinking. But more about the feminist perspectives later.

In the previous section, castration fear was discussed as motivating boys toward masculine identification whereas castration anxiety motivated girls toward feminine identification. These conceptions have been questioned and as a result discussions regarding the envy of women, breast envy, and envy of childbearing have ensued (see Horney, 1932; Klein, 1957; Lerner, 1978). The principal argument here is that the mother's role as primary caregiver encourages dependency that the child perceives as very powerful. The mother's perceived power, achieved through her role as the dispenser of love and gratification, could lead to a feeling of powerlessness and lack of control on the child's part. Ultimately, these feelings could manifest themselves through envy, anger, and fear and could lead to a devaluation of the mother (see Huston, 1983). It is in this manner that the young child becomes envious of women in general. The central point, however, seems to be that later, men assume dominant roles in their relationships with women by relegating them into positions of dependency. The woman "succumbs" to such dominance because she has accepted devaluation of her own gender (Huston, 1983).

Insofar as a direct treatment of the feminine Oedipus complex and sex role identity is concerned, Chodorow (1978) has fervently argued that the Oedipus complex is as much a mother/daughter issue as it is a father/daughter one and that the father/daughter relationship can only be understood within the context of the daughter's relationship with her mother. According to Chodorow, the girl's internal Oedipal complex is multifaceted. The girl's initial attachment to her mother remains intact, as her Oedipal attachment to the father comes into play. The emotional relationship to the father is equal to that of the mother. During Oedipal resolution, the young girl does not simply turn from mother to father but comes to include the father along with the mother in her early social relationships. Thus, the relationship can be viewed as triadic. However, because the father encourages stereotypic feminine behaviors toward him, the girl's Oedipal relationship toward her father is likely to consist of traditional feminine behaviors compared with the more affective-based and diverse involvement with the mother (Chodorow, 1978). For boys, the switch from one parent to the other is less pronounced. Moreover, boys appear to be in a better position to receive emotional gratification and heterosexual orientation from the mother than girls are likely to get from fathers; fathers are also less likely to be as available to girls as mothers are to boys. This, coupled with the socialization practices within the familial system, could contribute quite differently to the development of sex typing and dependency in boys and girls. This means that the achievement of an understanding of sex role development and gender identity—according to Freud's contemporaries (e.g., Chodorow, 1978)—is complex and intricately intertwined with the development of a sense of self.

Whether we pursue a traditional or more contemporary approach in our examination of the psychoanalytic perspective on sex role development, several issues remain unanswered. As Chodorow (1978) pointed out, object relations in children grow out of an individual's interactions within the family structure— and, we would add, a highly sex-delineated society—that are created by parents and children. Thus an argument can be advanced that gender personality, as defined by the psychoanalytic school of thought, does not necessarily have to come through the process of identification but can come through changes in ego development, which seem to be different for boys and girls (Chodorow, 1978).

The major weakness in the psychoanalytic perspective, though, lies in children's relationships with their fathers. Developmental psychologists (e.g., Lamb, 1979; Parke, 1979) have demonstrated that both boys and girls are attached to their fathers between 6 and 9 months of age, and that differential socialization by mothers and fathers occurs during infancy (see Roopnarine, 1986; Snow, Jacklin, & Maccoby, 1983). According to psychoanalysts, the father's role in sex role socialization and development of attachment seems to take shape around age five. Even though in traditional family structures the mother might assume the chief role in socialization, it is hard to believe that children achieve access to and identification with the father through the mother. Current findings (e.g., Lamb, 1977) suggest that mothers and fathers may assume qualitatively different but complementary roles in the early process of socialization.

How then do we view the psychoanalytic perspective on psychosexual development? On the one hand, we have the "anatomy is destiny" view and on the other, we have the "envy of women" hypothesis. Somewhere in the middle, from our standpoint, is the view that the inaccessibility of fathers to daughters and their differential treatment of sons and daughters might be a more plausible interpretation of the Oedipal resolution. Even this last point, however, must be taken with caution. The psychoanalysts did not place any importance on fathers until the phallic-urethral phase. It is our contention that the traditional psychoanalytic perspective has served as a stimulus for rather different conceptions on sex role socialization in a changing cultural milieu. The continued flogging of Freud's original tenets would lead to the stagnation of an emergent cognitive-social psychology of sex role development. Freud's formulations were largely nonempirical.

## FROM SOCIAL LEARNING TO COGNITIVE SOCIAL LEARNING THEORY

Although the psychoanalytic perspective may have provided the requisite foundation for a comprehensive theory of psychosexual development, it has always been difficult to prove or disprove. Consequently, it was viewed by social learning theorists as inadequate for explaining the process of sex role development. Though primarily concerned with reinforcements, the social learning theorists themselves have had to restructure their conceptual framework due to a variety of criticisms levied against them regarding the role of cognition in the acquisition of sex-typed behaviors. More recently, the role of cognition in children's learning has been worked into the theory (see Bandura, 1977). The aim here is to provide the reader with the general notions of social learning principles and then to outline the cognitive social learning perspective.

The social learning theorists believe that parents and significant other adults in the child's life shape gender-role behavior by rewarding or praising gender-appropriate behaviors while punishing or discouraging gender-inappropriate ones (Mischel, 1966; Maccoby & Jacklin, 1974). These theorists suggest that parents might reward aggressive, assertive behaviors and ignore doll play in their sons. Similarly, they might encourage and reward submissive, nurturant, and dependent behaviors and punish aggressive behaviors in daughters.

The evidence regarding the differential treatment of boys and girls is contradictory at best. While Snow, Jacklin, and Maccoby (1983) reported that fathers treated their infant sons and daughters differently, Roopnarine (1986) failed to find sex-of-parent effects in a study of mothers' and fathers' behaviors toward the sex-typed toy play of their infants. Likewise, while Fagot (1977) has reported differential parental reactions to the sex-typed activities of children, others (Margolin & Patterson, 1975; Smith & Daglish, 1977) have failed to find sex-related patterns of socialization. Other work (Baumrind & Black, 1967; Fagot, 1978), though, suggests that fathers were more likely to punish boys than girls but were more likely to encourage dependency in girls than in boys.

Children may also acquire gender-appropriate behavior through imitation of or identification with a model (Bandura & Walters, 1963; Sears, Rau, & Alpert, 1965). Both psychoanalytic and observational learning theorists propose that boys and girls initially imitate their mothers since they are usually the primary caregivers during the early years when gender identity is established. Girls continue to model their mothers' behaviors while boys shift to identification with their fathers. To observational learning theorists, this switch is motivated by the young boy's appraisal of the father's power and control over familial resources. This theory suggests that girls become feminine by modeling the behaviors of their mothers, while boys become masculine by renouncing their primary attachment figures and identifying with their fathers. The processes, though, are influenced by several important factors.

Seemingly, children show a tendency to imitate models that are powerful and have control over resources. The extent to which the father is viewed as being dominant and competent has been shown to be related to the son's masculinity, regardless of the father's own masculinity (Hetherington, 1965; Mussen & Distler, 1959). By contrast, parental dominance does not appear to be related to daughters' femininity (Hetherington, 1967). In related work it has been demonstrated that while masculinity in sons is positively related to the warmth and nurturance of fathers, the femininity in daughters seems to be related to the warmth and nurturance of either parent (Mussen, 1961; 1962; Mussen & Distler, 1959.

Despite the dominance of social learning principles in psychology research, and the influence of social learning conceptions on research in sex typing, the theory underwent a major revision within the last decade. Both Bandura (1977) and Mischel (1977) have emphasized the role of mental processes as mediating variables in learning and in the acquisition of behavior. This attempt at restructuring the early conceptions of social learning theory to make it more cognitively based is not surprising in view of the fact that a number of other social scientists have attempted to demonstrate patterns of covariation between cognitive and social functioning (see Emmerich, Cocking, & Sigel, 1979; Shantz, 1975; 1983). Furthermore, there is some evidence to show that cognitive functioning might facilitate social adaptation (Emmerich et al., 1979) and that social and cognitive functioning are related at different points in time (see Shantz, 1983).

Cognitive social learning posits that when children experience reinforcements and punishments, they tend to formulate certain expectancies that will direct how they respond to their social environments subsequently. Thus the individual's behavior is influenced by both internal and external factors, rather than being solely determined by external stimuli as has been previously suggested (Bandura, 1977). The theory now suggests that four factors appear central to the process of observational learning: attention, retention, motoric reproduction, and motivation.

The first, *attention,* is presumed to be influenced by expectations derived from the child's previous social commerce with the object-person-environment. The relevance of attention for sex role development lies in the gender of the child and of the model it observes. According to social learning theory, the child should pay more attention to same-sex than other-sex models, apparently because of prior reinforcements from same-sex adults and peers. Indeed, a sizable body of research suggests that same-sex reinforcements are more salient than other-sex reinforcements (see Chapters 5 and 7, this volume). Despite the strong tendency for peers and adults to reinforce same-sex over other-sex behaviors, the evidence regarding selective attention to same-sex models is rather sparse. In laboratory studies (Bryan & Luria, 1978; Grusec & Brinker, 1972; Slaby & Frey, 1975), the data do not seem to support the contention that children are more likely to attend to same-sex models than other-sex models. Clearly, more research is needed to delineate the role of attention in the acquisition of sex-typed behaviors. As we will see later on, however, the notion of attention to same-sex models will reappear in our discussions of cognitive developmental and gender schema theories.

The second issue, *retention,* deals with the child's ability to achieve some internal representation of the model's behavior. Not unlike other theoretical orientations (Piaget, 1970; Sigel & Cocking, 1977), the child's ability to form an internal representation of a model's behavior depends on its level of cognitive development and existing knowledge of particular constructs. Cognitive social learning theory, however, does not clearly explain why children might retain certain attributes of a model's behavior while ignoring or showing a tendency to drop others. Certainly the mental processes that are involved in retention must go through a series of modifications and/or transformations in order for the child to make some sense of the relevance of different aspects of the model's behavior. The crucial question here is, when does the model's sex or behavior become important enough for the child to attend to it and commit it to memory? (See Huston, 1983.) Previous research (Hetherington, 1965) has shown that the father's power and nurturance, regardless of his own masculinity, affects his son's masculinity. Why then should the sex of the parent become so potent in the recruitment of attention? The clue might be found in the child's understanding of and knowledge base of sex stereotypes.

Following the retention of a model's behavior, imitation will depend on the child's ability to *reproduce* the behavior *motorically. Motivation,* too, will determine motor reproduction. Motivation is largely a function of vicarious and direct reinforcement expectancies pertaining to the feedback received for reproducing or imitating particular behaviors.

It is clear from our discussion that the specific properties of cognitive social learning may pose several problems for researchers who are trying to explicate the features of the acquisition of sex typing in young children. While the reformulation of social learning theory has entailed modifying the purely external approach to the acquisition of behavior to include internal representation, the ancillary role cognition assumes in providing a conceptual and methodological framework for delineating the ontogeny of sex typing is quite apparent. The dominant theme of social learning theory in general still is that sex typing is largely shaped by the environment. The specific role of cognition as a mediating variable in children's production of sex-typed behaviors remains largely undefined and elusive within the mechanistic school of thought.

## COGNITIVE DEVELOPMENTAL THEORY

Although the learning theorists have now openly acknowledged the role of cognition in sex role development, conceptions of the roles of cognition in sex role development, or at least their theoretical assumptions, were first postulated by Kohlberg (1966).

To the cognitive developmental psychologists, an understanding of the child's conception of gender is the cornerstone of the growth of sex typing. Children's perceptions, organization of an internal representation of particular behaviors, and the differentiation of such behaviors as their cognitive development becomes increasingly complex—all are tied to the acquisition of gender identity. Therefore, it is presumed that changes in sex-typed behavior generally correspond to cognitive changes in logical thought development.

Kohlberg's (1966) theory is predicated on understanding of the constancy of one's own sex. Such an understanding occurs gradually between two and seven years of age and becomes irreversible during the concrete operational thought period. Apparently children can make discriminations about maleness and femaleness based on physical size, hairstyle, and other physical attributes. By classifying physical attributes that are appropriate for men and women, children are then able to categorize individuals as boys or girls. The ability to categorize children as boys and girls appears around three years of age. Gender constancy, the cognitive understanding that one's gender is invariant, is achieved in conjunction with the ability to conserve other properties.

Following the attainment of gender constancy—an understanding of maleness and femaleness—and certain activities that are akin to them, children imitate the model that is appropriate for their own sex. Because we live in a very sex stereotyped world, boys will show a strong tendency to imitate the masculine behavior of their fathers, while girls will show a keen tendency to imitate the feminine behaviors of their mothers. The sacrosanct values of the larger cultural milieu, then, will serve as the basis for children's decision making regarding the model they choose to imitate. The motives for acquiring sex-typed patterns of behavior seem to relate to the child's need to develop a sense of consistency and to boost self-esteem (Kohlberg, 1966).

Kohlberg's notion as to how children acquire sex-typed behaviors has often been misunderstood (see Huston, 1983). The theory predicts a curvilinear trend in children's understanding of sex role stereotypes. The rigidity with which children display or adhere to sex-stereotypic behaviors, therefore, should decrease after age seven. While Kohlberg and his colleagues (Kohlberg & Ullian, 1974; Ullian, 1976) have presented some data on flexibility in thinking regarding an understanding of social roles, others (Hartup & Zook, 1960; Venar & Snyder, 1966) have noted that boys' and girls' sex-typed preferences may be quite different over time. Boys seem to show a monotonic age increase in their preference for masculine activities, while girls display a steady increase for female-typed activities up to age five or six and then show a strong interest in male-typed activities (Hartup & Zook, 1960; Kohlberg & Zigler, 1967). Nevertheless, cognitive flexibility in middle childhood and adolescence is a contradictory one (see Carter & Patterson, 1982).

Cognitive developmental theory, as presented by Kohlberg (1966), is quite appealing in that the child's cognitive understanding of a phenomenon was detailed. Furthermore, scattered evidence (Brooks-Gunn & Lewis, 1975; Emmerich, 1977; Slaby & Frey, 1975) seems to support Kohlberg's developmental progression from the standpoint of the acquisition of an internal schema of the irreversibility of gender. But in effect a second look at Kohlberg's perspective reveals some problematic issues. A program of research spearheaded by Carter and his colleagues (Carter & Patterson, 1982; Carter & Taylor, in press; Carter & Levy, 1987; Levy, 1986), employing a multifaceted approach to the study of sex role stereotypes in young children, casts serious doubts about the age at which children acquire the understanding of the permanence of one's gender. First, Carter's earlier work suggested that sex stereotypes and social conventions may not be separate areas of social cognition. In fact, it was found that children's understanding of sex role stereotype flexibility corresponded to changes in their understanding of social conventions. If this is the case, then children's sex-typed behaviors and understanding of social conventions may show a more linear than curvilinear trend as children approach the concrete operational period (Carter & Patterson, 1982). Second, Carter (Carter & Taylor, in press; Carter & Levy, in press) demonstrated that gender constancy was unrelated to either stereotype knowledge or to sex-typed preferences.

These problems notwithstanding, Frieze, Parsons, Johnson, Ruble, and Zellman (1978) have been influential in incorporating a more "social-cognitive" approach to Kohlberg's original ideas. Basically, these social scientists' reformulation of cognitive-development theory considers cultural stereotypes and role divisions within the larger cultural context along with cognition as influencing how children become sex stereotyped. This articulation may indeed serve as a beacon in the evolution of a social-cultural-cognitive approach to sex typing. Again, we should warn that a social-cognitive perspective to the study of human behavior is not a new one (see Shantz, 1975). Psychologists are quickly realizing that cognitive and biological functioning may be the bases for a wide array of human behaviors. Whatever is arming children with nomenclature regarding sex-typing, we owe much to Kohlberg for the cognitively based orientation to sex role development.

## INFORMATION PROCESSING THEORIES: SELF SCHEMA AND GENDER SCHEMA

Concern about the role of cognition in the acquisition of sex-typed behaviors has led to the evolution of thinking in the direction of information processing models. Of course, the territory may seem new but the concept schema, inherent in the information-processing models of sex role development and representational thinking in general, is one of the hallmarks of Piaget's intellectual theory of development (Piaget, 1970). Instead of emphasizing sex-typed behaviors per se, schema theories (Bem, 1981; Martin & Halverson, 1981) highlight the child's internal conception of sex typing. The cognitive construct, the schema, consists of

a set of expectations or a network of associations that guide and organize an individual's perceptions. A schema functions as an anticipatory structure that leads the individual to search for certain information or to be ready to receive information consistent with the schema, (Huston, 1983; p. 399)

Note that the child develops certain expectations—a process that is somewhat similar to that outlined by cognitive social learning theorists. Nevertheless, during internal scanning, information that is incongruent with existing schemas may be ignored or used as a building block for the acquisition of other cognitive constructs.

### Self-Schema Theory

The proponents of self-schema theory (Martin & Halverson, 1981) suggest that sex role stereotypes have a clarifying and extending function in helping individuals develop schemas pertaining to social information. Children's knowledge and understanding of sex stereotypes are enlarged when the child evaluates perceptual information as appropriate or inappropriate for his or her own gender. In this way the child develops organizational structures (schemas) for sex-stereotyped behaviors that are more common to his/her own sex than for the other sex. Such a process offers the child an understanding of gender-relevant and gender-irrelevant activities. Subsequently, when the child encounters social activities that are appropriate for the self, she/he explores the activities and may search for information relevant to the activities. This is not in sharp contrast, then, to the processes of mediation, integration, modification, and so on that are central to the acquisition of other cognitive constructs.

Perhaps the dominant consideration in this approach is that gender constancy may not be a prevailing factor in enhancing sex-typed interests and behaviors and may not even be a prerequisite for children's early acquisition of sex-typed preferences. Despite current attempts to strengthen the schema-based conception to sex typing (e.g., Martin & Halverson, 1981, 1983), this model needs to be attuned not only to children's attention to sex-typed prescriptions but to changes in the processes involved in conceptual development-modification, extensions, and differentiation. How children come to acquire sex-typed behaviors is still a mystery in view of recent evidence demonstrating sex-typed preferences among infants (Roopnarine, 1986).

## Gender-Schema Theory

The organizational framework of gender-schema theory may seem similar but is different from that of self-schema theory. The focus of this theory (Bem, 1981) is that gender schemas are central to children's organization of information regarding sex-typed stereotypes, which accords well with self-schema theory. But there is one important departure: there is variability in the susceptibility to and importance of gender schemas among individuals. Those who are high on dimensions of sex typing tend to have a low tolerance for sex-typed concepts. By contrast, for androgynous individuals, gender-schemas are quite intact, but they do not form the primary basis of an individual's social functioning. It is expected, then, that androgynous individuals would use a wider range of constructs in judging others (Huston, 1983). In Bem's approach, therefore, the schemas serve to guide individuals' social functioning and the degree to which they engage in sex-typing behavior.

The formation of gender-schemas, according to this theory, emerges out of society's insistence that the sexes remain bipolar; that is, for practical and functional reasons masculinity and femininity should be at opposite ends of one dimension. It is essentially this emphasis that encourages the classification of objects and behaviors into gender schemas. Individuals begin with passive associations and then move into a more active process of assimilating and understanding social information from the environment. As for sex typing, it is derived from the individual's ability to incorporate and organize information that is consonant with the larger cultural definitions of the social roles we assume. The internal representations or schemas guide the individual to adjust his/her behaviors to meet societal definitions regarding sex-appropriate and sex-inappropriate behaviors (see Bem, 1984).

Given these propositions, one may legitimately ask why gender is such a salient characteristic in information processing and the cognitive organization of behavior. Bem (1984) argues that gender distinctions have come to assume a central role in social information processing because of the presumed importance attached to it by society. Thus gender, rather than race or size, becomes a more important basis for dichotomous categorization. The argument is persuasive but, in our judgment, nevertheless inadequate. Admittedly, children do assimilate information from the environment and modify it to fit existing schemas. But again we should point out that recent research (e.g., Roopnarine, 1986; Snow et al., 1983; Zelazo & Kearsley, 1980) has shown that children seem to display sex-typed toy use around the first birthday. While this propensity might relate to the "activation of hypotheses" in infancy, it is hard to believe that the infant is able to engage in gender-based dichotomous sorting. When does the child start to internalize gender-based schemas and what mechanisms are involved in the differentiation and incorporation process? These issues remain largely unexplored.

Both self-schema and gender-schema theories emphasize the role of cognition and the general readiness of individuals to respond to environmental stimuli based on ingrained cultural stereotypes. Even though these conceptions offer us an exodus out of the purely socialization approach and research does indicate that memory plays a role in schema processing (Carter & Levy, in press; Signorella & Liben, 1984, 1985), the challenge for cognition-based approaches is to delineate the emergence of an understanding of sex stereotypes (see Fagot, 1985) and the ideological/conceptual structure that provides the framework for devising or choosing particular behaviors that are or are not, sex-typed.

## ANDROGYNY

As the women's movement came to the forefront of American society, the inequitable treatment of women became a formidable issue. The foci of the women's movement and the disdain within academia with sexist and unsubstantiated and ill-defined theories of sex role development led to the emergence of androgyny. The view that men and women should assume different but complementary functions was soon questioned. Androgyny points to the need for the reconceptualization of the notion that masculinity and femininity are at opposite ends of the sex role domain. However, some differences do exist in the operational definition of psychological androgyny (see Table 2.2), and the concurrent development of several scales to assess the construct makes it even more difficult to achieve some synthesis of the area. Nonetheless, we will attempt to present the contrasting but sometimes closely related views on psychological androgyny.

### Bem's Conceptions

The conceptual framework of psychological androgyny, according to Bem (1974, 1975, 1981) lies in the assumption that individuals who are androgynous might "be *both* masculine and feminine, *both* assertive and yielding, *both* in-

rogyny

| | View | Emphasis |
|---|---|---|
| Bem (1974) | Individuals are both masculine and feminine, assertive and yielding, and expressive and instrumental (static view) | Restrictiveness and negative consequences of extreme sex typing |
| Spence, Helmreich, & Stapp (1975) | High on dimensions of both masculinity and femininity (static view) | Socially desirable masculine and feminine personality attributes show a weak association with sex role preferences |
| Rebecca, Hefner, & Oleshansky (1976) | Sex role development assumes a "stage-like" progression—from rudimentary conceptions of sex-typed behaviors toward conflict resolution and transcendence (nonstatic view) | Growth toward the transcendence of sex roles and sex typing through conflict resolution |
| Block (1973) | Also suggested that sex role development assumes a "stage-like" progression that is intertwined with the individual's level of ego development (nonstatic view) | Integration of masculinity and femininity toward higher levels of development |

Source: Compiled by authors.

strumental and expressive—depending on the situational appropriateness of these various behaviors." Furthermore, Bem (1974) explicitly states that strongly sex-typed individuals might be limiting the opportunities for exposure to the wide array of situations they would encounter if they were androgynous. Whereas the androgynous individual's orbit of knowledge and understanding might be enlarged due to the sensitivity and flexibility displayed in moving from situation to situation, the highly sex-typed person is restrictive, constantly referring to internalized sex role standards and therefore missing out on formidable social experiences (see Kagan, 1964; Kohlberg, 1966). The conceptual demands of high sex-typing may have undesirable consequences as well. For instance, high femininity in women has been shown to be related to anxiety, low self-esteem, and low social acceptance (see Cosentino & Heilbrun, 1964; Gale, 1969; Gray, 1957; Sears, 1970; Webb, 1963). Likewise, high masculinity in men has been shown to be related to high anxiety and low self-acceptance (Harford, Willis, & Deabler, 1967; Mussen, 1962). Among young children, boys and girls who are more sex-typed tend to have lower intelligence and appear less creative (Maccoby, 1966). For these and other reasons, non-sex-typed methods of exposition would maximize the opportunity for individuals to deepen their understanding of individual differences.

Bem (1974, 1975) developed her own scale (Bem Sex Role Inventory—BSRI) to assess psychological androgyny. In her earlier work, Bem (1974, 1975) classified individuals as androgynous if they scored similarly on the masculine and feminine dimensions of the inventory. Her assessments of psychological androgyny among college students were quite revealing. Androgynous individuals, both males and females, displayed ''masculine'' independence during a conformity exercise in a laboratory room and more ''feminine'' playfulness when asked to interact with a kitten. Nonandrogynous individuals did not display much ''feminine'' playfulness. To Bem, androgyny is tied to the relative lack of judgments based on sex. This view is in sharp contrast to those espoused by other social scientists (e.g., Spence, Helmreich, & Stapp, 1975).

### Spence et al.'s Perspectives

Like Bem (1974), Spence and her colleagues (Spence, Helmreich, & Stapp, 1975; Helmreich, Spence & Holahan, 1979) have developed their own scale (Personal Attributes Questionnaire—PAQ) to assess psychological androgyny and sex role flexibility. Although both the BSRI and the PAQ scales contain items on masculinity and femininity that are basically orthogonal (Helmreich, Spence, & Holahan, 1979), Spence and her co-investigators argue that androgyny should be characterized in terms of high scores on dimensions of both masculinity and femininity.

To understand the conceptual similarity between these two competing positions on androgyny, we need to examine the scales more closely. According to Helmreich et al. (1979), the PAQ is a ''self-report measure of socio-affective instrumental and expressive traits, the items making no mention of instrumental or expressive behaviors or the situations that elicit them.'' By comparison, not all items on the BSRI can be defined as expressive or instrumental. Nevertheless, both inventories appear to be validly assessing global indices of masculinity and femininity. The major complicating factor in the assessment of androgyny, however, according to Spence and Helmreich (1978), is embodied in the hypothesis that socially desirable masculine and feminine personality attributes might not show good associations with sex role preferences unless, of course, the behaviorial preferences are intimately interwoven in expressive and instrumental skills. Thus both the BSRI and the PAQ may be personality measures that do not assess sex roles among individuals. This argument receives further support when the findings of Helmreich et al. (1979) are considered. Among college students, measures of comfort and preference for sex-typed and neutral activities and performance on the PAQ showed weak associations. Whether psychological androgyny as assessed by either the BSRI or the PAQ is related to sex-typed behaviors or not must await further investigation. Society is only now becoming increasingly acquainted with the concept of androgyny.

### Sex Role Transcendence Model

Rebecca, Hefner, and Oleshansky (1976) have assumed a somewhat different approach to the concept of androgyny. Dismayed with the sluggish pace of changes in thinking within the social sciences in general, these psychologists proposed a model of sex role transcendence that is radically different from all of the views outlined in this chapter. To them, sex role development assumes a stage-like progression: from undifferentiated conception of sex roles (Stage I) to polarized oppositional views of sex roles (Stage II) to a flexible dynamic transcendence of sex roles (Stage III). This view is embedded in the stage-conception of models of development (e.g., Kohlberg, 1964; Piaget, 1970).

In Stage I, undifferentiated conception, the child is busy organizing perceptual information from the environment. He/She does not yet know that society has imposed a sex-delineated system whereby individuals make judgments on the basis of gender. However, the child soon learns, through a process of differentiation, that rudimentary biopolarity exists (e.g., big/small) before grasping that individuals are either male or female and that society has prescribed certain specific roles for each sex. This transition process occurs prior to the child's entry into school.

Subsequently, in the polarized Stage II, the child becomes cognizant of the need to behave and think according to the sex-delineated prescriptions. Furthermore, societal pressures and the chief agents of socialization aid and abet the child toward the acceptance of traditional sex roles. Presumably, such an adoption prepares the child for entry into the adult society where sex-differentiated roles are strictly sanctioned and reinforced. As in the previous stage, a transition occurs, only now the individual experiences a "crisis" that is in sharp contrast to prevailing modes of thinking. Apparently, the crisis is so severe that the individual is forced to make some comparison between his/her existing arsenal of sex-typed conceptions and some alternative view (e.g., the rights of women). Unfortunately this change in conceptual thinking is not given enough support in a society that is still very sex-typed (Rebecca et al., 1976).

Finally, in Stage III, sex role transcendence, the individual is supposedly flexible in his/her behaviors and attitudes regarding sex typing; reorganization of thought and behaviorial tendencies allows the individual to transcend rigorous stereotypes that pertain to employment, and expressive and instrumental functions (Rebecca et al., 1976). The struggle to maintain flexibility continues as the individual grapples with his/her own conscience and societal insistence on gender based distinctions. Stage III of sex role development reflects a process that is constantly undergoing metamorphosis as a person confronts a vastly sex-typed culture.

This view postulates that we move from fairly sex-typed conceptions to a stage in which introspection and "conflict resolution" assist us to confront and deal with ingrained gender dichotomies. As such, this conceptual framework parts company with Bem's (1974) more static notion of androgyny (Rebecca et al., 1976). Although these theorists suggested that moral development and cognitive competence might facilitate the transcendence of gender based norms, their importance remains undefined.

## Block's Conception

Block's (1973) view of androgyny is superimposed on Loevinger's (1966; Loevinger & Wessler, 1970) theory of ego development. Masculinity and femininity are perceived in terms of Bakan's (1966) conception of human existence: *agency*—the organism as a self entity that presents itself in modalities that reflect self-protection, self-assertion, and self-expansion; and *communion*—the recognition that we are part of a larger existence and we manifest ourselves as being at one with other individuals.

During the early stage of sex role conceptions, the infant begins to develop rudimentary notions of gender identity but these notions appear sexless. Behaviorally, the child is concerned with self-assertion, self-interest, and self-expression—attributes that have historically been described as masculine. Later, the child seems torn between the values espoused by a traditional system of socialization and the need for self-enhancement or maximizing "one's own gain." Nonetheless, the child conforms to the rules and prescriptions of society, and divergent patterns of socialization occur for boys and girls. For example, boys are taught to control their affective dispositions while girls are prohibited from displaying aggressive tendencies. Subsequently, introspection and self-criticism permit the child to temper masculine/feminine dispositions. This modification occurs when the child questions internalized values and ideas. Next, in a process of conflict-resolution, perhaps similar to that outlined in the previous section, the individual develops a degree of autonomy from traditional sex role prescriptions. Evidently the individual sees the system of inculcating bipolar, sex-delineated values as problematical. Eventually the individual integrates attributes that are both masculine and feminine into his/her personality. For Block (1973), the integration of roles that are conventionally considered feminine and those traditionally defined as masculine constitutes androgyny.

The prevailing assumption in Block's theory is that as the individual moves toward higher levels of ego development, he/she will be better able to deal with sex role discrepancies in a more androgynous manner. Although we agree that the resolution of sex role conflicts might involve higher levels of thinking and ego development, and Block (1973) provides ample evidence that the internalization of predominant societal values has differential effects on the personality development of males and females, there are several issues that warrant discussion. In general, it is difficult to explain gradients of change for any given developmental phenomenon. This assumption applies to Block's theory as well. The theory does not explain the motivational factors that are the catalysts for change even though there is ample cross-cultural evidence to suggest that socialization and cultural factors will impinge on an individual's ability to become androgynous. Obviously, children will form internal representations of highly stressed cultural and sex-typed or non-sex-typed values. Reconstructive memory will then assist the individual to connect the immediate issues facing him/her with the internalized cultural mores. This process seemingly suggests the strong contributions of cognitive factors.

To summarize, we have presented four different but related conceptions of androgyny. The construct is an appealing one in light of the negative consequences of high sex-typed preferences on personality development, and the stifling and demeaning impact of sex discrimination on both men and women. The infusion of more egalitarian conceptions of human development principles during socialization will be a tremendous asset to our children and society in the long run.

## FEMINIST PERSPECTIVES

There is no one single approach or perspective of feminist thinking on sex role development. A number of scholars, assuming different approaches, converge to question the assumptions of traditional theories of sex role development (e.g., Chodorow, 1978; Ruddick, 1980; Sayers, 1982). We should inform the reader that feminists have dealt with a wide range of issues dealing with women's roles in both traditional and nontraditional societies, sex discrimination, and other issues that are central to women's intellectual, social, economic, and political development. Our discussion will be narrow in focus in that it will deal with women and mothering—an issue that has received quite a bit of attention. To avoid redundancy and for other practical reasons, the views pertaining to androgyny and Chodorow's attack on psychoanalytic thinking will not be restated. As we have mentioned earlier, more egalitarian relationships between the sexes is an issue we can no longer afford to ignore.

While Chodorow (1978) argues that mothers, because they are the same sex as daughters, may have a closer alliance with daughters than with sons, some feminists (Benjamin, 1978; Rich, 1980) poignantly suggest that the mother-daughter relationship would serve to fight male tyranny and remove the father as a central figure in society. Yet others see the mother-infant relationship as the basis for the development of women's solidarity (Lieven, 1981). A majority of the attacks on traditional modes of socialization have been directed at Freud's Oedipal complex, however.

The central point in feminist discussions of the female Oedipal complex is that the father is accorded far too much importance. The movement of the daughter away from the mother toward the father could be on the child's own accord. The pain and frustration the child suffers during toilet training and weaning could lead him/her to turn to the father in the absence of any paternal encouragement (Klein, 1950; Sayers, 1984). This view is in contrast to that espoused by Irigaray (1980) who sees the pre-Oedipal phase as a facet of patriarchy that encourages distancing between women and themselves.

A more moderate approach to early socialization has been proposed by Sara Ruddick (1980). After systematically examining the plight of women in terms of maternal power and thinking, she proposed an excellent platform for reformation of traditional roles, one which might move us closer to androgyny. Her realistic proposal entertains changes in the institution of motherhood that include the participation of men equally in every aspect of child care. The exclusion of men in the care of children coupled with the manifestation of power dominance in other aspects of life can only lead to the inculcation of sexist orientations in children from very early in life (Ruddick, 1980). By contrast, involving men in child care would require them to relinquish power in other realms of life and move toward a more balanced division of labor. Reforms of this nature could penetrate into the highly structured work environment and could in turn lead to restructuring there as well. This would enable us to expose our children to models that value equality and behave in an egalitarian manner.

## DIRECTIONS FOR FUTURE RESEARCH

In a sense, the leitmotif of this chapter was coming to grips with thinking regarding the emergence and stability of sex-typed behavior. As such, a number of theories have attempted to explain the underlying processes that might be involved in this evolution. We were generally pleased with the social-cognitive direction the empirical work has taken. On the other hand, we were dismayed that so few of the theories have actually dealt with the emergence of sex-typed behaviors and their developmental progression. With the exception of the psychoanalytic school of thought, there has been limited interest in developing a comprehensive life-span theory of sex role development. The patterns of sex typing may indeed change as we progress through the lifespan. Such a model does not necessarily have to assume a stage-like progression.

With these concerns in mind, we would like to suggest the following issues as pertinent for future investigations.

1. We need to explore further the influence of extreme sex typing on the personality attributes and intellectual functioning of children and adults. Scattered evidence suggests a negative association between extreme sex typing and cognitive and social variables. Our message here is a political one as well as one that involves concern for the mental health of individual members of society.

2. Research on the influence of the media on modeling sex-typed behaviors and on internal representation and reconstructive memory processes is absolutely necessary. The media

present potent sex-typed messages, and sexist language is prevalent in television episodes.

3. We need to explore the effects of differing styles of parenting on children's manifestation of sex-typed behavior in the peer group. Given that a large number of children are raised in peer group settings, it would be of interest to assess the potency of peer and parental contributions to sex-typed behavior in the same model. It is plausible that as children spend more of their waking hours with peers than with parents, the peer group might assume a burgeoning role in the process of personality development.

4. The processes whereby children encode, store, and retrieve information regarding roles in society need to be outlined. To state that a child forms a schema of a behavior does not solve the issue of why the child attends more to the "sex" of an individual than to other features. Longitudinal studies of the processes of integration, differentiation, and modification of sex-typed information are badly needed.

5. An examination of nontraditional modes of socialization across cultures will enable us to understand the interlocking roles of social and cognitive factors in the emergence and saliency of sex typing.

We are quite certain that there are other recommendations on areas of investigation that other contributors to this volume will highlight as well. Our contention is that newer theories of sex role development are in their early stages of the process of substantiation and refinement. Hopefully, as we begin to understand the complex and interrelated factors that are the precursors to sex typing and the manifestation of sex-typed behaviors, our theoretical frameworks will become firmer and better grounded.

## CONCLUSION

We have attempted to provide an overview of some wide ranging but interrelated conceptions of sex role development. Most of the perspectives outlined herein suggest that both cognitive and social factors are involved in the acquisition of sex-typed behaviors. Intuitively, it stands to reason that changes in socialization practices should lead to corresponding changes in children's conceptions and internal representations of roles and behaviors that are central to human functioning. Unless we move toward a more egalitarian treatment of individuals, regardless of their sex, the emotional, intellectual, and economic costs to society will be tremendous.

## REFERENCES

Bakan, D. (1966). *The duality of human existence*. Chicago: Rand McNally.

Bandura, A. (1977). *Social learning theory*. Englewood Cliffs, NJ: Prentice-Hall.

Bandura, A. & Walters, R. (1963). *Social learning and personality development*. New York: Holt, Rinehart, & Winston.

Baumrind, D. & Black, A. E. (1967). Socialization practices associated with dimensions of competence in preschool boys and girls. *Child Development, 38,* 291–328.

Bem, S. L. (1974). The measurement of psychological androgyny. *Journal of Consulting and Clinical Psychology, 42,* 155–162.

Bem, S. L. (1975). Sex role adaptability: One consequence of psychological androgyny. *Journal of Personality and Social Psychology, 31,* 634–643.

Bem, S. L. (1981). Gender-schema theory: A cognitive account of sex typing. *Psychological Review, 88,* 354–364.

Bem, S. L. (1985). Androgyny and gender-schema theory: A conceptual and empirical integration. In T. B. Sonderegger (Ed.), *Nebraska Symposium on Motivation: Psychology and Gender.* Lincoln, NE: University of Nebraska Press.

Benjamin, J. (1978). Authority and the family revisited; or, a world without fathers. *New German Critique, 13,* 35–57.

Block, J. H. (1973). Conceptions of sex role: Some cross-cultural and longitudinal perspectives. *American Psychologist, 28,* 512–526.

Brooks, J. & Lewis, M. (1975). Person perception and verbal labeling: The development of social labels. Paper presented at the Society for Research in Child Development meeting, Denver, April.

Brooks-Gunn, J. & Matthews, W. S. (1979). *He and she: How children develop their sex role identity.* Englewood Cliffs, NJ: Prentice-Hall.

Bryan, J. W. & Luria, A. (1978). Sex role learning: A test of the selective attention hypothesis. *Child Development, 49,* 13–23.

Carter, D. B. & Levy, G. D. (in press). Gender schemata and sex role development: Relationships between knowledge, preferences, and processing of gender relevant information. *Child Development.*

Carter, D. B. & Patterson, C. J. (1982). Sex roles as social conventions: The development of children's conceptions of sex-role stereotypes. *Developmental Psychology, 18,* 812–824.

Carter, D. B. & Taylor, R. D. (in press). The development of children's awareness and understanding of flexibility in sex-role stereotypes: Implications for preferences, attitudes, and behavior. *Sex Roles.*

Chodorow, N. (1978). *The reproduction of mothering: Psychoanalysis and the sociology of gender.* Berkeley: University of California Press.

Cosentino, F. & Heilbrun, A. B. (1964). Anxiety correlates of sex role identity in college students. *Psychological Reports, 14,* 729–730.

Emmerich, W. (1977). Structure and development of personal–social behaviors in economically disadvantaged preschool children. *Genetic Psychology Monographs, 95,* 191–245.

Emmerich, W., Cocking, R., & Sigel, I. (1979). Relationships between cognitive and social functioning in preschool children. *Developmental Psychology, 15,* 494–504.

Fagot, B. I. (1977). Consequences of moderate cross-gender behavior in preschool children. *Child Development, 48,* 902–907.

Fagot, B. I. (1978). The influence of sex of child on parental reactions to toddler children. *Child Development, 49,* 459–465.

Fagot, B. I. (1985). Changes in thinking about early sex-role development. *Developmental Review, 5,* 83–98.

Frieze, I. H., Parsons, J. E., Johnson, P. B., Ruble, D. N., & Zellman, G. L. (1978). *Women and sex roles.* New York: W. W. Norton and Company.

Freud, S. (1905/1962). *Three essays on the theory of sexuality.* New York: Avon, 1962.

Freud, S. (1924/1964). The dissolution of the Oedipus complex. In James Strachey (Ed.), *The standard edition of the complete psychological works of Sigmund Freud, Vol. IX.* London: The Hogarth Press & Institute of Psychoanalysis, 1964.

Gale, M. D. (1969). The relationship between masculinity–femininity and manifest anxiety. *Journal of Clinical Psychology, 25,* 294–295.

Gray, S. W. (1957). Masculinity–femininity in relation to anxiety and social acceptance. *Child Development, 28,* 203–214.

Grusec, J. G. & Brinker, D. B. (1972). Reinforcement for imitation as a social learning determinant with implications for sex role development. *Journal of Personality and Social Psychology, 21,* 149–158.

Harford, T. C., Willis, C. H., & Deabler, H. L. (1967). Personality correlates of masculinity–femininity. *Psychological Reports, 21,*881–884.

Hartup, W. W. & Zook, E. A. (1960). Sex role preferences in three- and four-year-old children. *Journal of Consulting Psychology, 24,* 420–426.

Helmreich, R. L., Spence, J. T., & Holahan, C. K. (1979). Psychological androgyny and sex role flexibility: A test of two hypotheses. *Journal of Personality and Social Psychology, 37,* 1631–1644.

Hetherington, E. M. (1965). A developmental study of the effects of the dominant parent on sex role preferences, identification, and imitation in children. *Journal of Personality and Social Psychology, 2,* 188–194.

Hetherington, E. M. (1967). The effects of familial variables on sex typing, on parent-child similarity, and on imitation in children. In J. P. Hill (Ed.), *Minnesota symposia on child psychology,* (Vol. 1 (pp. 82–107). Minneapolis: University of Minnesota Press.

Horney, K. (1932). The dread of women. *International Journal of Psychoanalysis, 13,* 359.

Huston, A. (1983). Sex typing. In E. M. Hetherington & P. H. Mussen (Eds.), *Handbook of child psychology* (4th ed., Vol. 4). *Socialization, personality, and social development* (pp. 387–467). New York: Wiley.

Irigaray, L. (1980). When our lips speak together. *Signs, 6,* 69–79.

Kagan, J. (1964). Acquisition and significance of sex typing and sex role identity. In M. L. Hoffman & L. W. Hoffman (Eds.), *Review of child development research,* Vol. 1. New York: Russell Sage Foundation.

Klein, M. (1950). The Oedipus complex in the light of early anxieties. In, *Contributions to psychoanalysis.* London: Hogarth, (First published in 1934.)

Klein, M. (1957). *Envy and gratitude.* New York: Basic Books.

Kohlberg, L. (1964). Development of moral character and moral ideology. In M. L. Hoffman & L. W. Hoffman (Eds.), *Review of child development research,* Vol. 1. New York: Russell Sage Foundation.

Kohlberg, L. (1966). A cognitive-developmental analysis of children's sex role concepts and attitudes. In E. E. Maccoby (Ed.), *The development of sex differences* (pp. 82–172). Stanford: Stanford University Press.

Kohlberg, L. K. & Ullian, D. Z. (1974). Stages in the development of psychosexual concepts and attitudes. In R. C. Friedman, R. M. Richart, & R. L. Vande Wiele (Eds.), *Sex differences in behavior,* (pp. 209–222). New York: Wiley.

Kohlberg, L. & Zigler, E. (1967). The impact of cognitive maturity on the development of sex-role attitudes in the years 4 to 8. *Genetic Psychology Monographs, 75,* 89–165.

Lamb, M. E. (1977). The development of parental preferences in the first two years of life. *Sex Roles, 3,* 495–497.

Lamb, M. E. (1979). Parental influences and the father's role: A personal perspective. *American Psychologist, 34,* 938–943.

Lamb, M. E. & Urberg, K. (1978). The development of gender role and gender identity. In M. E. Lamb (Ed.), *Social and personality development.* New York: Holt, Rinehart, & Winston.

Lerner, H. E. (1978). Adaptive and pathogenic aspects of sex role stereotypes: Implications for parenting and psychotherapy. *American Journal of Psychiatry, 135,* 48–52.

Levy, G. (1986). *Gender schematization versus gender constancy: An investigation of developmental influences on sex stereotypes in young children.* Syracuse University: Unpublished master's thesis.

Lieven, F. (1981). Subjectivity, materialism, and patriarchy. In Cambridge Women's Studies Group (Eds.), *Women in society.* London: Virago.

Loevinger, J. (1966). The meaning and measurement of ego development. *American Psychologist, 21,* 195–206.

Loevinger, J. & Wessler, R. (1970). *Measuring ego development,* Vol. 1. San Francisco: Jossey-Bass.

Maccoby, E. E. (1966). (Ed.) *The development of sex differences.* Stanford, CA: Stanford University Press.

Maccoby, E. E. & Jacklin, C. N. (1974). *The psychology of sex differences.* Stanford, CA: Stanford University Press.

Margolin, G. & Patterson, G. R. (1975). Differential consequences provided by mothers and fathers for their sons and daughters. *Developmental Psychology, 11,* 537–538.

Martin, C. L. & Halverson, C. F. (1981). A schematic processing model of sex typing and stereotyping in children. *Child Development, 52,* 1119–1134.

Martin, C. L. & Halverson, C. F. (1983). Gender constancy: A methodological and theoretical analysis. *Sex Roles, 9,* 775–790.

Mischel, W. (1966). A social learning view of sex differences in behavior. In E. E. Maccoby (Ed.), *The development of sex differences.* Stanford, CA: Stanford University Press.

Mischel, W. (1977). On the future of personality measurement. *American Psychologist, 32,* 246–254.

Mussen, P. H. (1961). Some antecedents and consequences of masculine sex typing in adolescent boys. *Psychological Monographs, 75,* whole no. 506.

Mussen, P. H. (1962). Long-term consequents of masculinity of interests in adolescence. *Journal of Consulting Psychology, 26,* 435–440.

Mussen, P. H. & Distler, L. (1959). Masculinity, identification, and father–son relationships. *Journal of Abnormal and Social Psychology, 59,* 350–356.

Parke, R. D. (1979). Perspectives on father–infant interaction. In J. D. Osofsky (Ed.), *Handbook of infant development,* (pp. 549–590). New York: Wiley.

Parsons, T. & Bales, R. F. (1955). *Family, socialization, and interaction process.* Glencoe, IL: Free Press.

Piaget, J. (1970). Piaget's theory. In P. H. Mussen (Ed.), *Carmichael's manual of child development,* Vol. 2 (pp. 703–732). New York: Wiley.

Rebecca, M., Hefner, R., & Oleshansky, B. (1976). A model of sex role transcendence. *Journal of Social Issues, 32,* 197–206.

Rich, A. (1980). Compulsory heterosexuality and lesbian existence. *Signs, 5,* 631–660.

Roopnarine, J. L. (1986). Mothers' and fathers' behaviors toward the toy play of their infant sons and daughters. *Sex Roles, 14,* 59–68.

Ruddick, S. (1980). Maternal thinking. *Feminist studies, 6,* 342–367.

Sayers, J. (1982). Feminism and mothering: A Kleinian perspective. *Women's Studies International Forum, 7,* 239–241.

Sears, R. R. (1970). Relation of early socialization experiences to self concepts and gender role in middle childhood. *Child Development, 41,* 267–290.

Sears, R. R., Rau, N. & Alpert R. (1965). *Identification and child rearing.* Stanford, CA: Stanford University Press.

Shantz, C. U. (1975). The development of social cognition. In E. M. Hetherington (Ed.), *Review of child development research 5.* Chicago: University of Chicago Press.

Shantz, C. (1983). The development of social cognition. In J. H. Flavell & E. M. Markham (Eds.), *Handbook of child psychology.* (4th ed.) *3, Cognitive Development.* New York: Wiley.

Sigel, I. & Cocking, R. R. (1977). *Cognitive development from childhood to adolescence: A constructivist perspective.* New York: Holt, Rinehart, & Winston.

Signorella, M. & Liben, L. (1984). Recall and reconstruction of gender-related pictures. Effects of attitude, task, difficulty, and age. *Child Development, 55,* 393–405.

Signorella, M. & Liben, L. (1985). Recall and reconstruction of gender related pictures. Paper presented at the biennial meetings of the Society for Research in Child Development, Toronto, Canada, April.

Slaby, R. G. & Frey, K. S. (1975). Development of gender constancy and selective atttention to same-sex models. *Child Development, 46,* 849–856.

Smith, P. K. & Daglish, L. (1977). Sex differences in parent and infant behavior in the home. *Child Development, 48,* 1250–1254.

Snow, M., Jacklin, C., & Maccoby, E. E. (1983). Sex-of-child differences in father–child interaction at one year of age. *Child Development, 54,* 227–232.

Spence, J. T. & Helmreich, R. L. (1978). *Masculinity and Femininity. Their psychological dimensions, correlates and antecedents.* Austin: University of Texas Press.

Spence, J. T., Helmreich, R. L., & Stapp, J. (1975). Ratings of self and peers on sex role attributes and their relation to self-esteem and conceptions of masculinity and femininity. *Journal of Personality and Social Psychology, 32,* 29–39.

Sutton-Smith, B. & Rosenberg, B. G. (1972). *Sex and identity.* New York: Holt, Rinehart, & Winston.

Ullian, D. Z. (1976). The development of conceptions of masculinity and femininity. In B. Lloyd and J. Archer (Eds.), *Exploring sex differences,* (pp. 25–48). London: Academic Press.

Venar, A. M. & Snyder, C. A. (1966). The preschool child's awareness and anticipation of adult sex roles. *Sociometry, 29,* 159–168.

Webb, A. P. (1963). Sex role preferences and adjustment in early adolescents. *Child Development, 34,* 609–618.

Zelazo, P. & Kearsley, R. (1980). The emergence of functional play in infants: Evidence for a major cognitive transition. *Journal of Applied Developmental Psychology, 1,* 95–117.

# 3
# Measurement Issues in Sex Roles and Sex Typing
## Michael S. Windle

During the past 15 years we have witnessed the emergence of alternative conceptualizations and measurements of psychological constructs related to sex roles and sex typing (e.g., Bem, 1974; Constantinople, 1973; Spence & Helmreich, 1978). Whereas prior to 1970 most theoretical orientations tended to view masculinity and femininity as opposite ends of a single bipolar dimension, some recent alternative conceptualizations have tended to view these as two distinct, orthogonal dimensions (e.g., Bem, 1974; Spence & Helmreich, 1978). Paralleling this shift in alternative conceptual systems of sex roles and sex typing has been a revision in the way that instruments have been designed to measure masculinity and femininity.

The purpose of the present chapter is to provide an historical review of measurement approaches to sex roles and sex typing across the lifespan and to then critique these measurement approaches and their conceptual foundations in relation to several salient measurement issues. The chapter is organized into two parts. First, attention is directed toward a brief and primarily recent history of the conceptualization and measurement of sex roles and sex typing in the childhood, adulthood, and gerontological literatures. The second part of this chapter addresses some critical measurement issues in the study of sex roles and sex typing. The following three issues are focused upon, though they admittedly do not represent an exhaustive list: (1) psychometric issues associated with multidimensionality; (2) research designs and multivariate statistical models; and (3) measurement equivalence of psychological constructs across populations. Space limitations do not permit a complete elaboration with detailed examples from the sex roles and sex typing literature for each of the above measurement issues, though references are provided for more detailed study. The "meta-message" to be conveyed in this chapter is that the increasingly complex conceptual notions that have been advanced by many in the field of sex roles and sex-typing research require a higher level of sophistication in the application of research designs, measurement procedures, and statistical models. That is, if we seek to describe, explain, and predict complex, causally interdependent networks of variables associated with sex role behavior, it is necessary to employ tools (i.e., research designs, measurement techniques, and statistical models) that are adequate for such an undertaking.

## HISTORY OF CONCEPTUALIZATIONS OF SEX ROLES AND SEX TYPING

In providing a brief history of conceptualizations of sex roles and sex typing, Whitley's (1983) distinction of sex role models is utilized. Whitley referred to the congruence model of sex roles as one in which healthy development is indicated by the adoption of a masculine or feminine sex role consistent or congruent with one's biological gender. Therefore psychological growth in males is facilitated by the adoption of a masculine sex role and in females by the adoption of a feminine sex role. An alternative perspective on healthy sex role development is referred to as the androgyny model. This model suggests that optimal psychological growth is enhanced when individuals score highly on each of the two independent dimensions of masculinity and femininity. High scores on both of these dimensions presumably increase the range of adaptive responses to variable environmental demands (Bem, 1974 1975). A third perspective on healthy sex role development is referred to as the masculinity model. This model suggests that the masculine sex role is the most advantageous for both sexes, primarily due to the cultural demands and positive reinforcers for behavior consistent with what has been defined as masculine (e.g., high achievement). That is, the cultural context is structured such that masculine-type behaviors are often more highly valued and eventuate in more positive feedback in the form of monetary and social rewards.

During the following discussion on conceptualizations of sex roles and sex typing, the congruence model is used to characterize much of the research in the child development literature. The origins of this model's formulation are presented as well as a brief, general description of how measures were constructed to investigate theoretical notions regarding congruity. The androgyny model is used to characterize much of the research in the early adult literature, and major emphasis is directed toward the formulations of two of the major researchers in this area, Sandra Bem and Janet T. Spence. The gerontological literature also can more aptly be characterized by the androgyny model rather than the congruence or the masculinity model, though the origins of this androgyny formulation differ from those of the early adult literature. The origin of the androgyny model developed by gerontological researchers is provided along with a general description of the measurement procedures used to investigate personality changes in sex role functioning among older adults.

## Childhood Literature

Early perspectives of sex role development in childhood were largely influenced by Freudian based notions regarding the importance of identification with the same sex parent. According to Freud (1933), optimal psychosexual adjustment would be enhanced by the adoption of a sex role identity consistent with one's biological gender. Furthermore, deviations from this congruity between sex role identification and biological gender would result in conflictual issues for the individual and would adversely affect subsequent psychosexual development.

The theoretical notions of congruity between biological gender and sex role identification, and of the prominent role of parents in the development of sex role identity in their offspring, had a major influence on early theorizing about sex roles and sex typing and continues to influence much contemporary research both in terms of conceptualization and measurement. That is, although considerable controversy has transpired over the past 20 years regarding the causal dynamics underlying sex roles and sex typing, with several alternative theoretical models proposed to more adequately and/or more parsimoniously describe the behavior of interest, a central focus has continued to be on the antecedents and mechanisms involved in the adoption of same-sex identity (i.e., masculinity for males and femininity for females). For example, much of the early sex role research in social learning theory focused on processes of imitation by children and parental role modeling by parents to explain the adoption of sex role "appropriate" identities by males and females (see Block, 1983; Maccoby & Jacklin, 1974; for reviews). Similarly, Kohlberg's (1966) cognitive development theory sought to describe the sequence of cognitive stages that characterize the internalization and adoption of traditional sex roles. Thus, despite the divergence in theoretical orientations, there emerged a general consensus regarding the set of research questions to be pursued, namely, the dynamics involved in same-sex identification.

The significance of this consensus regarding what to study in sex roles and sex typing was manifested in the kinds of instruments developed, the scoring procedures used, and the interpretations provided. A wide variety of instruments were developed by a host of methods including projective techniques, picture preferences, toy preferences, teacher ratings, and parent ratings (see Beere, 1979; Huston, 1983; for reviews). One pervasive feature of virtually all these measures was the manner in which they were scored. Responses were scored along a single, bipolar dimension of masculinity/femininity. For example, a child selecting a truck to play with might be given a score of "1" on a unitary, masculinity/femininity continuum, whereas selecting a doll would result in a score of "7" along this same continuum. Typically, separate item responses were then summed to provide a single total scale score of masculinity/femininity. A further commonality among most of these bipolar measures was the criterion used for item selection. Constantinople (1973) reported that biological sex alone generally served as the sole criterion for the inclusion of items on many bipolar, masculinity/femininity scales. More specifically, items were selected only if they could be easily (i.e., with high frequency) classified into either masculine- or feminine-typed social categories, as prescribed by the extant cultural norms for sex role appropriate behavior. This kind of item selection procedure was consequential in that it maximized between group differences and conversely, minimized possible overlapping between group sources of variance.

## Early Adulthood Literature

The prominent role of bipolar, unidimensional conceptualizations and measurements of sex roles and sex typing was not exclusive to child development researchers. Rather, many of the major personality and vocational interest inventories such as the Minnesota Multiphasic Personality Inventory (MMPI), the California Psychological Inventory (CPI), the Guilford-Zimmerman Temperament Inventory (GZTI), and the Strong Vocational Interest Inventory (SVII) included a subscale that measured masculinity and femininity as a unidimensional, bipolar factor. However, in the early 1970s, within the historical/social/political context of the Women's Movement, alternative models of sex roles and sex typing were proposed (Bem, 1974; Constantinople, 1973; Spence & Helmreich, 1978).

The major feature distinguishing these alternative formulations of sex roles and sex typing from previous ones was that masculinity and femininity were conceptualized and measured as two distinct, orthogonal dimensions (Bem, 1974; Spence & Helmreich, 1978). In terms of measurement, this translated into the derivation of two separate subscale scores, one for masculinity and one for femininity, and provided the basis for median-split based typologies and for the androgyny model of mental health. Although alternative methods of scoring the masculinity and femininity dimensions to classify individuals into a typology of sex role orientations were proposed (e.g., see Sedney, 1981), four types were typically identified. Persons, of either sex, scoring high (e.g., above the sample median) on both masculine and feminine dimensions were classified as androgynous. Persons, of either sex, scoring high on the masculine dimension and low (e.g., below the median) on the feminine dimension were classified as masculine typed. Persons, of either sex, scoring high on the feminine dimension and low on the masculine dimension were classified as feminine typed. Persons, of either sex, scoring low on both masculine and feminine dimensions were classified as undifferentiated.

Much research ensued regarding the psychological significance of these sex role classifications in regard to theory-based expectations (for reviews, see Taylor & Hall, 1982; Whitley, 1983). The fundamental theoretical notion guiding this research was that androgynous persons would provide a psychologically healthier prototype than sex-typed persons (i.e., either masculine- or feminine-typed males and females). This psychological healthiness was proposed to be the result of the greater flexibility afforded to androgynous persons (relative to sex-typed) in meeting the multiple demands necessitated by living conditions. For instance, many situations in life may require masculine-typed behaviors such as self-reliance or assertiveness, while others may require feminine-typed behaviors such as nurturance and compassion. It was proposed that the person able to respond effectively to situational specificities would have an advantage over those people whose behavioral response repertoires were restricted. That is, the greater latitude of response alternatives afforded androgynous persons would enhance their effectiveness in dealing with the diverse situations of a variable, multiple role demand context. Implicit also was the idea that androgynous persons were actualizing a greater range of inherent potential, integrating various facets of their personalities.

These theory-based expectations of androgyny/psychological health relations differed from those of previously described congruence models of sex role development. The congruence model formulation suggested that congruity between biological gender and sex role orientation would facilitate psychological health. The androgyny model is not antithetical to the congruence model, but rather suggests that high levels of both masculinity and femininity results in greater psychological health than simple congruence between biological sex and sex role orientations. The measurement procedures developed by Bem (1974) and Spence and Helmreich (1978) were able to be used to investigate theoretical notions about the androgyny model formulation.

## Gerontological Literature

A third and distinct body of research concerned with sex roles and sex typing has been the gerontological literature. Whereas the childhood literature may be broadly characterized as concerned with the antecedents and mechanisms of same-sex role identification, the early adulthood literature with the relationships between androgyny and mental health indices, the gerontological literature may be characterized as concerned with intrapsychic developmental transformations and their consequences for successful aging.

Formalized interest in sex roles and aging has theoretical origins dating back to Jung (1933). Jung suggested that the surfacing of opposite-sex behavior was an intrinsic feature of the psychological transformation that takes place in the second half of life, a surfacing that provides the context for personality integration. According to Jung, males become inwardly aware of feminine components of their psyche (anima) and females become inwardly aware of masculine components of their psyche (animus). Within the research literature, Neugarten and Gutmann (1958) reported what were, at the time, unexpected differences among groups of younger (subjects aged 40–54) and older (subjects aged 55–70) males and females in response to a picture from the Thematic Apperception Test (TAT). The picture consisted of a family scene with an older man and woman and a younger man and woman apparently discussing something. In analyzing the responses to this picture, younger men and women consistently described the older man in the picture as the authority figure, whereas the older men and women consistently characterized the older woman in the picture as dominant and the older man in the picture as submissive. These responses of the older men and women were reversed in terms of stereotyped sex role patterns that were expected. Gutmann (1977) reported similar findings among older adults in diverse cultures, further suggesting that sex role reversibility or sex role flexibility may be a concomitant of the aging process.

A number of other investigations into the internal dynamics of personality functioning among older adults have tended to converge on the finding of a decrease in sex role differentiation occurring with older adults (e.g., Neugarten, Crotty, & Tobin, 1964; Reichard, Livson, & Peterson, 1962; Williams & Wirth, 1965). Furthermore, the sex role differentiation was associated with greater behavioral flexibility and successful aging. It is of interest to note that in most of these studies the primary purpose was not the investigation of androgynous sex role functioning, but rather into possible disengagement process among older adults or of various patterns of aging. The two principal methods of data collection used in these studies were semi-structured interviews and projective techniques. These more open-ended and less structured methods, relative to some behavioral observation methods or forced-choice tests, may have facilitated the emergence of patterns not predicted by theory. Quite different findings and interpretations might have resulted from using instruments embedded within a bipolar, unidimensional conceptualization of sex roles.

The general trends of these early gerontological personality studies have led many researchers to theorize about and a few to test the androgyny model as a useful guide for the lifespan study of sex role development (e.g., Hefner, Rebecca, & Oleshansky, 1975; Hyde & Phillis, 1979; Sinnott, 1977, in press; Windle & Sinnott, 1985). Although there are differences among these theoreticians regarding specific features of their androgyny formulations, they do, in general, suggest that an androgynous sex role may be especially advantageous to older adults who are in transition and who may be experiencing multiple, age-associated contextual demands regarding the nature of the self to the world. Sinnott (in press) has noted the limitations of unidimensional, acontextual models of sex role development, and has articulated a living systems model to aid in the conceptualization and measurement of multiple demand features that influence and are influenced by sex role behavior.

There have been few empirical studies of the androgyny model for older adults. In fact, to the author's knowledge there is no standard measure currently available to measure sex role functioning among older adults. Windle (in press) reports some of the limitations of using an instrument normed on college-aged samples, such as the BSRI, with older adults. High priority must be given to the development of sound measures of sex roles for older adults in order to pursue lifespan theoretical notions on sex role development.

In summary, we have reviewed the conceptualizations and measurement assumptions of sex roles and sex typing within the childhood, young adult, and gerontological literatures. Different questions pursued within each of these literatures influenced the manner in which sex roles and sex typing were conceptualized and measured. The congruence model most adequately described the childhood literature, whereas the androgyny model most adequately described the young adult and gerontological literatures. Given this general historical backdrop, we are now going to delve into some more specific issues related to measures and measurement.

## ON THE MEASUREMENT OF SEX ROLES AND SEX TYPING

In the previous sections various conceptualizations of sex roles and sex typing were provided along with the general manner in which instruments were designed to measure the constructs of these alternative models. Evidence for consistency between theoretical model and method of measurement was illustrated for both congruence and androgyny models. The next three sections focus on the following topics: (1) multidimensionality within the sex role and sex typing literature; (2) research design considerations in measuring sex role development; and (3) issues concerning the equivalent measurement of constructs across populations.

### Multidimensionality Issues

Two distinct issues related to multidimensionality have often been raised within the sex role and sex typing literature. The first pertains to the more traditional psychometric concern with the underlying dimensional structure of attributes such as masculinity and femininity. As noted previously, reconceptualizations of sex roles by investigators in the early adulthood literature (e.g., Bem, 1974; Spence & Helmreich, 1978) have consisted of proposals for two relatively orthogonal dimensions of masculinity and femininity. These bidimensional perspectives were contrasted with previous theorizing and instrument development procedures, which viewed masculinity and femininity as bipolarities of a unitary dimension.

However, differences exist regarding the adequacy of bidimensional measures such as the BSRI or PAQ to account for the variable range of behavior encompassed by the terms masculinity and femininity (Bem, 1981; Pedhazur and Tetenbaum, 1979; Spence, 1985; Spence & Helmreich, 1978; Windle & Sinnott, 1985). Spence and Helmreich (1978) have argued for a much more restrictive definition of the two traits measured by the PAQ and have preferred to describe the traits measured by the PAQ as instrumentality and expressivity. Spence (1985) has further suggested that the expectation of high predictive validity for these two specific traits in regard to global outcome variables is not very probable, due to the multi-causal nature of much human behavior. Others (e.g., Pedhazur & Tetenbaum, 1979; Windle & Sinnott, 1985) have applied factor analysis procedures to data collected on the BSRI and have found a two-factor solution to be inadequate. Rather, the number of factors tended to vary from 4 to 9 and the solutions differed for males and females. It appears therefore that masculinity and femininity may each be composed of multiple dimensions, suggesting that a multifactorial representation may facilitate the conceptualization and measurement of sex roles and sex typing (Spence, 1985; Windle & Sinnott, 1985).

A second issue relevant to multidimensionality has evolved from the plethora of constructs measured under the rubric of sex roles and sex typing, but which manifest consistent patterns of low intercorrelations among themselves (Huston, 1985; Orlofsky, 1981; Spence, 1985; Worell, 1981). Various classification schemes have been proffered to organize the numerous constructs in the sex role and sex typing literature (e.g., Huston, 1983), and for purposes of illustration, the following three construct classes are used: self-perception of personality; preferences and attitudes; and behavioral enactments or overt behavior. It is suggested that these three construct classes are probably better characterized as reflecting different but related content domains of human functioning, which in the past have, at least implicitly, been assumed in the sex role and sex typing literature to behave in a unitary, integrated fashion.

However, the empirical literature has not supported this unitary-function assumption (see Spence, 1985; Worell, 1981). One of the principal objectives of a study conducted by Orlofsky (1981) was to investigate the interrelationships among measures of sex role personality traits, sex role attitudes, and stereotypic masculine and feminine interests and role behaviors. The general finding was that a low correspondence characterized the interrelationships among the three domains. Furthermore, the few low-to-moderate relationships that were found tended to be more highly associated with biological sex rather than masculinity or femininity of personality traits, attitudes, or interests and role behaviors. A second point of interest in this study was the finding of larger differences between males and females regarding their sex role behaviors in comparison to their personality traits. Orlofsky (1981) proposed that powerful social contingencies (i.e., social norms) may contribute to the development and maintenance of identifiable sex-appropriate overt behavior, whereas personality traits, as abstract qualities, are not as subject to public scrutiny and influence. This theoretical proposal demonstrates the necessity for explicit formulations of differential causal agents involved in the development and maintenance of different features of sex role behavior.

In a separate study, Feather and Said (1983) used the BSRI with a sample of college students to investigate the interrelationships between personality, sex role traits, biological sex, and occupational preference. The general finding was that biological sex, rather than masculinity or femininity, was associated with occupational preference. The authors of the study concluded that in the investigation of occupational preferences, a clear distinction should be made between normatively based generalized expectations about sex role functioning in a given context (e.g., occupational preference), and the impact of specific personality traits related to instrumental and expressive skills. These conclusions are in accord with those of Spence and Helmreich (1978) regarding a more restrictive definition of masculinity and femininity.

Additionally, Feather and Said (1983) highlight the significance of considering the context in designing studies and anticipating relationships among variables. More specifically, the authors propose a need to understand features of a context (e.g., other salient characteristics or dimensions) that may moderate the expected sex role/outcome-variable relationships. Orlofsky (1981) raised a similar issue, in a somewhat different vein, when discussing expectations for cross-situational and, by extension, cross-temporal relations among sex role behaviors. Because individuals behave in a highly sex-typed manner in one aspect of their lives (e.g., vocational interests) cannot be construed to mean that they will behave in a similar way in other aspects (e.g., dating behavior). The more general issue here is that the psychological constructs developed by sex role researchers (as well as psychological constructs in other research domains) have a limited predictive scope and are constrained by features of the context. A future direction for sex role researchers to consider is how to incorporate some of the constraining features of various demand contexts into research designs so as to increase the explanatory and predictive power of sex role constructs.

As noted at the outset of this section and further illustrated by the two sample studies presented, the content domain of sex roles and sex typing cannot be characterized as homogeneous. Classification schemes such as Huston's (1983) are useful in distinguishing among the constructs associated with different content domains. Although there is no necessary reason why these content domains need to be highly interrelated and to function in a unitary fashion, it does seem that with appropriately developed measures, some moderate or even high interrelationships should be found for some specific constructs. One systematic way of addressing this issue would be to use, for example, a three-dimensional table (with axes such as sex role personality traits, attitudes, and overt behaviors) to organize various studies that have used sex role constructs. Studies of related sex role constructs could then be tabulated both within and between dimensions and thus serve as a heuristic device for integrating past and future research. This would be useful both in terms of identifying significant (and nonsignificant) relationships within and between construct classes, and in facilitating meta-analytic investigations.

## Research Design Considerations

Single occasion, one sample and cross-sectional research designs and univariate statistical models (e.g., one-way ANOVAs) have most frequently been used in research conducted within the sex role and sex typing literature. While these procedures may provide useful information about sex roles and sex typing, each is limited in addressing many of the salient theoretical and measurement issues previously discussed. A few examples will illustrate some of these limitations. First, single occasion one sample and cross-sectional research designs provide samples of behavior only at one point in time and thus restrict interpretations to descriptive age differences. That is, differences in occupational interests for males and females at various age levels do not provide an adequate data source for the developmental explanation for these differences. These same individuals might provide quite different occupational interests if measured at a second (and/ or third) occasion of measurement, and the differences between age levels may increase, decrease, or stay the same. Furthermore, from a substantive perspective, the rapidly changing social conditions that influence and are influenced by sex role expectations of appropriate behavior indicate that not only may individual patterns of sex role behavior undergo change, but that variation may be expected among birth cohorts. Schaie (1977) has proposed several research designs to disentangle some of the major sources of variance that must be accounted for in any comprehensive theory of development, including sex role.

Univariate statistical models are limited in applications to sex roles and sex typing for at least three reasons. First, many questions pertinent to the utilization of longitudinal research designs necessitate the use of some kind of multivariate model. For instance, if a research question arises pertinent to changes in the covariance relations of some manifest or latent sex role variables, univariate statistical models may be of little assistance. Second, to address issues associated with the dimensionality of constructs, such as masculinity and femininity, some multivariate model (e.g., factor analysis) is needed to investigate the dependency structures. In addition, to the extent that researchers seek to answer questions about the simultaneous influence of sex role behaviors on more than one dependent variable, it is appropriate to use a multivariate model representation (e.g., multivariate regression model). Third, multi-trait, multi-method (MTMM) techniques may be especially useful in pursuing issues relevant to the interrelationships of constructs within and between content domains of sex roles and sex typing. By using the MTMM methodology, it may be possible to obtain convergent relations among some measures for a given construct as well as providing discriminant validity for these same measures through their lack of association with other measured constructs.

## Measurement Equivalence

Measurement equivalence concerns the likelihood that a given measure is assessing corresponding manifest or latent variables when applied to multiple populations (Labouvie, 1980). For example, are the constructs of masculinity and femininity measured by the BSRI tapping similar latent constructs for males and females? For younger adults and older adults? Can we assume that responses to TAT cards are measuring similar psychological constructs among people of Western technological societies and primitive tribes in Africa?

Questions concerning measurement equivalence have for a long time been on the horizon of cross-cultural investigators. Increasingly, developmental psychologists have become sensitized to the issue in attempting to interpret findings in which tests normed on one sample are administered to other samples who are dissimilar on one or more dimensions (e.g., age). Windle and Sinnott (1985) investigated the issue of measurement equivalence in the application of the BSRI to an older adult sample. Confirmatory factor analytic techniques were used to investigate the probability that the factor structure of the BSRI for the older adult sample was similar to the two-dimensional model proposed for younger adults (Bem, 1974). The two-factor model did not result in an adequate fit for the older adult sample and subsequent exploratory factor analyses indicated that eight and nine-factor models fit better for older adult males and females, respectively. Thus, according to the statistical modeling approach used in this study to investigate measurement equivalence, the BSRI is measuring much more highly differentiated features of personality sex role traits among older, than among younger, adults. In addition, for the older adult sample structural differences were found between males and females, indicating that measurement was not completely equivalent between genders. Windle (in press) expands upon some of the issues involved in measurement equivalence and one method for addressing such issues.

The measurement equivalence issue merits more attention from researchers seeking to integrate literature from various phases of the life cycle and conducting research within a lifespan development perspective. Given the range of biological, psychological, and social/cultural forces influencing sex role development over the course of one's life, critical thought on the equivalence of measures at different points in the lifespan is essential.

## SUMMARY

A brief historical review of conceptualizations and measurements of sex roles and sex typing has been presented for literatures associated with childhood, early adulthood, and older adulthood. The childhood literature generally supports the congruence model of healthy psychological development, emphasizing the importance of sex role identification with the parent of the same biological sex. The origins of the congruence model were traced to Freud's theory of psychosexual development. A reconceptualization of sex roles emphasizing the orthogonality of the dimensions of masculinity and femininity was selected for review in the young adulthood literature. The androgyny model proposes that healthy psychological development results from high levels of both masculinity and femininity, and the associated flexibility of the behavioral repertoire in handling the variable demands of the environment. An androgyny model also characterizes the literature reviewed for older adults. Increasing sex role flexibility has been associated with greater life satisfaction and more successful aging for older adults.

Two separate issues of multidimensionality have been discussed. The first pertains to the multidimensionality of the constructs of masculinity and femininity. The second pertains to the multidimensionality of the content domain subsuming the many constructs studied in sex roles and sex typing. A three-dimensional matrix, reflecting the content domains of personality, sex role traits, sex role attitudes, and sex role behaviors is proposed as one way to organize and direct this variegated literature. Longitudinal research designs and multivariate statistical models were proposed as additional and often preferable means of conducting research on sex roles and sex typing. Finally, the importance of considering issues relevant to the equivalent measurement of constructs across populations was presented along with an application in the sex role literature.

## REFERENCES

Beere, C.A. (1979). *Women and women's issues: A handbook of tests and measures.* San Francisco: Jossey-Bass.

Bem, S.L. (1974). The measurement of psychological androgyny. *Journal of Consulting and Clinical Psychology, 42,* 155–162.

Bem, S.L. (1975). Sex role adaptability: One consequence of psychological androgyny. *Journal of Personality and Social Psychology, 31,* 634–643.

Bem, S.L. (1981). The BSRI and gender schema theory: A reply to Spence and Helmreich. *Psychological Review, 88,* 369–371.

Block, J.H. (1983). Differential premises arising from differential socialization of the sexes: Some conjectures. *Child Development, 54,* 1335–1354.

Constantinople, A. (1973). Masculinity–femininity: An exception to the famous dictum? *Psychological Bulletin, 80,* 389–407.

Feather, N.T. & Said, J.A. (1983). Preference for occupations in relation to masculinity, femininity, and gender. *British Journal of Social Psychology, 22,* 113–127.

Freud, S. (1933). *New introductory lectures on psychoanalysis.* New York: Norton.

Gutmann, D. (1977). The cross-cultural perspective. Notes on a comparative psychology of aging. In J.E. Birren & K.W. Schaie (Eds.), *Handbook of the psychology of aging.* New York: Van Nostrand.

Hefner, R., Rebecca, M., & Oleshansky, B. (1975). Development of sex-role transcendence. *Human Development, 18,* 143–158.

Huston, A.C. (1983). Sex typing. In P.H. Mussen & E.M. Hetherington (Eds.), *Handbook of child psychology* (Vol. 4, 4th ed.) *Socialization, personality, and social behavior.* New York: Wiley.

Huston, A.C. (1985). The development of sex typing: Themes from recent research. *Developmental Review, 5,* 1–17.

Hyde, J.S. & Phillis, D.E. (1979). Androgyny across the life-span. *Developmental Psychology, 15,* 334–336.

Jung, C.G. (1933). The states of life. In *Modern man in search of a soul.* (Trans. by W.S. Dell & C.F. Baynes). New York: Harcourt, Brace.

Kohlberg, L. (1966). A cognitive-developmental analysis of children's sex role concepts and attitudes. In E. Maccoby (Ed.), *The development of sex differences.* Stanford, CA: Stanford University Press.

Labouvie, E.W. (1980). Identity versus equivalence of psychological measures and constructs. In L.W. Poon (Ed.), *Aging in the 1980's: Selected contemporary issues in the psychology of aging.* Washington, D.C.: American Psychological Association.

Maccoby, E.E. & Jacklin, C.N. (1974). *The psychology of sex differences*. Stanford, CA: Stanford University Press.

Neugarten, B.L. & Gutmann, D.L. (1958). Age–sex roles and personality in middle age: A thematic apperception study. *Psychological Monographs: General and Applied, 17,* whole no. 470.

Neugarten, B.L., Crotty, W.F., & Tobin, S.S. (1964). *Personality in middle and late life*. New York: Atherton Press.

Orlofsky, J.L. (1981). Relationship between sex role attitudes and personality traits and the Sex Role Behavior Scale-1: A new measure of masculine and feminine role behaviors and interests. *Journal of Personality and Social Psychology, 40,* 927–940.

Pedhazur, E.J. & Tetenbaum, T.J. (1979). Bem Sex Role Inventory: A theoretical and methodological critique. *Journal of Personality and Social Psychology, 37,* 996–1016.

Reichard, S., Livson, F., & Peterson, P. (1962). *Aging and personality*. New York: Wiley.

Schaie, K.W. (1977). Quasi-experimental research designs in the psychology of aging. In J.E. Birren & K.W. Schaie (Eds.), *Handbook of the psychology of aging*. New York: Van Nostrand Reinhold.

Sedney, M.A. (1981). Comments on median split procedures for scoring androgyny measures. *Sex Roles, 7,* 217–222.

Sinnott, J.D. (1977). Sex-role inconstancy, biology, and successful aging. *Gerontologist, 17,* 459–463.

Sinnott, J.D. (In press). *Sex roles and aging: Theory and research from a systems perspective*. New York: S. Karger.

Spence, J.T. (1985). Gender identity and its implications for the concepts of masculinity and femininity. In T.B. Sonderegger (Ed.), Nebraska Symposium on Motivation, 1984: *Psychology and gender*. Lincoln: University of Nebraska Press.

Spence, J.T. & Helmreich, R.L. (1978). *Masculinity and femininity: Their psychological dimensions, correlates, and antecedents*. Austin: University of Texas Press.

Taylor, M.C. & Hall, J.A. (1982). Psychological androgyny: Theories, methods, and conclusions. *Psychological Bulletin, 92,* 347–366.

Whitley, B.E. (1983). Sex role orientation and self-esteem: A critical meta-analytic review. *Journal of Personality and Social Psychology, 44,* 765–778.

Williams, R. & Wirth, C. (1965). *Lives through the years*. New York: Atherton Press.

Windle, M. & Sinnott, J.D. (1985). A psychometric study of the Bem Sex Role Inventory with an older adult sample. *Journal of Gerontology, 40,* 336–343.

Windle, M. (In press). Methodological and statistical considerations in the measurement of sex roles and aging. In J.D. Sinnott (Ed.), *Sex roles and aging: Theory and research from a systems perspective*. New York: S. Karger.

Worell, J. (1981). Life-span sex roles: Development, continuity, and change. In R.M. Lerner & N.A. Busch-Rossnagel (Eds.), *Individuals as producers of their development: A life-span perspective*. New York: Academic Press.

# PART II
# LIFESPAN DEVELOPMENTAL
# ISSUES IN SEX ROLES AND SEX
# TYPING

# 4
# The Ontogeny and Phylogeny of Sex Differences in Development: A Biopsychosocial Synthesis

Kathryn E. Hood
Patricia Draper
Lisa J. Crockett
Anne C. Petersen

The universality of identification as female or male provides a salient focus for the reconstruction of theories about biological and behavioral interactions in development. The study of sex roles, in particular, stands to benefit from a creative integration that will go beyond the view that a well-adapted person must happily accept the limits of one's sex role proscriptions. Contemporary views of human potential are expanding the limited views of mechanistic science and the biased perspectives of implicitly male science, toward the goal of an integrative developmental account of the evolutionary, social, and historical forces that produce sex-related differences in behavior. To fully achieve this goal, a process of consistent and methodological comparison and synthesis must be applied to the new discoveries of biobehavioral science, in the separate fields of developmental psychology, evolutionary theory, cognition, comparative physiology, and neuroscience.

In this chapter we present a selective review of issues related to sex-typed development. We will use biological development as a framework within which to understand behavioral development. The review is necessarily far ranging, including topical issues from diverse fields of scientific activity. To present a biopsychosocial perspective that balances this changing array of biological, experiential, and social factors shaping individual development, we present an example from the study of cognitive development, focused on sex-related differences in specific skill areas. In our view, this model of biopsychosocial synthesis may be fruitful for understanding other areas of sex-role development, for example, achievement, aggressive behavior, parenting relationships, family roles, and lifespan employment patterns. Finally, we consider biological aspects of sex roles from an evolutionary perspective, introducing issues of individual and group adaptation, alternative strategies in reproduction, and the uniquely human aspects of social evolution that are critical for understanding our possible future sex-role adaptations.

A consideration of the biological aspects of sex differences in human behavior requires posing two key questions. First, how do biological factors promote sex differences in behavior in the course of individual development? Are there genetic, hormonal, or brain-related differences in the sexes that create sex differences in behavior? Second, how and why would gender differences in behavior evolve in the human species? These two questions involve different time frames: In the first, we are interested in the emergence of sex differences during ontogeny; in the second, we are interested in the evolution of sex differences over successive generations. Different kinds of answers are prompted by the two questions. Answers to the first question typically address proximal causes, because they specify the processes or means by which sex differences emerge. Answers to the second question may relate to issues of ultimate causation. For example, they may specify the process by which sexually dimorphic characteristics in a species are selected in the course of evolution.

Explanations for human behavior that come from different levels or theoretical perspectives (such as those of the social sciences) are not incompatible with or contradictory to those which come from evolutionary biology. Indeed, the different approaches each aim to determine what combination of factors in some causal sequence accounts for a given phenomenon. Tinbergen (1963) suggested that questions about the causation of behavior can be subdivided into four categories, each of which reflects a different level of analysis: immediate causation, ontogeny, ultimate causation, and phylogeny. The four differ in terms of specifying proximate versus more distal causes, and also differ in the time-frame presumed to operate in the causal sequence.

1. *Immediate causation.* What is the immediate cause of a behavior, in the most proximate sense? For example, are boys more aggressive than girls because agents of socialization are more tolerant of aggressive behavior in boys, or because boys have higher testosterone levels than girls?

2. *Ontogeny.* What are the maturational factors in the individual's life history that account for the behavior? Is it possible that boys are more aggressive than girls because, over the course of fetal and juvenile development, the central nervous system of the male is exposed to testosterone, which may produce an individual in whom aggressive behavior is more readily elicited? Alternatively, the behavioral difference may result from high activity levels, characteristic of boys, in combination with same-sex peer preferences, which are reinforced by social and educational developmental structures.

3. *Ultimate causation.* Did the behavior (in the past eons of the evolutionary environment) increase the probability that an individual will leave more offspring (who may carry the trait, if it is genetically based) than other individuals? The issues having to do with sex differences in patterns of reproductive success are crucial in order for a particular form or constellation of sex-related behaviors to evolve and become genetically fixed in populations of diverse species.

4. *Phylogeny*. Why, in the phylogenetic development of human species, would natural selection have favored the development of sex dimorphism with respect to some features, such as distribution of facial hair or body size?

The various disciplines that study human sex roles and sex typing can be classified in terms of their preference for the various levels of explanation. Because for the most part sociologists, psychologists, and anthropologists are concerned with change and continuity in the lives of individuals, they typically ask questions that are appropriate to the levels of ontogeny and immediate causation.

The phylogenetic perspective on sex differences in social development is concerned with change and continuity in a species whose antecedents stretch back millions of years. Evolutionary theorists, therefore, are naturally concerned with levels of explanation that address phylogeny and ultimate causation (Chisholm, 1980; Daly & Wilson 1983; vanden Berghe, 1979). The field of sociobiology offers a very different view of the "meaning" or the "reason" for sex differences in humans. The most salient aspects of sociobiological theory for this essay have to do with sex differences in reproductive function and the consequences of the functional difference for behavioral strategies on the part of the two sexes (Alexander, 1974; Trivers, 1972).

## Sexual Differentiation

Sexual differentiation refers to the biological processes governing the development of male and female individuals and leading to characteristic physical differences between the two. Multiple levels of causation underlie the process of sex differentiation in behavior: particularly, genes, hormones, and brain organization. Because these factors are themselves intertwined in the process of sexual differentiation, we begin with a discussion of sexual differentiation and then move to gender differences in gonadal hormones and brain organization and, finally, review the evidence relating these factors to gender differences in behavior. Thus, biological sex differences may occur at four levels: genes, hormones, morphology, and brain organization.

*Genes*. In normal development, sexual differentiation begins with an individual's complement of genes. Individuals inherit 23 pairs of chromosomes from their parents, including one pair of sex chromosomes. The identity of the sex chromosomes differs for males and females: in mammals, genetic females have two X chromosomes; genetic males have one X and one Y. The identity of the sex chromosomes determines whether male or female reproductive glands will develop from the undifferentiated gonadal tissue present in both sexes. Ovaries develop unless an individual carries an X and a Y chromosome; in that case, testes develop. Experimental studies using animals have demonstrated that the ovaries are not required for female reproductive structures to develop: even if the female gonads are surgically removed, at an early age, normal female development proceeds (Goy & McEwen, 1980). Similarly, humans having only a single X chromosome and in whom neither ovaries nor testes develop, are born with normal female external genitalia. If the XY complement is inherited, then the primitive gonads differentiate into testes during the sixth fetal week in humans. This process is guided by surface markers on each cell that code for genetic sex, the H-Y antigens (Wachtel, 1977). The events that follow are caused by the action of the testes. Male hormones, testosterone and other androgen metabolites, are secreted by the newly-differentiated testes and perfuse the local area to influence the differentiation of the reproductive tracts, producing the vas deferens, epididymis, urethra, and prostate, instead of the fallopian tubes, uterus, and vagina. A yet unidentified substance secreted by the testes causes the degeneration of the rudimentary female reproductive tracts.

As the circulatory system develops further, androgens are carried to the external genitalia, which form into the male structures, penis and scrotum, instead of clitoris and labia. The last stage in fetal sex differentiation involves specific brain structures in areas of the hypothalamus, which are sensitive to the presence of sex hormones. When the circulatory system is adequately developed, hormones from the testes reach the brain, and permanently alter the biochemical sensitivity of specific brain areas. Morphological differences in female and male brains are limited to the preoptic area of the hypothalamus, in humans found to be larger, with more neurons, in males than in females (Swaab & Fliers, 1985). In animals, this area of hypothalamus is sexually dimorphic, and associated with reproductive behaviors. In addition, a recent study of human brains reports a sex difference in the shape of the corpus callosum—the bundle of nerve fibers connecting the two hemispheres. The hind portion of this structure was reported to be larger and rounder in females than in males (de Lacoste-Utamsing & Holloway, 1982). Because this same area is known to play a role in the transfer of visual information between hemispheres, the authors speculate that the larger size of the area in females is related to the finding that females are more likely than males to process visual-spatial tasks bilaterally (that is, drawing equally on both hemispheres). However, the relationship between anatomical differences and sex-related differences in cognitive functioning has not been clearly established (McGlone, 1980). Furthermore, Witelson (1985) failed to replicate the earlier finding of a larger corpus callosum in females and felt that the earlier result was due to sampling artifact (also see Hier, 1981).

It appears, then, that the male is the induced phenotype. Prenatal development of female sexual structures is primarily under genetic regulation, and no gonadal hormones are necessary for female development to occur. In contrast, the organizing action of prenatal testicular androgens is necessary to produce male differentiation. In other words, sex differences in androgen secretion prenatally appear to be responsible for sexual dimorphism in genital morphology. During a critical period of early development, the bisexual potential of an individual is to become either a female or an androgen-induced male. Changes at puberty will again produce sex differences in gonadal hormones, which will cause the second active phase of sexual differentiation, activating sex differences in morphology and in behavior. There is wide variation, both between species and within species, in the forms of gonadal hormones that are active during development. For example, in different strains of mice, some use testosterone, others use aromatized testosterone (estradiol), and others use dihydrotestosterone as the inducing agent in neonatal sex differentiation (Ward, 1984; Whalen & Simon, 1984). For reviews of these aspects of development, useful sources are Feder (1984), Forest (1983), Goy and McEwen (1980), Jost (1970), Mackinnon (1979), Money and Ehrhardt (1972), Parsons (1980), Stumpf (1975), and Wilson, George, and Griffin (1981). In particular Moore (1985) emphasizes that the brain is only one possible target for sex hormones; peripheral sensory systems are also hormone responsive, and may produce sex differentiated responses to social and contextual stimuli.

*Endocrine Systems.* One consequence of genetic sex is the development of a sex-differentiated endocrine system, including the gonads, mammary glands, the pituitary gland, and specific brain areas in the hypothalamus. The development of either ovaries or testes is a crucial step in sexual differentiation because these glands produce gonadal hormones that organize further physical and neural development as male or female, the "organizational" effects of hormones (e.g., Gorski, 1980; Phoenix et al., 1959). Both prenatally and in adulthood, clear sex differences can be found in the average concentrations of sex hormones, with males having much higher levels of androgen than do females, on the average, and females having far more estrogen than do males. Actually, both males and females produce small amounts of the gonadal hormones associated with the other sex, so that the important sex difference is in the ratio of androgen to estrogen. Furthermore, since hormones are inactive when they are bound to other substances in the blood, it is technically the ratio of "free" androgen to estrogen that produces male/female differences.

In females, with lower levels of neonatal androgen (and no testes), the typical female pattern of cyclic responsiveness to sex hormones emerges at puberty, eventuating in ovulation and menstruation, paced by the hypothalamic-pituitary feedback system. In studies of nonhumans, prenatal exposure of females to androgen results in a male-type tonic, or steady-state, response pattern. Moreover, in the period just prior to and after birth, hormonal levels undergo a dramatic increase, temporarily reaching adult concentrations and producing an extreme sex difference in hormonal levels. Thus there are at least two points during fetal development when hormones might be expected to affect the brains of males and females differentially. The "organizing" effect of androgens, which changes the responsiveness of specific brain areas, ensures that appropriate adult patterns will occur at puberty, when increased levels of sex hormones will activate these organized structures (Phoenix, Goy, Gerall, & Young, 1959). Two conclusions can be drawn from this: female development is the basis from which male patterns deviate; and fetal development includes an organizing effect on the brain by sex hormones from the fetal gonads, which is expressed at puberty when sex hormones activate the organized tissues. These conclusions are based on animal studies, for example the work with nonhuman primates by Goy (1970) and Resko (1974). The extent to which these findings also apply to human development is presently unknown. (For a discussion of these issues, see Ehrhardt, 1985; Ward, 1984.)

At puberty, males and females are further distinguished by the development of secondary sex characteristics, which are also a function of gonadal hormones. During childhood, the levels of these hormones are kept low through the operation of a negative feedback system (Grumbach, 1980; Grumbach, Roth, Kaplan, & Kelch, 1974). At puberty the suppression of the system is gradually released, so that higher levels of gonadal hormones are tolerated. The large amounts of gonadal hormones produced at puberty exert an "activational" effect on body tissues, bringing about the development of secondary sex characteristics (Tanner, 1972). Increased levels of androgen produce voice deepening, facial hair growth, and further genital development in boys; increased androgens also stimulate the growth of pubic and underarm hair in both sexes. Increased estrogen levels lead to breast development and widening of the hips in girls (Petersen & Taylor, 1980). Both boys and girls undergo a spurt in height and weight during puberty, which is in part dependent on gonadal hormones (Tanner, Whitehouse, Hughes, & Carter, 1976). After puberty, males tend to be taller than females, broader through the shoulders (relative to the hips), and to have more facial and body hair. Females have larger breasts and broader hips (relative to shoulders).

Endocrine factors are clearly involved in the pacing of social developmental patterns in nonhuman animals. The appearance of sexual behaviors and changes in the intensity and frequency of aggressive interactions are salient features associated with the onset of puberty. From experimental manipulations of hormone levels in female and male animals, we know that the hormonal changes at puberty enhance sexual solicitation. In the case of aggressive behaviors, there is an opposite pattern by sex: marked pubertal enhancement of fighting in males and suppression in females (Barkley & Goldman, 1977; Beeman, 1947; Bronson & Desjardins, 1968; Edwards, 1969; McKinney & Desjardins, 1973). Patterns of female aggression during the ovulatory cycle of females, when hormone levels show large changes, support the proposition that gonadal hormones, such as progesterone, may actively inhibit the aggressiveness of females at puberty (Hood, 1984; Kislak & Beach, 1955).

These developmental patterns have led investigators to postulate that these same relationships obtain in human development (but see Benton, 1983, for a discussion of this phylogenetic leap). Going beyond developmental changes, some descriptive work has shown a relationship to exist in humans between individual differences in social status or aggressiveness and individual differences in androgen levels (e.g., Olweus, Mattsson, Schalling, & Low, 1980; Purifoy & Koopmans, 1980). The interpretation of these findings is complicated by the fact that androgen levels are responsive to environmental and social stress (for examples, see Harding, 1981; Kreuz, Rose, & Jennings, 1972; Mazur & Lamb,

1980). Obtained correlations between hormone levels and aggressive behavior may result from bidirectional influences. Environmental factors (or perceptions of environmental factors) alter both behavior and circulating androgen levels (e.g., Leshner, 1978, p. 324; Roche & Leshner, 1979). Simultaneously, changes in circulating androgens may change an individual's behavior, or an individual's interpretation of the social or physical environment. This bidirectional pattern of influences precludes an obvious causal inference from correlational findings.

Recent findings suggest, however, that pubertal development is one factor "driving" sexual behavior (e.g., Dorn, Petersen, & Crockett, 1986; Udry et al., 1986). The Udry research has identified testosterone level as more important than pubertal status (which also has a social stimulus effect). Social factors are, nevertheless, implicated as well because: (1) of variation among gender and racial groups in the importance of endocrine factors relative to somatic characteristics; (2) of greatest predictive power in the combination of biological and social influences; and (3) of finding that most young black males in their sample first experience intercourse prepubertally.

Ehrhardt (1985) offers a consideration of the interaction of hormone–behavior relationships in the context of structures provided by the social environment.

Thus, a hormonal factor at one point in development is surely not the determinant of a complex behavior at a much later point in the life course. However, it may present one of the links in a long chain of events leading to the expression of a specific trait. But even if that kind of developmental sequence can be analyzed for a specific behavior set, it clearly does not mean that there is only one pathway for the expression of the same behavior. For instance, while prenatal androgen may predispose to rough-and-tumble play, it requires special social environmental reinforcement for the behavior expression to occur. The same behavior pattern may be developed in an individual with a relatively low level of prenatal androgens with a different, more strongly reinforcing social environment. The pliability of the human organism is such that *many* pathways during the life course lead to similar behavior sets.

Research conducted by Crockett (1986) found exactly such an environmental contingency. In observations of school-age children at play, the extent to which girls and boys segregated into same-sex groups was dependent on the social structure provided by the school environment, curriculum, and tradition. Some schools fostered same-sex play groups; others had only mixed-sex groups. Environmental contingencies clearly overwhelmed any sex-related preference.

*Brain.* The development of sex-related differences in behavior in nonhuman animals is mediated by specific brain structures that, in adults, are structurally or functionally differentiated because of early exposure to sex hormones. For example, areas of the hypothalamus that are involved in sexual behavior are altered by the organizing effects of neonatal gonadal hormones. The female hypothalamus in adults shows a cyclic pattern of responsiveness, which paces ovulation, while the male hypothalamus, which had been exposed to a neonatal androgen surge, shows in adulthood a tonic pattern of response. Female differentiation, and female brain development, occurs in the presence of XX sex chromosomes, or in the absence of gonads. In order for male brain development to occur, there must be an androgen surge from the fetal testes, during a specific period in brain development. From experimental studies with animals, we know that this period of brain sensitivity to androgen occurs well after physical structures have been formed (Goy & McEwen, 1980). At this later stage, the circulatory system is extensively developed, and exposure to androgens produces a permanent change in the ultrastructure and function of the medial preoptic area (MPOA), a specific brain area in the anterior portion of the hypothalamus in animals (Gorski, 1980). In humans, a similar sex difference in the MPOA has been reported (Swaab & Fliers, 1985). This should be interpreted in light of the fact that, while humans are sex-differentiated in brain-endocrine-reproductive function, there are no exclusively masculine or feminine motor patterns of copulation. Among humans, sexual behavior is not highly sex dimorphic (Beach, 1978).

## Human Clinical Syndromes

Clinical syndromes, in which there is some discrepancy between genetic sex, gonadal hormones, and sex of rearing, can help elucidate the role of genes and hormones in the development of gender identity and gender dimorphic behavior. Three syndromes are of particular interest to our discussion: androgen insensitivity or testicular feminizing syndrome, Turner's syndrome, and adrenogenital syndrome. Landmark work on these syndromes was conducted by a research team at Johns Hopkins University (e.g., Money & Ehrhardt, 1972).

*Androgen insensitivity.* The androgen insensitivity syndrome is a rare disorder affecting genetic males. Because of a genetic defect, the bodies of these individuals cannot utilize androgen. Thus, although their testes produce androgen both prenatally and postnatally, the androgen has no effect on body tissue, including brain. Under these circumstances, the external genitalia differentiate as female. Because of their feminine appearance, these individuals are typically assigned and raised as female. At puberty, the small amounts of estrogen produced by normal testes are sufficient to induce breast growth and the development of a feminine body contour. Of course, these women cannot menstruate or bear children.

A study of 10 girls and women with androgen insensitivity (Money & Ehrhardt, 1972) indicated that these individuals conformed strongly to the feminine cultural stereotype. In clinical interviews, most reported a positive interest in raising a family and in caring for infants, and as adults, two adopted and reared children. Most also reported having played primarily with dolls and other "feminine" toys as children. Among the adults, sexual activity was exclusively heterosexual, and most reported average libido and a tendency to be the passive partner. Most liked feminine clothing and reported a strong interest in personal adornment. Importantly, almost all rated themselves as being happy with the female role.

Thus, despite their genetic sex and their male gonads, these individuals appeared feminine in gender identity and gender role. There was no evidence that genetic sex in any way masculinized these individuals. Rather, the combination of female morphology and being reared as a girl produced a feminine individual.

*Turner's syndrome*. A second syndrome involves individuals who develop with only a single "X" chromosome, rather than a pair of sex chromosomes. In such individuals, neither ovaries nor testes develop, with the result that gonadal hormones are entirely absent. Prenatally, these individuals differentiate as female, and at birth they are assigned as female. Estrogen therapy allows them to undergo a normal female puberty.

One study compared 15 girls with Turner's syndrome to matched controls (Money & Ehrhardt, 1972). There was no significant difference between the two groups in perceptions of being a tomboy (this was rare in both groups), in satisfaction with the female role, in preference for female playmates, or in preferred clothing. Turner's syndrome girls and controls also appeared similar on childhood indicators of interest in romance, marriage, and the maternal role. Where differences did appear between the two groups, Turner's syndrome girls appeared to be more feminine than the normal controls: they were less athletic, fought less as children, and had a greater interest in jewelry, perfume, and other aspects of personal adornment. Overall, then, these girls were highly feminine despite genetic and hormonal abnormalities. Based on these girls, feminine gender identity and gender role appear to be dependent neither on the presence of two "X" chromosomes nor on the presence of prenatal estrogen.

*Adrenogenital syndrome (AGS)*. A third syndrome involves genetic females who are exposed to androgens in utero. Under the influence of androgen, the external genitalia of these females become partially masculinized with varying degrees of clitoral enlargement and labial fusion. In AGS proper, the excess androgen results from a genetically based malfunctioning of the fetal adrenal glands; instead of producing cortisol, the adrenals produce androgen. Similar masculinization of the external genitalia can result from the administration of certain pregnancy-saving drugs having androgenergic properties. In the latter cases, masculinization ceases at birth, whereas in AGS individuals, virilization continues postnatally unless cortisone therapy is introduced. In either instance, the infant is usually assigned as female, and corrective surgery performed to give the genitalia a normal female appearance. Both parents and patients were informed that childbearing would be possible but complicated for these girls.

The importance of AGS (and drug-induced masculinization) is that the prenatal androgens that masculinize the external genitalia may also have had an effect on brain pathways. Thus the gender identity and behavior of these girls is especially interesting. Two samples of fetally androgenized girls were studied initially: one group of 15 for whom hormonal masculinization ceased at birth, and an older group of 23 AGS girls and women who continued to be virilized until adolescence because earlier treatment was not available (Money & Ehrhardt, 1972). The findings for both groups are similar, although more divergence from normal girls was found among those with postnatal as well as prenatal exposure to androgen.

Compared to matched controls, the prenatally androgenized girls were more likely to be considered tomboys; they showed a greater preference for physically energetic play, for boys as playmates, and for cars and guns over dolls. Interestingly, however, they did not differ from controls in level of aggressiveness or in childhood sex play (according to maternal report). Several differences appeared between the groups in life plans and fantasies. Whereas control girls focused on marriage and having children as life goals, androgenized girls generally subordinated marriage to career (or wanted both); many also lacked certainty about their desire to have children. Consonant with these preferences, they were somewhat late in starting to date and in marrying.

Girls and women who had been exposed to androgen prenatally and postnatally were substantially virilized, with dark body hair and deep voice tone. Behaviorally, they were similar to the first sample in that they recalled being tomboys and preferred to have a career outside the home. In addition, they reported a high incidence of homosexual fantasies along with heterosexual fantasies. A few reported homosexual experiences, and many were not actively considering having children. Still, none felt she should have been raised as a male. Moreover, the majority eventually married and several had children.

The studies of these girls indicate that some aspects of childhood behavior (e.g., play preferences) may be sensitive to prenatal androgen. The interpretation of these clinical observations is complicated, however, by the fact that statistical and methodological procedures are not strong in these studies and other investigations have not replicated these findings (McGuire, Ryan, & Owen, 1975). The girls' parents were informed at birth that their children were abnormal, with ambiguous genitalia at birth. Many families had more than one intersex child. The influence of this situation on parental attitudes and childrearing practices is potentially important in accounting for these children's development. The anticipation of unusual difficulties in childbearing may have influenced the girls' future role interests involving marriage, career, and childbearing. In addition, many of the children underwent genital reconstruction by surgery, and they were maintained on treatment regimens of cortisone. Increased activity level is one side effect of cortisone, which may have produced the male-type play patterns observed in these patients.

In summary, the evidence suggests that neither prenatal nor postnatal androgen exposure necessitates the adoption of a masculine gender role or identity. Any "masculine" preferences of AGS girls appeared to become incorporated into a feminine gender identity.

*Five-"alpha" (5–"alpha") reductase deficiency.* A recently described metabolic disorder offers unique insights into biological and social perspectives of sex role development. In two small villages in the Dominican Republic, 18 persons have been studied who carry a genetic deficiency that blocks dihydrotestosterone, DHT, a metabolite of testosterone, and prevents the development of male-type genitalia. At birth, these genetic males looked like girls, and they were raised as girls, with feminine household tasks and female socialization, in a highly sex-segregated social setting. At puberty, the development of secondary sexual characteristics was not prevented by the genetic condition, and these "girls" suddenly developed into boys, with deep voices, enlarged penile and testicular structures, erections, and ejaculations from a urethral opening at the root of the penis (Imperato-McGinley, Peterson, Gautier, & Sturla, 1979). The outcome of this incongruous developmental pattern has been that 16 of the 18 people studied successfully reversed their sex roles at puberty. After more than 10 years of training in female sex-role patterns, they switched to the male pattern, selected women for marriage partners, and fully assumed male roles in their society. This developmentally delayed, yet complete change of sex role could result from the characteristically human flexibility in adapting to a changing set of social demands. Alternatively, it could result from early brain organization in a male pattern due to the normal levels of testosterone circulating during fetal development, in this syndrome. The causal sequence is undetermined, but apparently, early male-type socialization and genital development are not necessary for adult male sex-role socialization to be completely successful.

The evidence from clinical syndromes provides limited support for the notion that some aspects of gender dimorphic behavior reflect biological predispositions. Although chromosomal or genetic sex per se appears to have no effect on either gender identity or gender role behavior, there is some evidence that prenatal (and perhaps postnatal) hormones play a role, presumably through effects on the brain. Importantly, the influence of prenatal androgens appears to shape, but not to determine, masculine role behavior. Genetic females, some of whom received enough androgen exposure to almost completely masculinize their external genitalia, developed a feminine gender identity and performed many feminine role behaviors despite the fact that they exhibited more "masculine" play preferences and interests than did control girls. Thus, at least at the doses received by these girls, it appears that androgen may affect only a limited number of behaviors. Any other effects are evidently overridden by postnatal social experience, with the result that, in most cases, behavior and identity conform fairly well to sex of rearing.

## Sex Differences in Behavior: The Case of Cognition

In humans, very few behaviors show clear sex differences. In their important review of research on gender differences, Maccoby and Jacklin (1974) concluded that there were four areas in which there was evidence for gender differences in behavior: aggressiveness, spatial ability, mathematics achievement, and verbal ability. The evidence on cognition suggested that males excel in spatial ability and mathematics achievement and that females excel in verbal ability.

In a recent meta-analysis, Linn and Petersen (1985) found that only two aspects of spatial ability show reliable sex differences: horizontality/verticality and mental rotations (also see Hyde, 1981). The effects with horizontality/verticality exist as early as this test has been given, by about age seven. In mental rotations the magnitude of the gender difference is one standard deviation (or 8 percent of the total variance) with a three-dimensional task; the size of the effect with a two-dimensional task is about one-fourth of a standard deviation. The difference exists as early as the test has been given, which is about eleven years of age. Performance on mental rotations tasks, and the obtained gender difference, appears to result from differences in the speed of visual image rotation; this difference could result from differential brain processing capacity, or alternatively, from the use of different cognitive strategies such as attention deployment or cautiousness. Studies with older adults find that the gender difference disappears after one training trial (e.g., Krauss, 1985; Willis, 1985). We should note that some test constructors use gender differences as a validation criterion; when creating tests of spatial ability, they deliberately select items on which males excel.

## Biological Hypotheses about Sex Differences

The primary hypotheses that have been pursued to explain individual and gender differences in cognition involve biological influences. The proposed biological hypotheses have referred to such factors as genetic influences, hormonal influences, the timing of maturation, and differences in brain organization to explain differences in cognitive ability. A more complex causal model (Petersen, 1981), however, must include a broader set of factors, including sociocultural hypotheses, with sex role socialization, sex typing of intellectual areas, and differences in experience as factors producing differences in cognitive abilities. We will briefly review the current status of evidence in these areas.

Genetic explanations have frequently been invoked to account for individual and sex differences in cognitive performance. Traits that are X-linked show a distinctive pattern of parent-to-child correlations, because in males the X chromosome (and hence the gene) is only inherited from the mother, whereas females can inherit the gene from either parent. With X-linked traits, correlations between mother and son are highest, mother-daughter and father-daughter correlations similar and intermediate, and father-son correlations are lowest. The main cognitive trait for which some evidence of X linkage has been reported is spatial visualizing ability—the ability to mentally rotate three-dimensional figures. The early evidence (Bock & Kolakowski, 1973; Hartlage, 1970; Stafford, 1961) has not been confirmed in later studies (Boles, 1980; Vandenberg & Kuse, 1979); therefore the possibility of X linkage for cognitive abilities remains controversial.

Hormonal influences have also been identified as possible correlates of cognition (cf. Petersen, 1979, 1980, 1983; Petersen & Wittig, 1979). The evidence for hormonal influence comes primarily from two sources: (1) studies correlating hormonal levels with cognition in normal individuals, and (2) studies examining cognition in subjects with genetic/endocrine anomalies.

The main finding of this literature is that some forms of spatial ability (that is, spatial visualization) are related to androgen levels. Presumably, androgens exert their effect on the same brain areas potentially affected by prenatal and pubertal hormones. It may be that a sensitivity to androgens in these areas is established prenatally and is subsequently maintained by adult hormone levels.

The fact that males tend to outperform females on tests of spatial ability and also tend to have higher androgen levels leads to the expectation that higher androgen levels would be associated with better spatial skills. Given this expectation, the findings with respect to postpubertal androgen levels are somewhat surprising. When men and women are arranged by androgen level along a single continuum, those individuals whose androgen levels are in the intermediate range tend to do best on spatial tasks (reviewed in Petersen, 1979). Because women tend to have low androgen levels and men tend to have high levels, it is the women with high androgen levels relative to other women and men with low levels relative to other men who seem to do best (Petersen, 1976). The same pattern emerged in a recent replication study (Berenbaum & Resnick, 1982), although the finding did not reach statistical significance. A similar pattern was observed when androgen concentrations were directly measured in the blood, and, in this case, the curvilinear relationship reached statistical significance (Cantoni, Pellegrino, & Hubert, 1981). Finally, the association was replicated when self-ratings of body shape were used to estimate hormone levels (Petersen & Gitelson, forthcoming). The fact that the pattern emerged with even this crude a measure indicates that the relationship is robust. The strength of the association between androgen and spatial ability has been greater in males than in females, although it varies somewhat depending on the particular measures employed.

Alternatively, it has been hypothesized that in adults cognition is affected not so much by absolute hormone levels as by periodic fluctuations in the levels of these hormones. Such fluctuations are typical of the female menstrual cycle. However, cyclic fluctuations in hormone levels have not been linked to consistent changes in cognitive performance (reviewed in Dan, 1979), and even though some aspects of behavior may vary over the menstrual cycle (for example, activity level, sensory threshold), these changes seem to have little effect on cognitive performance (Golub, 1976; Sommer, 1982). Thus it is unlikely that hormonal fluctuations could account for sex-related differences in cognition.

It has been hypothesized that pubertal hormones have an analogous effect on important aspects of brain development. Specifically, Waber (1976, 1977) proposed that the upsurge in hormones at puberty curtails brain lateralization—the progressive specialization of the cerebral hemispheres for differing cognitive functions. Because boys on the average reach maturity two years later than girls, the lateralization process may continue that much longer in boys, with the result that at maturity males would tend to be more lateralized than females. Waber's hypothesis fits the research finding of greater laterality or asymmetry of function in males. Moreover, Waber found that later maturers of both sexes tended to score higher on measures of spatial ability relative to measures of verbal ability. If greater lateralization is assumed to improve efficiency and hence performance, Waber's data would support her contention that the timing of puberty affects both brain organization and cognition. The sex difference in performance on cognitive (at least spatial) tests could then be explained as a secondary effect of a sex-related difference in the typical age at which maturity is reached.

Some subsequent studies have replicated the association between later maturation and better spatial performance (Carey & Diamond, 1980; Newcombe & Bandura, 1983; Petersen & Gitelson, forthcoming), although other studies have failed to confirm it (Herbst & Petersen, 1979; Petersen, 1976). For the most part, the effect of timing on cognitive performance appears to be a weak one most likely observed when extreme groups (for example, very early versus very late developers) are compared. No study, however, has replicated Waber's second finding of an association between timing of maturation and degree of lateralization. Individuals who reach maturity relatively late do not seem to show more asymmetric functioning than those who mature early. Moreover, sex differences in laterality are not always observed (for example, Kail & Siegel, 1978; Petersen, 1981).

The evidence linking brain structure to spatial ability is limited, with the further qualification that what we know is based on human clinical data (Luria, 1966; for a discussion, see Crockett & Petersen, 1984). Even when a sex difference is found, the magnitude is likely to be small. In many ways, then, the brain organizations of males and females are more similar than they are different.

## Effects of Experience on Brain Development

Recent research in brain development has stimulated a radical revision of our conception of the developmental interactions of brain structure, behavior, and experience. There is very exciting research that demonstrates the plasticity of the brain and the multiple levels of influence of experience on brain differentiation and growth (for a review, see Lerner, 1984). Brain growth, like growth in other organs, is genetically programmed to take place within a particular range of environments. Growth can be enriched by providing an enriched environment, or limited by an impoverished environment. The occurrence of changes in brain structure in response to experience in animals of very advanced age supports the case that plasticity in brain structure persists throughout the life span (Buell & Coleman, 1979; Greenough & Schwark, 1984). A significant part of brain growth and development occurs after birth. Postnatal brain growth primarily involves growth in size and complexity of neurons and of their dendritic and axonal support cells and synaptic connections. Preliminary reports of studies of avian brain development suggest that, contrary to the previously accepted dogma, neural regeneration and replacement may be a process that is active throughout the life span (Nottebaum, 1984; for a survey of contemporary findings on adult brain plasticity, see the special issue of *Science, 225,* 1984). It is neural pathways in the brain that provide for complexity and flexibility of behavior. In humans, the major expansion in the neural dendritic and synaptic network takes place in the first two years of life. Growth continues to adulthood, and the ability to form new connections persists throughout most of the lifespan (for a review, see Greenough & Green, 1981; Lynch & Gall, 1979; Rozenzweig, 1984).

The significance of this pattern in neural growth is that especially in humans a substantial amount of brain growth occurs under the influence of, and in functional interaction with, the environment. Indeed, input from the external world is essential for many aspects of normal brain development and function to occur. For example, the psychosocial environment of rearing affects brain development in monkeys (Prescott, 1975).

## THE BIOPSYCHOSOCIAL SYNTHESIS

In every study of human gender differences, biological sex is completely confounded with social and psychological sex. There have been few investigations of socialization effects on gender differences in cognitive abilities, and relatively many investigations seeking biological explanations for the small gender difference in spatial ability. Sex is a simple variable in that it is easy to measure; however, as an explanatory referent, it is inherently complex and difficult to interpret. Until these levels of interactions have been studied, including social and experiential factors, any speculation about biological causes of gender differences in cognitive abilities is premature.

We wish to propose the possibility that developmental differences in spatial ability derive substantially from sex-differential experiences. Humans are born with relatively immature brains. The different experiences of boys and girls are consistent, pervasive, and continual from the moment of birth. It seems plausible that the effects of differential experience could accumulate to produce slight differences in brain development and test performance. Together with sex-differential contributions to social interactions and sex-differentiated responses to stimulation (Draper, 1985), many other factors operate, probably in a synergistic fashion, to produce gender differences in performance.

Several lines of research demonstrate that the kinds of experiences one has can affect performance on tests of ability and cognitive achievement generally. It may be that sex-typed socialization sufficiently constrains the activities and experiences of girls and boys to produce sex-typed cognitive performance. The emergence of gender differences in cognition and achievement during development has been investigated in the context of socialization and academic training. From a separate line of research, we know that specific experiences can alter the course of brain development. However, there has been little integration of these areas in understanding the development of gender differences in cognition. Until the evidence from such research exists, further speculation about biological causes of gender differences in cognition and achievement is pre-mature, and possibly misleading.

The cumulative effects of consistent sex-related differences in training ex-periences that promote spatial ability may be sufficient to produce gender dif-ferences on psychological tests for spatial ability (Coates, Lord, & Jakabovics, 1975; Connor & Serbin, 1977; Fagot & Littman, 1976; Houston, 1985; Serbin & Connor, 1979; Sherman, 1980). The effects of such experience may even produce physiological effects in the brain (see below). However, by this model, the primary cause of gender differences in spatial ability may be not sex, but rather the sex-stereotyped socialization patterns in which individuals participate.

It is possible that the different experiences of boys and girls *cause* different kinds of biological development. The practice that boys get playing football and other team sports may enhance their spatial skills, both because of the practice in traversing spatial areas as well as because of the possible enhancing effects on brain development. This hypothesis, first proposed by Tobias (1978), merits further exploration (also see Halpern, 1986).

## Indirect Effects of Sex-Related Characteristics

Whether or not biological factors are found to have a direct effect on cognitive functioning, they enter into the educational experience of boys and girls in other, less obvious ways. Genes and hormones are the primary determinants of each individual's physical appearance, and certain physical attributes, particularly those related to size and gender, function as important social signals. In our culture and in many others, tallness seems to engender a response of awe or even fear; thus it lends a measure of prestige. Similarly, physical characteristics that signal the approach of reproductive maturity become symbols of soon-to-be-attained adult status that may affect both social expectations, and self-per-ceptions. Both the responses or expectations of others and self-perceptions can affect behavior in important achievement domains (Jones, 1965).

An individual's mature height (assuming optimal nutrition) may be genetically programmed, but the program is carried out partly through the influence of pubertal hormones. At puberty, the rise in gonadal hormones initiates a skeletal growth spurt in both boys and girls, but the same hormones ultimately curtail growth by causing the bones to fuse with their terminal joints. This fusing, called the closure of the epiphyses, prevents further bone growth. Adult height is thus partly a function of the timing of puberty; the later puberty arrives, the more time before hormone levels rise, and the longer the individual has before his or her growth is curtailed. The timing of puberty is a particularly important factor in the emergence of sex differences in stature. Before puberty, the average height of girls and boys is roughly the same. Girls and boys also grow approximately equal amounts during their pubertal growth spurts. Boys, however, reach puberty about two years later than girls and thus have two extra years in which to grow before their bones fuse. It is the extra years of prepubertal growth in boys more than differential height gain during the pubertal growth spurt that produces the adult sex difference in height (Petersen & Taylor, 1980).

In our culture as well as in most others, height seems to be a symbol of status. Among adult males, height has been found to correlate with social class, the likelihood of being hired, starting salary, and occupational prestige (Freedman, 1979). Height may also influence the achievement expectations adults have for children. In one experiment, taller children were assigned more difficult tasks than were shorter children of the same age, even when the tasks did not require physical strength (Brackbill & Nevill, 1981). In other words, taller children were assumed to be cognitively superior.

In the same way, differences in height may contribute to sex differences in school achievement. Brackbill and Nevill (1981) note that in elementary school, girls are slightly taller than boys and also receive better grades. In adolescence, boys surpass girls in height and begin to surpass them in high school subjects. In adulthood, men are often higher achievers than women academically and professionally. Unfortunately, these findings do not permit us to disentangle the effects of height from those of gender. If parents have higher achievement expectations for boys than for girls, they would on the average appear to have higher expectations for taller children, since after adolescence males are taller than females. In our estimation, a child's gender is at least as potent an organizer of adult expectations for him or her as is the child's height.

Between the sexes, but also among individuals, size is likely to figure in dominance relations, although it is unlikely to be the sole determining factor. Dominance status may in turn affect access to and use of educational facilities, which may then create sex differences in behavior. At a recent conference, one of the authors overheard an anecdote that aptly illustrated this situation. Girls in one junior high school had been observed to use the computers less frequently than boys; on this basis it was assumed that the girls had less interest in computer work. On closer inspection, however, it was found that girls tried to use the computer but were frequently physically ousted by some of the boys. Once use was determined by sign-up rather than dominance, the sex difference in computer use disappeared. The dominance factor, then, contributed to the gender difference in computer use. While it might be assumed that dominance was based primarily on gender (boys having higher dominance status), this is not necessarily the case: when size is controlled for, sex differences in dominance disappear (M. Lockheed, personal communication, 1982).

## SUMMARY

Gender is a biologically based social category. Because of its salience as a social stimulus, gender can affect educational experience by influencing social expectations concerning abilities and appropriate behavior and by influencing the child's own values and performance standards. From an early age, boys and girls sex-type academic and social domains and, especially in adolescence when pubertal changes increase the salience of gender, tend to pursue sex-appropriate activities. Sex-typing of academic areas can thus become a major force channeling the adolescent's achievement strivings and academic interests.

If there are sex differences in brain structures or patterns of functioning, such as lateral specialization, that influence cognitive skills, such as spatial ability of language fluency, those structures develop in a context of socialization practices that can alternatively enhance sex differences or equalize them. Specific skill training, practical experience, social expectations, and life goals may shape developing brain structures as strongly as these structures influence complex behaviors. If brain structures are plastic and responsive to environmental and experiential changes, then the constraints on differences in reproductive and social behavior that follow from this asymmetry of energetic investment are most fully developed in sociobiological theory (Daly & Wilson, 1983; also see Hamburg, 1974; Lancaster, 1985; LeBoeuf, 1978).

In particular, the theory specifies that the sexes will partition reproductive effort (composed of mating effort and parenting effort) differently (Kurland & Gaulin, 1984). The implications of reproductive asymmetry are clearest for the majority of mammalian species in which males play little or no role in parenting. Because a female is biologically committed to the energetically costly parental role, she realizes few advantages in competing with other females for access to fertile males. In general, her fitness is enhanced by nurturing offspring until they are viable on their own (Trivers, 1972). From this standpoint, access to resources becomes critical for a female to support herself and her offspring. Competitive-aggressive interactions involving females are therefore more likely to involve offspring defense and aggression directed at other females and unrelated juveniles who impinge upon critical resources (Altmann, 1980; Silk et al., 1981; Wrangham, 1981).

Male reproductive anatomy entails no obligatory parental role. For males to successfully reproduce, they must compete with other males for access to females who are the parental specialists. In this sense, the biological and behavioral structures of each sex are intertwined. The difference between the sexes are not simply gonadal and genital. For a male to leave more offspring than another male, various behaviors having to do with agonistic encounter (bluff, intimidation, competition, assertiveness) must be practiced and consolidated over the life course, to gain access to fertile females. The presence of other males is a major component of a sex-specific selective filter in natural selection. For males, engaging in such high risk behaviors can have high payoffs because of the mating advantage associated with high status in a male dominance hierarchy.

Alternative views of male reproductive strategy include the possibility that the lifespan reproductive success of nondominant males may be equal to that of dominant males. Multiple, equally advantageous methods of bypassing the male dominance filter, by sneaking copulations or, alternatively, by helping closely related kin instead of producing offspring (West Eberhard, 1975; Williams, 1981), are theoretically possible (Caro & Bateson, 1986; Dunbar, 1983).

The empirical support for these alternative strategies is limited; few investigations have attempted to measure reproductive success over the lifespan. Because social structure in a species may change in response to environmental factors (Lott, 1984), and because social dominance is a dynamic quality of social structure (Rowell, 1974), it is not surprising that studies of the reproductive advantage of dominant males have yielded mixed results (Dewsbury, 1982). For example, in one frequently cited study of yellow baboons (Hausfater, 1975), observations of free-ranging animals over 400 days showed that the dominance rank of every one of the 14 males changed during this period. The top-ranked three males accounted for about 50% of observed copulations, with animals in all ranks achieving some copulatory success. It appears that female choice of males for mating accounts for much of the variance in male copulatory success, with females preferentially soliciting less dominant males, in some cases (Dewsbury, 1982; also see Chapais, 1983; Chapais & Schulman, 1980; Vining, 1986).

Female reproductive success is not determined solely by her ability to conceive and gestate, but also by her ability to secure resources over a long time period while sequential sets of offspring are reared. Because her major reproductive effort is parenting and not mating and because of the relatively long time period over which parental effort is spread, high risk behaviors by females do not confer an immediate payoff in reproductive advantage. However, dominance in these long-term relationships does appear to enhance fitness for females, as well as for males (Chapais & Schulman, 1980; Hrdy, 1981; Lancaster, 1985).

In the few mammalian species in which the sexes form monogamous pair bonds, evolutionary theory predicts that the sexes will test each other for the value of their potential parental investment. This testing takes different forms in the two sexes. Females often delay mating for some time period, during which the mate's potential parenting qualities are assessed; males attempt to guard females and to drive away other males. These are thought of as behavioral patterns that assure the male that his future mate produces offspring that are genetically his own. If males were unable to ascertain the paternity of their mate's offspring, they would sometimes rear offspring who were sired by other males who were not prepared to do the work of fathering. To the extent that paternal effort is genetically based, these offspring would not be likely to parent their own young successfully.

Similarly, females who mate indiscriminately with males regardless of their willingness to commit resources are, according to the predictions of this theory, in a less favorable position in terms of fitness. Their sisters who delay matings and "test" their partners may leave more offspring who will reproduce themselves because their offspring receive the benefits of bi-parental care. If these coy behaviors are genetically based, they will be associated with enhanced reproductive success, and they will become characteristic of all females in the family.

## CONCLUSION

A perspective that takes into account evolutionary factors that have shaped our species makes it possible to consider human sex differences in a framework that includes multiple levels. Some aspects of sex differences are clearly arbitrary, depend upon experience, and show great variability from one society to the next. Proximal socialization experiences account for such differences. Other sex differences, having to do with endocrine effects on the organization of tissue, are the result of the interaction of biological systems and are also accounted for by proximal factors, in this case the influence of certain chemicals in the development of an individual organism.

Other sex differences, for example in the realm of cognitive abilities, are more difficult to categorize and appear to involve both biological and cultural factors. For example, in the area of visual-spatial abilities, males appear to have an advantage. It is also apparent that certain attributes of the socialization experience of males reinforce these capabilities. In cases like these, it is not clear what is driving what. Boys may be differentially attracted to games and pursuits that have the effect of reinforcing visual-spatial skills. Such activities may also be pleasing to individuals whose underlying capabilities lead them in this direction.

Other examples of biology and socialization working in concert come in the case of early acquisition of verbal fluency in girls. Females apparently show mastery in fluent production at earlier ages than boys. One may reason that as a consequence they find interaction with adults (usually women) more stimulating and as a result girls enter into a socialization track that emphasizes closer cooperation with adults and more pressure for obedience. Spending time in such socialization environments will expose girls at early ages to social and parenting skills that are advantageous to adult women (Draper, 1975). Such scenarios are plausible, "after the fact" reconstructions and have in common the assumption that certain sex differences that occur reliably have been selected for in our ancestry because they promoted individual fitness. In actual fact, such assumptions are usually untestable in humans. Various difficulties are encountered when attempting to explain factors with reference to ultimate causation.

First, the finding of sex differences may be epiphenomenal—in other words, it may be an accidental outcome of some other factor and have no relationship to reproductive advantage. Second, the original evolutionary contexts in which the sex differences were consolidated are no longer available for inspection. Therefore, it is not possible to determine empirically what selective advantage is provided by a particular trait or behavior. Moreover, the current environment may have changed, with the result that an originally advantageous trait is no longer related in any obvious way to considerations of fitness.

Satisfactory field or laboratory tests of the relationship between a given behavior or trait and consequences for fitness are better conducted on short-lived species in which the generation time is short compared to the period of scientific observation. Humans have such long generation times that many predictions from evolutionary theory cannot be tested directly.

Certainly humans are unique in the evolutionary sequence, because of the size and complexity of the brain and because of the development of culture. Social scientists have built a conception of human cultural variation that stresses that culture is learned and highly arbitrary. Humans are seen as relatively "free" of biology because their extra-somatic symbolic adaptation, language, is the agency by which they maintain their hold on the physical world and by which humans regulate relations among themselves (Washburn, 1978). Yet the ability to learn language, for example, is based on features of brain organization, while the particulars of what sound system and grammar is learned remains "open" to environmental conditioning. Indeed, in humans the evolved biologically based capacity for learning has resulted in a situation of remarkable symbiosis between learned response and generality at the level of biological and psychological potential.

In the area of sexual behavior and gender roles, we know that some degree of variability exists in the different learning environments provided by different cultures. On the basis of sociobiological theory, we can expect that culturally acquired systems of behavior that impinge most closely upon considerations of reproductive fitness will show limited variability and that systems of behavior more removed from fitness issues will show more variation. For example, the types of clothing worn by people in different cultures are diverse; whereas modesty conventions regarding the acceptability of female versus male postures which expose the genitals are uniform (Ford & Beach, 1952; Guthrie, 1970).

Probably the single most important outcome of the application of evolutionary theory to understanding human behavior was that it forced a telescopic view of human diversity. In the case of scientists working in the area of socialization and sex role acquisition, the evolutionary viewpoint caused people to realize that paying too much attention to the proximate causes of behavior could obscure an underlying behavioral structure or predisposition. Once alerted to the existence of structure, one can infer how males and females might perform differently, even under conditions of identical environmental stimulus.

In our present state of the science, we have many pieces of information about *how* the sexes differ. Examples have been discussed above of endocrine, genetic, and experiential factors that are involved in producing these differences. This area of the topic is relatively well researched and consensus is building among scientists of various types regarding the dynamics of biological sexual differentiation. More controversial are the findings about sex differences in behavior. Scientists who stress the role of exogenous variables point to real world events that shape the behavior of individuals differently *because of* their gender. Other scientists argue that as a result of the biological processes of sexual differentiation, inclinations or proclivities of the sexes to respond to exogenous influences are different. This position, which emphasizes "prepared learning" in contrast to "social learning" stressed by others, blurs the convenient opposition between biological and environmental bases of gender differences.

If the sexes respond differently, the natural question is, "Why?" This is a question that addresses issues of ultimate rather than proximal causes.

Presumably, some aspects of male and female differences in our species have been selected for because in past evolutionary contexts they promoted individual fitness. Conventional and ubiquitous sex differences in sex role assignments have evolved at the cultural level in response to underlying pressures on fitness. For example, the exclusive male role in warfare receives widespread endorsement in human societies. The greater male propensity to competition and aggression makes men likelier recruits than women. The minimal role played by the male in reproduction renders at least some males of a group expendable in conflict, so long as a portion of the male population is spared.

Women in contrast make less efficient warriors and are expensive to field since they must either suspend their reproductive functions while in combat or jeopardize immature offspring. In these perhaps obvious ways, some cultural roles bear more than an arbitrary relation to biology. The intriguing question for the future is: In the new social and technical forms of society which lie ahead, how will the relationship between biological sex and sex-related social roles be constructed?

# REFERENCES

Alexander, R. D. (1974). The evolution of social behavior. *Annual Review of Ecological Systems, 5,* 325–383.

Altmann, J. (1980). *Baboon mothers and infants*. Cambridge, MA: Harvard University Press.

Barkley, M. S. & Goldman, B. D. (1977). The effects of castration and silastic implants of testosterone on intermale aggression in the mouse. *Hormones and Behavior, 9,* 32–48.

Beach, F. A. (1978). Sociobiology and interspecific comparisons of behavior. In M. S. Gregory, A. Silvers, & P. Sutch (Eds.), *Sociobiology and human nature*. San Francisco: Jossey-Bass.

Beeman, E. A. (1947). The effect of male hormone on aggressive behavior in mice. *Physiological Zoology, 20,* 313–405.

Benton, D. (1983). Do animal studies tell us anything about the relationship between testosterone and human aggression? In G. C. L. Davey (Ed.), *Animal models of human behavior*. New York: Wiley.

Berenbaum, S. & Resnick, S. (1982). Somatic androgyny and cognitive abilities. *Developmental Psychology, 18,* 418–423.

Bock, R. D. & Kolakowski, D. (1973). Further evidence of sex-linked major-gene influence on human spatial visualizing ability. *American Journal of Human Genetics, 25,* 1–14.

Boles, D. B. (1980). X-linkage of spatial ability: A critical review. *Child Development, 51,* 625–635.

Brackbill, Y. & Nevill, D. D. (1981). Parental expectations of achievement as affected by children's height. *Merrill-Palmer Quarterly, 27,* 429–441.

Bronson, F. H. & Desjardins, C. (1968). Neonatal androgen administration and adult aggressiveness in female mice. *General and Comparative Endocrinology, 15,* 320–325.

Buell, S. J. & Coleman, P. D. (1979). Dendritic growth in the aged human brain and failure of growth in senile dementia. *Science, 206,* 854–856.

Cantoni, V. J., Pellegrino, J. W., & Hubert, L. J. (1981). *The relationship between testosterone levels and human spatial abilities.* Unpublished manuscript, University of California, School of Education, Santa Barbara.

Carey S. E. & Diamond, R. (1980). Maturational determination of the developmental course of face encoding. In D. Caplan (Ed.), *Biological studies of mental processes.* Cambridge: MIT Press.

Caro, T. M. & Bateson, P. (1986). Organization and ontogeny of alternative tactics. *Animal Behavior, 34,* 1483–1499.

Chapais, B. (1983). Reproductive activity in relation to male dominance and the likelihood of ovulation in rhesus monkeys. *Behavioral Ecology and Sociobiology, 12,* 215–228.

Chapais, B. & Schulman, S. R. (1980). An evolutionary model of female dominance relations in primates. *Journal of Theoretical Biology, 82,* 47–89.

Chisholm, J. S. (1980). Development and adaptation in infancy. In C. Super & S. Harkness (Eds.), *Anthropological perspectives on child development.* San Francisco: Jossey-Bass.

Coates, S., Lord, M., & Jakabovics, E. (1975). Field dependence-independence, social-non-social play and sex differences in preschool children. *Perceptual and Motor Skills, 40,* 195–202.

Connor, J. M. & Serbin, L. A. (1977). Behaviorally based masculine-and-feminine-activity-preference scales for preschoolers: Correlates with other classroom behavior and cognitive tests. *Child Development, 48,* 1411–1416.

Crockett, L. J. (1986). Peer-group interaction and the development of sex-typed social skills in middle childhood. Unpublished doctoral dissertation, University of Chicago, Chicago.

Crockett, L. & Petersen, A. C. (1984). Biology: Its role in gender-related educational experiences. In E. Fennema & M. M. Ayer (Eds.), *Women and education.* Berkeley, CA: McCutchan.

Daly, M. & Wilson, M. (1983). *Sex, evolution, and behavior.* Boston: Willard Grant Press.

Dan, A. J. (1979). The menstrual cycle and sex-related differences in cognitive variability. In M. A. Wittig & A. C. Petersen (Eds.), *Sex-related differences in cognitive functioning: Developmental issues.* New York: Academic Press.

de Lacoste-Utamsing, C., & Holloway, R. L. (1982). Sexual dimorphism in the human corpus callosum. *Science, 216,* 1431–1432.

Dewsbury, D. A. (1982). Dominance rank, copulatory behavior, and differential reproduction. *The Quarterly Review of Biology, 57,* 135–159.

Dorn, L., Petersen, A. C., & Crockett, L. (1986). *Pubertal effects in early adolescence.* Manuscript to be submitted for publication.

Draper, P. (1975). Cultural pressure on sex differences. *American Ethnologist, 2*(4), 602–616.

Draper, P. (1985). Two views of sex differences in socialization. In R. Hall (Ed.), *Male female differences: A bio-cultural perspective* (pp. 5–25). New York: Praeger.

Dunbar, R. I. M. (1983). Life history tactics and alternative strategies of reproduction. In P. Bateson (Ed.), *Mate choice.* Cambridge: Cambridge University Press.

Edwards, D. A. (1969). Early androgen stimulation and aggressive behavior in male and female mice. *Physiology and Behavior, 4,* 335–338.

Ehrhardt, A. (1985). The psychobiology of gender. In A. Rossi (Ed.), *Gender and the life course*. New York: Hawthorne.

Fagot, B. I. & Littman, F. (1976). Relation of preschool sex-typing to intellectual performance in elementary school. *Psychological Reports, 39,* 699–704.

Feder, H. H. (1984). Hormones and sexual behavior. *Annual Review of Psychology, 35,* 165–200.

Ford, C. S. & Beach, F. A. (1952). *Patterns of sexual behavior*. London: Eyre & Spottiswoode.

Forest, M. G. (1983). Role of androgens in fetal and pubertal development. *Hormone Research, 18,* 69–83.

Freedman, D. G. (1979). *Human sociobiology: A holistic approach*. New York: Free Press.

Golub, S. (1976). The effect of premenstrual anxiety and depression on cognitive functioning. *Journal of Personality and Social Psychology, 34,* 99–104.

Gorski, R. A. (1980). Sexual differentiation of the brain. In D. T. Krieger & J. C. Hughes (Eds.), *Neuroendocrinology* (pp. 239–247). Sunderland, MA: Sinauer Associates.

Goy, R. W. (1970). Early hormone influences on the development of sexual and sex-related behavior. In F. O. Schmitt (Ed.), *The neurosciences: Second study program*. New York: Rockefeller University Press.

Goy, R. W. & McEwen, B. S. (1980). *Sexual differentiation of the brain*. Cambridge, MA: MIT Press.

Greenough, W. T. & Green, E. J. (1981). Experience and the changing brain. In J. L. McGaugh, J. G. March, & S. B. Kiesler (Eds.), *Aging: Biology and behavior*. New York: Academic Press.

Greenough, W. T. & Schwark, H. D. (1984). Age-related aspects of experience effects upon brain structure. In R. N. Emde & R. J. Harmon (Eds.), *Continuities and discontinuities in development*. New York: Plenum.

Grumbach, M. M. (1980). The neuroendocrinology of puberty. In D. T. Krieger & J. C. Hughes (Eds.), *Neuroendocrinology* (pp. 249–258). Sunderland, MA: Sinauer Associates.

Grumbach, M. M., Roth, J. C., Kaplan, S. L., & Kelch, R. P. (1974). Hypothalamic–pituitary regulation of puberty: Evidence and concepts derived from clinical research. In M. M. Grumbach, G. S. Grave, & F. E. Mayer (Eds.), *The control of the onset of puberty* (pp. 115–166). New York: Wiley.

Guthrie, R. D. (1970). Evolution of human threat display organs. *Evolutionary Biology, 4,* 257–302.

Halpern, D. F. (1986). A different answer to the question, "Do sex-related differences in spatial abilities exist?" *American Psychologist, 41,* 1014–1015.

Hamburg, B. A. (1974). The psychobiology of sex differences: An evolutionary perspective. In R. C. Friedman, R. M. Richart, & R. L. Vande Wiele (Eds.), *Sex differences in behavior*. New York: Wiley.

Harding, C. F. (1981). Social modulation of circulating hormone levels in the male. *American Zoologist, 21,* 223–231.

Hartlage, L. C. (1970). Sex-linked inheritance of spatial ability. *Perceptual and Motor Skills, 31,* 610.

Hausfater, G. (1975). Dominance and reproduction in baboons *(Papio cynocephalus):* A quantitative analysis. *Contributions to primatology* (Vol. 7). New York: S. Karger.

Herbst, L. & Petersen, A. C. (1979). *Timing of maturation, brain lateralization and cognitive performance in adolescent females.* Paper presented at the Fifth Annual Conference on Research on Women and Education, Cleveland, OH.

Hier, D. B. (1981). Sex differences in brain structure. In A. Ansara, N. Geschwind, A. Galaburda, M. Albert, & N. Gartrell (Eds.), *Sex differences in dyslexia.* Towson, MD: Orton Dyslexia Society.

Hood, K. E. (1984). Aggression among female rats during the estrous cycle. In K. J. Flannelly, R. J. Blanchard, & D. C. Blanchard (Eds.), *Biological perspectives on aggression.* New York: Alan R. Liss.

Hrdy, S.B. (1981). *The woman that never evolved.* Cambridge, MA: Harvard University Press.

Huston, A. C. (1985). The development of sex-typing: Themes from recent research. *Developmental Review, 5,* 1–17.

Hyde, J. (1981). How large are cognitive gender differences? *American Psychologist, 36,* 892–901.

Imperato-McGinley, J., Peterson, R. E., Gautier, T., & Sturla, E. (1979). Androgens and the evolution of male-gender identity among male pseudohermaphrodites with 5α-reductase deficiency. *New England Journal of Medicine, 300,* 1233–1237.

Jones, M.C. (1965). Psychological correlates of somatic development. *Child Development, 36,* 899–911.

Jost, A. (1970). Hormonal factors in the sex differentiation of the mammalian foetus. *Philosophical Transactions of the Royal Society of London, 259,* 119–131.

Kail, R. V., Jr. & Siegel, A. W. (1978). Sex and hemispheric differences in the recall of verbal and spatial information. *Cortex, 14,* 557–563.

Kislak, J. W. & Beach, F. A. (1955). Inhibition of aggressiveness by ovarian hormones. *Endocrinology, 56,* 684–692.

Krauss, I.K. (August, 1985). Rotating a spatial image: The sex by angle interaction. Paper presented at the annual meetings of the American Psychological Association, Los Angeles.

Kreuz, L. E., Rose, R. M., & Jennings, J. R. (1972). Suppression of plasma testosterone levels and psychological stress. *Archives of General Psychiatry, 26,* 479–482.

Kurland, J. A. & Gaulin, S. J. C. (1984). The evolution of male parental investment: Effects of genetic relatedness and feeding ecology on the allocation of reproductive effort. In D. Milton (Ed.), *Primate paternalism.* New York: Van Nostrand Reinhold.

Lancaster, J. B. (1985). Evolutionary perspectives on sex differences in the higher primates. In A. S. Rossi (Ed.), *Gender and the life course.* Hawthorne, NY: Aldine.

LeBoeuf, B. J. (1978). Sex and evolution. In T. E. McGill, D. A. Dewsbury, & B. D. Sachs (Eds.), *Sex and behavior: Status and prospectus* (pp. 3–33). New York: Plenum.

Lerner, R. M. (1978). Nature, nurture, and dynamic interactionism. *Human Development, 21,* 1–20.

Lerner, R. M. (1984). *On the nature of human plasticity.* New York: Cambridge University Press.

Leshner, A. I. (1978). *An introduction to behavioral endocrinology.* New York: Oxford University Press.

Linn, M. C. & Petersen, A. C. (1985). Gender differences and spatial ability: Emergence and characterization. *Child Development, 56,* 1479–1498.

Linn, M. C. & Petersen, A. C. (1986). A meta-analysis of gender differences in spatial ability: Implications for mathematics and science achievement. In J. Hyde & M. C. Linn (Eds.), *The psychology of gender: Advances through meta-analysis*. Baltimore: The Johns Hopkins University Press.

Lott, D. F. (1984). Intraspecific variation in the social systems of wild vertebrates. *Behaviour, 88,* 266–325.

Luria, A. R. (1966). *Higher cortical functions in man*. New York: Basic.

Lynch, G. & Gall, C. (1979). Organization and reorganization in the central nervous system: Evolving concepts of brain plasticity. In F. T. Falkner & J. M. Tanner (Eds.), *Human growth. Vol. 3. Neurobiology and nutrition*. New York: Plenum.

Maccoby, E. E. & Jacklin, C. N. (1974). *The psychology of sex differences*. Palo Alto: Stanford University Press.

Mackinnon, P. (1979). Sexual differentiation of the brain. In F. Falkner & J. M. Tanner (Eds.), *Human growth III: Neurobiology and nutrition*. New York: Plenum.

Mazur, A. & Lamb, T. A. (1980). Testosterone, status, and mood in human males. *Hormones and Behavior, 14,* 236–246.

McEwen, B. S. (1980). The brain as a target organ of endocrine hormones. In D. T. Krieger & J. C. Hughes (Eds.), *Neuroendocrinology* (pp. 33–42). Sunderland, MA: Sinauer Associates.

McGlone, J. (1980). Sex differences in human brain asymmetry: A critical survey. *The Behavioral and Brain Sciences, 3,* 215–227.

McGuire, L. S., Ryan, K. O., & Owen, G. S. (1975). Congenital adrenal hyperplasia. II. Cognitive and behavioral studies. *Behavior Genetics, 5,* 175–188.

McKinney, T. P. & Desjardins, C. (1973). Postnatal development of the testis, fighting behavior and fertility in the house mouse. *Biology of Reproduction, 9,* 274–294.

Money, J. & Ehrhardt, A. A. (1972). *Man and woman, boy and girl: Differentiation and dimorphism of gender identity from conception to maturity*. Baltimore: The Johns Hopkins University Press.

Moore, C. L. (1985). Another psychobiological view of sexual differentiation. *Developmental Review, 15,* 18–55.

Newcombe, N. & Bandura, M. M. (1983). Effect of age at puberty on spatial ability in girls: A question of mechanism. *Developmental Psychology, 19,* 215–224.

Nottebaum, F. (1984). Birdsong as a model in which to study brain processes related to learning. *Condor, 86,* 227–236.

Olweus, P., Mattsson, A., Schalling, D., & Low, H. (1980). Testosterone, aggression, physical, and personality dimensions in normal adolescent males. *Psychosomatic Medicine, 42,* 253–269.

Parsons, J. (1980). *The psychobiology of sex differences and sex roles*. New York: Hemisphere.

Petersen, A. C. (1976). Physical androgyny and cognitive functioning at adolescence. *Developmental Psychology, 12,* 524–533.

Petersen, A. C. (1979). Differential cognitive development in adolescence. In M. Sugar (Ed.), *Female adolescent development*. New York: Brunner/Mazel.

Petersen, A. C. (1980). Biopsychosocial processes in the development of sex-related differences. In J. Parsons (Ed.), *The psychobiology of sex differences and sex roles*. New York: Hemisphere.

Petersen, A. C. (1981). Sex differences in performance in spatial tasks: Biopsychosocial influences. In A. Ansara, N. Geschwind, A. Galaburda, N. Albert, & N. Gartrell (Eds.), *Sex differences in dyslexia*. Towson, MD: Orton Dyslexia Society.

Petersen, A. C. (1983). Pubertal change and cognition. In J. Brooks-Gunn & A. C. Petersen (Eds.), *Girls at puberty: Biological and psychosocial perspectives*. New York: Plenum.

Petersen, A. C. & Gitelson, I. B. (Forthcoming). *Toward understanding sex-related differences in cognitive performance*. New York: Academic Press.

Petersen, A. C. & Hood, K. E. (in press). The role of experience in cognitive performance and brain development. In E. Tobach & B. Rosoff (Eds.), *Genes and gender IV: Women's work and changing technology*. New York: Guardian Press.

Petersen, A. C. & Taylor, B. (1980). The biological approach to adolescence: Biological change and psychological adaptation. In J. Adelson (Ed.), *Handbook of adolescent psychology* (pp. 117–155). New York: Wiley.

Petersen, A. C. & Wittig, M. A. (1979). Sex-related differences in cognitive functioning: An overview. In M. A. Wittig & A. C. Petersen (Eds.), *Sex-related differences in cognitive functioning: Developmental issues*. New York: Academic Press.

Phoenix, C. H., Goy, R. W., Gerall, A. A., & Young, W. C. (1959). Organizational action of prenatally administered testosterone propionate on the tissues mediating behavior in the female guinea pig. *Endocrinology, 65,* 369–382.

Prescott, J. W. (1975). Developmental neuropsychophysics. In J. W. Prescott, M. S. Read, & D. B. Coursin (Eds.), *Brain function and malnutrition*. New York: Wiley.

Purifoy, F. E. & Koopmans, L. H. (1980). Androstenedione, T and free T concentrations in women of various occupations. *Social Biology, 26,* 179–188.

Resko, J. A. (1974). The relationship between fetal hormones and the differentiation of the central nervous system in primates. In W. Montagna & W. A. Sadler (Eds.), *Reproductive behavior*. New York: Plenum.

Roche, K. E. & Leshner, A. I. (1979). ACTH and vasopressin treatments immediately after a defect increase future submissiveness in male mice. *Science, 204,* 1343–1344.

Rowell, T. E. (1974). The concept of social dominance. *Behavioral Biology, 11,* 131–154.

Rozenzweig, M. R. (1984). Experience, memory, and the brain. *American Psychologist, 39,* 365–376.

Serbin, L. A. & Connor, J. M. (1979). Sex-typing of children's play preferences and patterns of cognitive performance. *Journal of Genetic Psychology, 134,* 315–316.

Sherman, J. A. (1980). Mathematics, spatial visualization and related factors: Changes in girls and boys, grades 8–11. *Journal of Educational Psychology, 72,* 476–482.

Silk, J., Samuels, A., & Rodman, P. (1981). The influence of kinship, rank, and sex on affiliation and aggression between adult and immature Bonnet Macaques (*Macaca radiata*). *Behaviour, 78,* 111–137.

Sommer, B. (1982). Cognitive behavior and the menstrual cycle. In R. C. Friedman (Ed.), *Behavior and the menstrual cycle*. New York: Marcel Dekker.

Stafford, R. E. (1961). Sex differences in spatial visualization as evidence of sex-linked inheritance. *Perceptual and Motor Skills, 13,* 428.

Stumpf, W. E. (1975). The brain: An endocrine gland and hormone target. In W. E. Stumpf & L. D. Grant (Eds.), *Anatomical neuroendocrinology*. Basel, Switzerland: Karger.

Swaab, D. F. & Fliers, E. (1985). A sexually dimorphic nucleus in the human brain. *Science, 228,* 1112–1115.

Tanner, J. M. (1972). Sequence, tempo, and individual variation in growth and development of boys and girls aged twelve to sixteen. In J. Kagan & R. Coles (Eds.), *Twelve to sixteen: Early adolescence.* New York: Norton.

Tanner, J. M., Whitehouse, R., Hughes, P., & Carter, B. (1976). Relative importance of growth hormone and sex steroids for the growth at puberty of trunk length, limb length, and muscle width in growth hormone-deficient children. *Journal of Pediatrics, 89,* 1000–1008.

Tinbergen, N. (1963). On aims and methods of ethology. *Zeitschrift für Tierpsychologie, 20,* 410–433.

Tobias, S. (1978). *Overcoming math anxiety.* New York: Norton.

Trivers, R. L. (1972). Parental investment and sexual selection. In B. Campbell (Ed.), *Sexual selection and the descent of man.* Chicago: Aldine.

Udry, J. R., Talbert, L. M., & Morris, N. M. (1986). *Biosocial foundations for adolescent females sexuality.* Manuscript submitted for publication.

Vandenberg, S. G. & Kuse, A. R. (1979). Spatial ability: A critical review of the sex-linked major gene hypothesis. In M. A. Wittig & A. C. Petersen (Eds.), *Sex-related differences in cognitive functioning: Developmental issues.* New York: Academic Press.

vanden Berghe, P. (1979). *Human family systems.* New York: Elsevier.

Vining, D. R., Jr. (1986). Social versus reproductive success: The central theoretical problem of human sociobiology. *Behavioral and Brain Sciences, 9,* 167–216.

Waber, D. (1976). Sex differences in cognition: A function of maturation rate. *Science, 192,* 572–574.

Waber, D. (1977). Sex differences in mental abilities, hemisphere lateralization and rate of physical growth at adolescence. *Developmental Psychology, 13,* 29–38.

Wachtel, S. S. (1977). H–Y antigen and the genetics of sex determination. *Science, 198,* 797–799.

Ward, I. L. (1984). The prenatal stress syndrome: Current status. *Psychoneuroendocrinology, 9,* 3–11.

Washburn, S. L. (1978). Human behavior and the behavior of other animals. *American Psychologist, 33,* 405–418.

West Eberhard, M. J. (1975). The evolution of social behavior by kin selection. *The Quarterly Review of Biology, 50,* 1–33.

Whalen, R. E. & Simon, N. G. (1984). Biological motivation. *Annual Review of Psychology, 35,* 257–276.

Williams, B. J. (1981). A critical review of models in sociobiology. *Annual Review of Anthropology, 10,* 163–192.

Willis, S. L. (1985). Towards an educational psychology of the older adult learner: Intellectual and cognitive bases. In J. E. Birren & K. W. Schaie (Eds.), *Handbook of the psychology of aging* (2nd Ed.), 818–846. New York: Van Nostrand Reinhold.

Willis, S. L. & Schaie, W. K. (1986). Training the elderly on the ability factors of spatial orientation and inductive reasoning. *Psychology and Aging, 1,* 239–247.

Wilson, J. D., George, F. W., & Griffin, J. E. (1981). The hormonal control of sexual development. *Science, 211,* 1278–1284.

Witelson, S. F. (1976). Sex and the single hemisphere: Specialization of the right hemisphere for spatial processing. *Science, 193,* 425–427.

Witelson, S. F. (1985). The brain connection: The corpus callosum is larger in left-handers. *Science, 229,* 665–668.

Wrangham, R. W. (1981). Drinking competition in vervet monkeys. *Animal Behaviour, 29,* 904–910.

# 5
# Sex Role Development and Early Educational Experiences
## Ruth L. Wynn
## Christine Fletcher

Nursery schools and daycare centers are frequently the settings for the child's first introduction into the wider social world that exists outside of the immediate family. The presence of numerous age-mates marks such programs as distinctly different from family rearing environments. While adults have always been involved, either overtly or implicitly, in teaching children what is appropriate and inappropriate for their genders, the early exposure to age-mates and the opportunity for daily interaction with them enlarges the social context in which sex role socialization occurs. For children attending these programs, the influence of peers becomes an important adjunct to the sex role influences that originate within the family.

Although it has been customary for adults to organize early childhood programs only by age, the age stratified groups manage their world conventionally by gender. The sex segregation that has been observed in the society of children is not formalized in any way, but appears almost as soon as boys and girls are brought together. Little evidence to the contrary has emerged in the research literature over the past fifty years. In an attempt to trace the development of this phenomenon to its source, La Freniere, Strayer, and Gauthier (1984), observing very young daycare children, discovered that boys and girls did not discriminate according to gender before 27 months of age. At 27 months, however, the first evidence of the sex cleavage in the social group appeared as girls began directing affiliative behaviors to other girls well above the level expected by chance. This preference for same-sex social companions remained stable among girls observed in the older age groups. About a year later, the preference for same-sex social interactions developed among boys, and steady increases in same-sex affiliation were found in each older age group. The majority of studies (e.g., Fagot & Patterson, 1969; Fagot, 1977; Lamb & Roopnarine, 1979) have found sex-segregated play among three- and four-year-old boys and girls, but not all of the research supports these developmental trends. Three studies (Eisenberg-Berg, Boothby, & Matson, 1979; Goldman, 1981; Roopnarine, 1984) report that three-year-old girls did not discriminate between boys and girls in their social interactions, while four-year olds did. Although developmental studies are too few and inconsistencies too many to establish firm developmental trends, it has been generally accepted both that the preference for same-sex playmates increases with age during the preschool years and that sex-differentiated behavior becomes the norm.

This conclusion is compatible with the development of social play (Bakeman & Brownlee, 1980; Parten, 1933). Immediately after infancy, children's play is primarily solitary but with age shifts to ever greater social participation. At age three, when there are inconsistencies in the data in regard to same-sex preference, transitions to more advanced forms of play generally take place (Bakeman & Brownlee, 1980). These occurrences may be connected in some way. Thus, results pertaining to gender differences in developmental timing remain inconclusive, although given the precocity of females compared to their male age-mates, such differences seem reasonable.

Sex segregation implies that children are forming into gender exclusive groups. Now children rarely come together to do nothing. Rather, they interact for the purpose of doing something. The choice of activities then intersects with the choice of playmates. It is difficult to determine whether children select playmates and then decide what they will do, or the reverse—select an activity and then find someone to share it with. There is some indication, although the data are only correlational, that the latter best describes the sequence of social interaction, at least for four-year olds who demonstrate same-sex preferences in the group setting (Eisenberg, Tryon & Cameron, 1984). Children usually both approached play materials alone and chose those toys that were not in the possession of another child. In part, the lack of more sophisticated skills in organizing social play and of sharing may be a consequence of preschool teachers giving more direct instruction about not interfering with another's play by taking that child's toy than they give about initiating social interaction. Boys and girls, however, who select sex-appropriate toys find that other children of the same gender will play with them, while children who choose sex-inappropriate toys are left alone (Fagot & Patterson, 1969; Fagot, 1977; Eisenberg et al., 1984; Eisenberg-Berg et al., 1979). Both boys and girls respond to the positive attention shown them primarily by same-sex peers for sex-appropriate play by prolonging the activities (Lamb & Roopnarine, 1979; Lamb, Esterbrooks, & Holden, 1980; Roopnarine, 1984). In comparison, sex-inappropriate play, which may be either criticized or ignored, is abandoned sooner than sex-appropriate play. Children in group settings thus spend more time in and are more likely to play with same-sex peers in sex-appropriate activities than sex-inappropriate ones. The end result is the sex-segregated play that characterizes social interaction in early childhood programs. The social arbiters are the children themselves.

As socializing agents, children have determined which activities are masculine and which are feminine by their play behaviors. For example, boys prefer blocks, play with transportation toys, and hammering. Girls show a preference for art activities, and doll and domestic play. The sex cleavage, in large part, is an artifact of these sex-typed activities in which the participation of either boys or girls is dominant. The children's designations correspond to the sex-role stereotypes of the adult world (Connor & Serbin, 1977). Children delivering social reinforcements and punishments shape each other's sex-typed behavior. In a series of studies, Lamb and his associates (Lamb et al., 1980; Lamb & Roopnarine, 1979; Roopnarine, 1984), noting that positive attention was more effective when it was contingent on sex-appropriate rather than sex-inappropriate play, advanced the suggestion that the social pressure functioned mainly to remind children of expectations about sex roles learned previously.

It is not unreasonable to assume that children have detected the regularities governing traditional sex roles and having done so, will interpret them as rules to be applied even in their play. Piaget (1932/1965) investigated rule-following behavior in children's play. He wrote that young (preoperational) children regard rules as external to themselves, as ''sacred realities . . . external and imbued with the spirit of the Elders or the Gods.'' Accordingly, children believe that rules are unchangeable, and any modification would be wrong. Children do not begin to see rules as arbitrary and changeable until late middle childhood. The ability to make up new rules appears later still. Applied to sex role socialization, children's respect, even veneration, of rules and customs may be the conservative influence perpetuating sex role stereotyping even as society slowly moves to sex role convergence. Recent studies of the development of children's understanding of social rules have considered the sex role regularities as a form of social rule, the social convention (Carter & McCloskey, 1983; Carter & Patterson, 1982; Damon, 1977; Turiel, 1977). With increasing age, children come to recognize the arbitrary nature of sex role conventions, but preschool and young school-age children consider all social rules binding. They adhere strictly to sex role conventions, deferring to group pressure to avoid the disagreeable consequences of peer disapproval (Carter & McCloskey, 1984).

Other explanations for sex segregation and sex typing in play, some based on behavioral compatibility and others on cognitive consonance, have been advanced. Like direct peer reinforcement, however, neither explanation alone nor in combination is able adequately to account for the stereotyping of activities. Behavioral compatibility implies, among a number of possibilities, gender differences in activity level. It has been shown that activity level is not related to male and female toy preferences in girls (Eisenberg-Berg et al., 1979), and when gross motor equipment is involved, boys do not engage in more rough-and-tumble play than girls (Blurton-Jones, 1972). Another component of the behavioral compatibility explanation invokes gender differences in maturation, but neither male nor female stereotyped activities make greater maturity demands than the other. Similarity in verbal fluency has also been considered in accounting for same-sex affiliations as girls are more fluent than boys (e.g., Field, 1982; La Freniere et al., 1984). Same-sex affiliation, however, occurs among deaf as well as hearing children (Lederberg, Chapin, Rosenblatt, & Vandell, 1986).

The cognitive consonance approach is even more problematic, for it rests on children's knowledge of gender identity of self and others. Common sense would argue that gender identity should precede the appearance of same-sex preferences. Through interviews with 24-, 30-, and 36-month-old toddlers, Thompson (1975) found that the ability to apply gender labels correctly to one's self and others and preferential behaviors did not become stable phenomena until 36 months of age. Both phenomena were preceded by an awareness of sex-role stereotyping, which was evident at 24 months and became more pronounced at 30 months. It appears that as children try to make sense of their social world, they rely on whatever rules they are able to discover operating in their environment.

Studies of the development of gender identity and its final stage of gender constancy raise some provocative issues. A number of investigators have claimed that gender characteristics provide the viewer with salient and easily discernible cues for assigning gender labels (e.g., Damon, 1977). In an era that has popularized the unisex style, however, this is not always possible. Moreover, there has been a long tradition dating from the Middle Ages (Aries, 1965) of nondifferentiation of young children's attire and hair style. Then, both wore dresses, now both tend, at least in preschool programs, to wear jeans, overalls, or slacks. Certainly, gender is more difficult to distinguish when children are not allowed to run about naked. Early childhood programs, however, have integrated "toileting time," which permits children to observe and discuss genital differences. The recognition that genital differences are the sole criterion for gender assignment, however, does not happen until the preschool period is well passed (McConaghy, 1979). If human sexuality is kept shrouded in mystery for the young, the sex-stereotyped characteristics are all that remain for the identification of gender. With few exceptions (e.g., McConaghy, 1979; Thompson and Bentler, 1971, 1973)), assessments of the development of gender identity have omitted genital differences and concentrated on the attributes of appearance and activities.

The relationship between sex-typed activities as used in children's judgments of gender constancy and as seen in sex-segregated play has rarely been considered. Gender constancy refers to knowing that gender assignment is invariant even, for example, in the face of participation in sex-inappropriate activities. Uncertainty about gender constancy is not unusual among three- and five-year olds, and even those who make constancy judgments fail to give explanations or simply refer to sex-stereotypic norms (Wehren & DeLisi, 1983). Should we accept that children believe what they tell us when they say that a boy (girl) playing with a girl's (boy's) toy becomes a girl (boy)? If it is accepted, there should be an absence of sex-segregated play as children would not consider gender a stable attribute. That this is not the case leads to an assumption that perhaps sex-inappropriate activities are being avoided for fear of a change in gender. More probably, the inconsistency between what children say and how they act is related to the time lag between verbal theoretical judgments and the concrete evaluations that operate in action (Piaget, 1932/1965). Martin and Halverson (1983) found that many children approach questions about gender constancy as if they referred to a pretend situation. When asked to respond in a "for real" manner, they exhibited gender constancy as early as 3–4 years of age. The basis for both children's thought and their behavior appears to be the determination that certain activities are sex-typed. Upon discovering the rules governing sex roles, children unquestioningly follow them by adjusting their behavior to conform. Smetana and Letourneau (1984) suggest that at least for girls who have not fully attained gender constancy, same-sex social interactions provide a way of acquiring and practicing sex-appropriate behavior.

At one time, sex role learning was considered an appropriate goal of socialization. With the move to greater equality between the sexes, however, this assumption is being questioned. Although unintended, some ideological biases are present in the studies of sex role socialization. One such bias that has come to be accepted almost as gospel is to treat changes and differences that occur with age as advances. Thus four-year olds who show more sex-stereotypic behavior have been presented as developmentally ahead of three-year olds, and threes ahead of twos, without considering whether the behavior is valued, especially for later adjustment. There are those individuals who would prefer that activities and toys be gender neutral. While much less attention has been focused on this aspect of the preschool environment, it is possible to ascertain from data given on time spent in sex-typed activities that children spend about half of their time in gender neutral play (Fagot & Patterson, 1969; Lamb et al., 1980). In studies that report on gender neutral activities, both boys and girls have been observed to spend a greater proportion of time with neutral toys than sex-typed ones (Cameron, Eisenberg, & Tryon, 1985; Eisenberg et al., 1984) and neutral toys were preferred by children engaged in solitary play (Smetana & Letourneau, 1984). Positive attention from peers also has been found to occur for children engaged in neutral activities (Roopnarine, 1984). Three-year-old boys received more positive attention from peers for gender neutral than for sex-typed activity, and three-, and four-year-old girls received amounts almost equal to that received for feminine activities. Peer pressure for four-year-old boys to conform was much greater.

Because the focus of the research has emphasized conventional sex role development, gender neutral behavior is under-reported. This may be viewed as another bias in the research literature. Even more problematic, however, is the fact that the educational philosophy of the programs under study is rarely explicitly stated. As a discipline, preschool education has not uniformly adopted any one position on the continuum of sex role socialization attitudes. Since conventional socialization practices have changed unevenly, it would be important to have this information.

For those who would encourage cross-gender play with gender neutral toys, the potential for change is enormous. Naturally occurring cross-sex play is rare

(Fagot, 1977). Keeping in mind that there are numerous inherent dangers in comparing studies, some change may be taking place. Fagot and Patterson (1969) reported that girls and boys spent 7.6 and 13.5 percent of the time, respectively, in cross-gender play, whereas it can be determined from Lamb's data (Lamb et al., 1980) that girls and boys spent 23 and 18 percent of the time in cross-sex activities. A modest cross-gender preference is tolerated in girls, but boys are treated differently (Fagot, 1977). Boys received less positive attention and more criticism from age-mates than their peers and were often ignored and apt to play alone. By way of illustrating how extreme this can be is the case of a boy who spent many hours in his preschool class playing with the doll house and furniture. He played alone. Because of parental concern, the teacher inquired what he was doing, only to learn that he was playing "moving man." No one—children, teachers, or parents—could see the sex-appropriate truck for the sex-inappropriate doll house and furniture.

Experimental manipulations to change the low level of cross-gender play have been undertaken (Serbin, Connor, & Iler, 1979; Serbin, Tonick, & Sternglanz, 1977). These experimental studies have demonstrated that positive attention from teachers that is contingent on cross-sex play and the introduction of new toys in a non-sex-stereotyped manner, both singly and in combination, are effective in increasing cross-gender play. Perhaps the main conclusion that can be drawn from this work is that teachers take a conventional approach to sex role socialization and do not naturally encourage the adoption of more egalitarian behavior among boys and girls. If it were otherwise, the increases that are found when teachers are instructed to respond in a non-sex-stereotyped manner would not have occurred, and the children's cross-gender play would not have returned to baseline levels after the experimental treatment ended.

While much has been written outlining the potential benefits of a nonsexist curriculum and detailing steps to be taken in setting up such a program (e.g., Sprung, 1975, 1978; McCune & Matthews, 1976), there has unfortunately been very little research done in this area. Two studies (Bianchi & Bakeman, 1978; Koblinsky & Sugawara, 1984) that have attempted to measure the influence of nonsexist curriculums have found that there is indeed a significant difference in the amount of sex role stereotyping exhibited by children exposed to a traditional versus a nonsexist curriculum. Bianchi and Bakeman (1978) observed children during their freeplay time in two preschools that were similar in the population served but differed in their philosophies. One school, designated "open" in its approach, emphasized individual development and took deliberate steps, including the hiring of both male and female teachers, to avoid perpetuating sex role stereotypes. The staff of the second school believed in the appropriateness of traditional sex roles and often grouped the children by gender. It was found that while children in both programs spent the same amount of time playing with others, those in the "open" school were far more likely to engage in mixed-sex play than were those in the traditional program. In the traditional program a greater proportion of the play was restricted to same-sex peers. Boys and girls were equally likely to participate in same-sex groups in both programs.

Koblinsky and Sugawara (1984) examined sex role stereotyping and same-sex preference at the beginning and end of a six month period in which three- to five-year-old children were exposed to either a nonsexist or a control curriculum led by either a male or a female teacher. The nonsexist curriculum was modeled on a program developed by the Women's Action Alliance (Sprung, 1975) and involved the presentation of nonsexist stories and activities. The control program also received new materials, but they were unrelated to sex roles. Children were tested on the SERLI and ITSC 80 as program differences precluded assessment by direct observation. Exposure to the nonsexist curriculum had the desired effect, reducing sex stereotyping to a greater extent than did exposure to the control curriculum.

While the type of curriculum can have an effect on sex typing, it is likely that parents select programs that are consonant with their stance on the sex role socialization issue. This would be a potentially confounding factor in studies comparing two different programs.

The empirical studies of social play in early childhood programs reveal that in the group setting, children have demonstrated a rather rigid adherence to sex role stereotypes. Moreover, non-sex-typed programs may eventually lead to a diminishment of socially prescribed sex-based differences and thus to a reduction of the actual differences. At the moment, it is important to recognize that differences exist, and that they are a reflection of the larger society.

Sex roles are being redefined, and sex role socialization is bound to change as a result. With 52 percent of mothers of preschool children in the labor force, increasing numbers of children are spending a large portion of their waking day in the company of peers and teachers in daycare programs. Others are attending half-day nursery school programs, some because the hours are sufficient for mothers working only part-time, but more than likely because parents have come to believe the experience is important for their child's social and cognitive development. Where parents were once the primary socializing influence for their young child, they are now sharing this aspect of child rearing with others. While this in itself is one indication of change, perhaps an even more profound change related to the fact of women's employment out of the home is the blurring of the traditional boundaries of sex roles. Many occupations no longer require the advantage of male strength, and the feminist movement has made headway in eliminating some of the stereotyping of occupations. There is also greater participation of men in childcare and domestic tasks, especially in families where the mother works. The most recent generations of children will have to deal with the expansion and greater equality of sex roles.

An example of how these two changes intersect is offered in the following episode, which took place at a university daycare center. A teacher explained to the children that her husband, who had stopped by, could not stay to play with them because he had to go to work. She was immediately corrected by a not-quite three-year-old boy, who stated emphatically, "No—mommies work, daddies go to school." All of the other children present concurred with their classmate. From this incident, it would appear that very young children spontaneously use gender as an organizing principle in constructing their social world. Furthermore, the gender schema spontaneously used by young children is not necessarily stereotyped but reflects their narrow personal experience. Finally, it is of interest to note that children in the company of peers have no difficulty in resisting adult points of view. Children are able to perceive when the practical conditions of male and female work have changed and when the stereotypic notions that specify the place and role of females only in relation to their functions within the home and males in the workplace are no longer valid. Sex-stereotypic behavior will most likely disappear in preschool programs when adult society is no longer regulated in this fashion. Stereotypes are always a generation out of date—that is their nature.

## REFERENCES

Aries, P. (1965). *Centuries of Childhood*. New York: Vintage Books.

Bakeman, R., & Brownlee, J. (1980). The strategic use of parallel play. A sequential analysis. *Child Development. 51*, 873–878.

Bianchi, B. D., & Bakeman, R. (1978). Sex-typed affiliation preferences observed in preschoolers: Traditional and open school differences. *Child Development. 49*, 910–912.

Blurton-Jones, N. (1972). Categories of child-child interaction. In N. Blurton-Jones (Ed.), *Ethological Studies of Child Behavior*. Cambridge: Cambridge University Press.

Cameron, E., Eisenberg, N., & Tryon, K. (1985). The relations between play and preschoolers' social behavior. *Sex Roles. 12*, 601–615.

Carter, D. B., & McCloskey, L. A. (1984). Peers and the maintenance of sex-typed behavior: The development of children's conceptions of cross-gender behavior in their peers. *Social Cognition. 2*, 294–314.

Carter, D. B., & Patterson, C. J. (1982). Sex roles as social conventions: The development of children's conceptions of sex-role stereotypes. *Developmental Psychology. 18*, 812–824.

Connor, J. M. & Serbin, L. A. (1977). Behaviorally based masculine- and feminine-activity-preference scales for preschoolers: Correlates with other classroom behaviors and cognitive tests. *Child Development, 48*, 1411–1416.

Damon, W. (1977). *The Social World of the Child*. San Francisco: Jossey-Bass.

Eisenberg-Berg, N., Boothby, R., & Matson, T. (1979). Correlates of preschool girls' feminine and masculine toy preferences. *Developmental Psychology, 15*, 354–355.

Eisenberg, N., Tryon, K., & Cameron, E. (1984). The relation of preschoolers' peer interaction to their sex-typed toy choices. *Child Development, 55*, 1044–1050.

Fagot, B. I. (1977). Consequences of moderate cross-gender behavior in preschool children. *Child Development, 48*, 902–907.

Fagot, B. I. & Patterson, G. R. (1969). An in vivo analysis of reinforcing contingencies for sex-role behaviors in the preschool child. *Developmental Psychology, 1*, 563–568.

Field, T. (1982). Same-sex preferences of preschool: An artifact of same-age grouping? *Child Study Journal, 2*, 151–159.

Goldman, J. A. (1981). Social participation of preschool children in same-versus mixed-age groups. *Child Development, 52*, 644–650.

Koblinsky, S. A. & Sugawara, A. I. (1984). Nonsexist curricula, sex of teacher, and children's sex-role learning. *Sex Roles, 10*, 357–367.

La Freniere, P., Strayer, F. F., & Gauthier, R. (1984). The emergence of same-sex affiliative preferences among preschool peers: A developmental/ethological perspective. *Child Development, 55*, 1958–1965.

Lamb, M. E., Easterbrooks, M. A., & Holden, G. W. (1980). Reinforcement and punishment among preschoolers: Characteristics, effects, and correlates. *Child Development, 51*, 1230–1236.

Lamb, M. E. & Roopnarine, J. L. (1979). Peer influences on sex-role development in preschoolers. *Child Development, 50*, 1219–1222.

Lederberg, A. R., Chapin, S. L., Rosenblatt, V., & Vandell, D. L. (1986). Ethnic, gender, and age preferences among deaf and hearing preschool peers. *Child Development, 57*, 375–386.

Martin, C. L. & Halverson, C. F. (1983). Gender constancy: A methodological and theoretical analysis. *Sex Roles, 9*, 775–790.

McConaghy, M. J. (1979). Gender permanence and the genital basis of gender: Stages in the development of constancy of gender identity. *Child Development, 50*, 1223–1226.

McCune, S. D. & Matthews, M. (1976). Toward a nonsexist education for all children. *Childhood Education, 52*, 178–186.

Parten, M. (1933). Social play among preschool children. *Journal of Abnormal and Social Psychology, 28*, 136–147.

Piaget, J. (1932/1965). *The Moral Judgment of the Child.* New York: Free Press.

Roopnarine, J. L. (1984). Sex-typed socialization in mixed-age preschool classrooms. *Child Development, 55*, 1078–1084.

Serbin, L. A., Connor, J. M., & Iler, I. (1979). Sex-stereotyped and nonstereotyped introductions of new toys in the preschool classroom: An observational study of teacher behavior and its effects. *Psychology of Women Quarterly, 4*, 261–265.

Serbin, L. A., Tonick, I. J., & Sternglanz, S. H. (1977). Shaping cooperative cross-sex play. *Child Development, 48*, 924–929.

Smetana, J. G. & Letourneau, J. (1984). Development of gender constancy and children's sex-typed free-play behavior. *Developmental Psychology, 20*, 691–696.

Sprung, B. (1975). *Non-sexist Education for Young Children: A Practical Guide.* New York: Citation Press.

Sprung, B. (ed.). (1978). *Perspectives on Non-Sexist Early Childhood Education.* New York: Teachers College Press.

Thompson, S. K. (1975). Gender labels and early sex role development. *Child Development, 46*, 339–347.

Thompson, S. K. & Bentler, P. M. (1971). The priority of cues in sex discrimination by children and adults. *Developmental Psychology, 5*, 181–185.

Thompson, S. K. & Bentler, P. M. (1973). A developmental study of gender constancy and parent preference. *Archives of Sexual Behavior, 2*, 379–385.

Turiel, E. (1977). The development of concepts of social structure. In J. Glick & A. Clarke-Stewart (Eds.), *Personality and Social Development,* Vol. 1. New York: Gardner Press.

Wehren, A. & DeLisi, R. (1983). The development of gender understanding: Judgments and explanations. *Child Development, 54,* 1568–1578.

# 6
# Socialization of Sex Roles within the Family
## Beverly I. Fagot
## Mary D. Leinbach

Common sense and observation tell us that the world is not the same for boys and girls, but the importance we place on the different worlds boys and girls inhabit depends upon our theoretical biases, our own experiences, and to some extent, on having grown up male or female. Our views on sex role development are suggested by the title of this chapter: although we do not question the importance of the child's own cognitive self-socialization as boy or girl, we assume that the sex typing encountered in everyday life provides the material upon which cognition feeds and that the family is the matrix within which the earliest sex role socialization takes place. There the child first learns who is male and who female, what males and females are and do, and that the whole business of being one or the other somehow matters a great deal. Research has been slow to document, however, what Freud established more or less by fiat: parental input and power over a young child's world do make a difference in how the child grows up, male or female.

The question of socialization of sex roles within the family has been somewhat controversial for the past decade. In their landmark review of the literature on sex differences, Maccoby and Jacklin (1974) concluded that there were surprisingly few differences in the socialization of boys and girls within the family. This view went largely unchallenged until Block (1976, 1978) took a harder look at the information Maccoby and Jacklin had summarized and pointed out a number of shortcomings. Most of the studies had considered only young children, methodological adequacy was not evaluated, and many studies reviewed were not really designed to investigate sex differences. Block held that a more rigorous appraisal of this literature indicated differences in socialization with far-reaching consequences for the development of boys and girls. More recently, Huston (1983) concluded that the evidence for sex-differentiated socialization was stronger than it had been 10 years earlier and that converging data from observational and laboratory studies suggest that parents consistently promote sex differences in activities and interests and, somewhat less consistently, react to boys' and girls' personal and social behaviors in different ways. As with the studies considered by Maccoby and Jacklin, most of the work Huston reviewed was done with young children from intact families—a reflection, perhaps, of an impoverished data base from which to draw conclusions about familial sex typing.

The question of differential socialization within the family has been asked as if sex role socialization represents a single dimension of behavior, but the relationship of parents and children is both multidimensional and bidirectional; the answers we find will vary depending upon which aspects we choose to study. Moreover, we often speak of parental behaviors as if mothers and fathers act as a unit, although we know that they react to their children in different ways. We believe it is useful to look at mothers' and fathers' behaviors toward boys and girls in three different domains—cognitive, affective, and behavioral—and to examine, where possible, the child's contribution to the interaction in each domain. Of course, we must keep in mind that these domains, though conceptually separable, are interdependent.

Much of the work on parental socialization has focused on the cognitive domain. Via questionnaire or interview (without the child present and under nonstressful conditions), parents have been asked what they do or would do, and why. Parents have many values and attitudes concerning childrearing that are available to contemplation and amenable to investigations of this type; in a rational, controlled setting one tends to get rational, controlled answers. Unfortunately, as we know, what parents say they have done, do, or will do, and what they have done, do, or will do may be quite discrepant (Fagot, 1978). Older children and adolescents have also been questioned and interviewed as to what they and their parents believe and do, and these studies are subject to the same limitations one finds with parent interview data. With younger children, sex typing has often been approached as if it involved only the child's own cognition, irrespective of parental influence. Emotional reactions are usually not so accessible to consciousness, and the affective side of parental influence on sex typing has received little attention. Yet parents undoubtedly react to their children's behavior in positive and negative ways, often without benefit of conscious decision making or even knowing why certain patterns of behavior please or annoy them; even subtle approval or disapproval may promote or retard sex typing in the child. As for the behavioral domain, there are laboratory analog studies of parent–child interaction, but observational studies of what parents actually do with their children within the home and family are confined almost entirely to infants and preschoolers.

Block (1983) reported results from both parent report and observational studies of sex-differentiated socialization, but, because more data are available, her review is skewed toward younger children. After careful consideration of the findings, however, she concluded that (1) there is evidence for sex-differentiated socialization; (2) there are specific sex-of-parent and sex-of-child interaction effects; (3) emphasis on sex differentiation appears to increase as children get older; and (4) sex-related values of mothers and fathers appear relatively consistent across socioeconomic and educational levels and cultural backgrounds. Parents, particularly fathers, emphasize achievement and task orientation more for boys than for girls. In doing so, they provide boys with more contingent feedback and give them more opportunity to experiment with toys and other objects and to explore the physical world. Girls tend to be kept under closer supervision and given more help in solving problems. They are provided a more structured and predictable environment, where feedback is more positive and reassuring, but less instructive, than for boys; they are given toys that encourage imitation and repetition rather than innovation. Thus, boys are directed toward understanding the more logical physical world, while girls are directed toward engagement in the interpersonal or social world.

Block (1983) spelled out a number of implications differential socialization has for the cognitive and emotional development of boys and girls. In her view, the physical world promotes active problem solving and mastery because its laws are generally orderly and discoverable, while the social world is more complex and variable, governed by rules and relationships that are not readily comprehended. Consequently, boys learn to examine and understand the world in which they live and develop a greater sense of efficacy or mastery over the environment. Boys are encouraged to change their perspective when new problems or challenges are encountered, or, in Piagetian terms, to accommodate. In their focus on action and change, accommodation or the creation of new adaptive modes may become their preferred way of meeting new situations. Girls, on the other hand, are taught to focus on the right answer or the end product, rather than the process of solving problems; they are encouraged to stay within bounds or to assimilate what is new to what is known, to the detriment of their creativity and problem solving abilities.

Have the 1980s provided new evidence to support Block's view of sex role socialization within the family? One finding stands out clearly: as more investigators have come to include fathers in their samples, we see that it is fathers more than mothers who treat boys and girls differently. It is true that not every study finds differential treatment of boys and girls, but the differences that are found tend to be consistent with each other and with society's sex-typed rules and values. They are also, in general, consistent with Block's hypotheses, but we feel that her rather negative view of girls' socialization misses something important in female development. During childhood, it is girls, not boys, who seem to be less affected by the upsets of divorce (Hetherington, Cox, & Cox, 1982), difficulties in parents' marital adjustment (Emery & O'Leary, 1984), and maternal problems (Sameroff & Seifer, 1983). Even if our childrearing practices are detrimental to girls' cognitive development, as Block suggested, they may still provide advantages in the social realm. Conversely, boys' apparent advantage with regard to cognitive development and mastery should not blind us to the possibility that their socialization could lead to social and emotional deficits.

## DIFFERENTIAL SOCIALIZATION IN THE FIRST FEW YEARS OF LIFE

Huston's (1983) review of the literature on sex typing devoted just one short paragraph to differential treatment of boys and girls during the first year of life. Huston noted that, within the overall similarity of caregiving, a few consistent differences could be seen, but, like Maccoby and Jacklin (1974), she concluded that patterns of parental interaction are similar for boy and girl babies. What parents do for and with baby boys and girls may be similar, but perhaps we have not looked carefully enough at family interactions to document subtle differences and have ignored differences that are too familiar to seem noteworthy.

We all have beliefs about what males and females are like, and sex-typed expectations may blind us to things in one sex that we would see in the other— or lead us to see things that aren't there. Parents of newborns actually appear to perceive their sons and daughters differently. Rubin, Provenzano, and Luria (1974) found that new parents, especially fathers, tended to describe their babies sex-stereotypically. Even though the infants themselves did not differ in birth weight, length, or Apgar scores, fathers were more likely to describe daughters as softer, finer-featured, more awkward, less attractive, weaker, and more delicate, and sons as firmer, larger-featured, better coordinated, more alert, stronger, and heavier. Mothers' ratings, though less extreme, were in the same directions, but mothers rated sons as cuddlier, and fathers rated daughters as cuddlier.

What an infant does may also be interpreted differently, depending on its sex. Haviland (1977) chose videotape segments showing babies with four different facial expressions, so that each expression was displayed by both a boy and a girl. Young adults—some of whom were told the infants' sex correctly, some incorrectly, and some not at all—were asked to judge the emotion shown; those not told the babies' sex were asked to guess. Babies perceived or designated as boys were seen as expressing fear, anger, and distress much more often than those who were, or were presumed to be, girls, who, conversely, were seen as joyful twice as often. Condry and Condry (1976) similarly found that subjects who saw a child labeled a boy displaying an ambiguous negative response interpreted the response as anger, while those who saw the same videotape with the child labeled a girl saw the emotion as fear. Mislabeling the babies caused them to be judged differently in ways that are congruent with adult sex role stereotypes.

Adults also vary their actions toward infants according to the perceived sex of the child. For example, an infant is more likely to be given a sex-appropriate toy and more encouragement for motor activity when labeled as a boy than when identified as a girl (Frisch, 1977; Smith & Lloyd, 1978). Similar differences are found in parents' treatment of their own children. Mothers talk more to their daughters and imitate the infant's vocalizations, but provide more tactile and visual stimulation to sons (Lewis, 1974; Moss, 1967). Fathers, especially with firstborns, stimulate and talk more to sons and, as the boys get older, interact in a hearty, playfully rough manner; daughters are more likely to be cuddled (Lamb, 1978; Parke & Sawin, 1976). Snow, Jacklin, and Maccoby (1983) also found fathers more likely to hold 12–month-old daughters and give them toys; although girls were handed trucks and dolls equally often, dolls were seldom given to boys.

It is possible that boy and girl babies differ in ways that bring about different reactions from parents and thus help shape their own sex typing. Newborn girls, for example, have been shown to maintain eye contact over longer time intervals than newborn boys, and to respond to postural change with increased eye contact (Hittleman & Dickes, 1979). Boys, on the other hand, may find prolonged eye contact too arousing, as their emotional states tend to be more labile, building up more rapidly than those of girls (Osofsky & O'Connell, 1977); gaze aversion may be a way of moderating over-arousal (Haviland & Malatesta, 1981). Since eye contact appears to be a source of pleasure to both caregiver and infant, even a slight difference could alter the course of parents' interactions with their babies in the direction of more social responsiveness for girls. Gunnar and Donahue (1980) found greater reciprocity in mother-daughter than in mother-son dyads. By six months of age, girls were more responsive when their mothers spoke to them and initiated more interactions with the mother than did boys. However, Block (1983) concluded that, even in infancy, boys' vocalizations received more *contingent* responding from both parents and tended to elicit more physical and gross motor stimulation. Perhaps parents perceive boys' greater tendency to avert gaze as a sign that they need to try harder to communicate or interact with sons.

When we look at the real world, we find boys and girls, literally from birth, lovingly enfolded in trappings that both befit and proclaim their sex. Shakin, Shakin, & Sternglanz (1985) observed 1– to 13–month olds in suburban shopping malls and found that the infants' clothing or accessories clearly proclaimed the child's sex. Interestingly, when parents were asked what they considered in choosing clothing for their infants, they did not spontaneously mention sex-appropriateness, but they dressed baby girls in pink, puffed sleeves, ruffles, and lace (even on tiny sox), while boys wore blue or sometimes red, but nothing ruffled or pink. We might add that, in our laboratory, ruffles on girls' overalls are common, and we have even seen beruffled jogging suits! Shakin et al. (1985) noted that sex-typed clothing serves very well to announce the child's sex and thereby ensures sex-appropriate treatment even from strangers. In addition, clothing is functional as well as decorative, and girls' more delicate and restrictive apparel can inhibit active play and promote "ladylike" (i.e., sex-stereotyped) behavior. In the home, too, the stage is set differently for boys and girls. Children's bedrooms are nearly always sex-typed; ruffles and pink are not found in a boy's room. Parents also provide sex-typed toys for their children (Rheingold

& Cook, 1975). The father who rushes out to buy a football for his brand new son is a cliche figure, to be sure, but he does exist.

The sex typing begun in infancy continues as the baby becomes a toddler and then a preschooler. Parents tend to agree on toys' appropriateness to one sex or the other and expect their children to choose sex-appropriate toys when given a choice (Schau, Kahn, Diepold, & Cherry, 1980). Expectations continue to color interpretation. Condry and Ross (1985) presented college students with a video-taped sequence showing two children, dressed in snowsuits so that they could not be identified as boys or girls, involved in aggressive play. Subjects were told that the children were both boys, both girls, or one of each, and asked to rate the behavior of one of the children. Those who thought they were judging two boys saw the behavior as significantly less aggressive and more affectionate than those who thought they were seeing two girls or a boy and a girl. As Condry and Ross interpret their results, "if we see two children 'roughhousing' and we think the two are boys, we say 'boys will be boys' . . . If we do not approve of aggression in our children, we might well stop the girls from 'fighting,' but leave the boys to 'play' roughly but affectionately" (p. 231). They considered parents likely to share this bias in perception, as it was stronger in students who had had more experience with children. We believe parental intervention is more likely to go in the opposite direction. We have found that playgroup caregivers, some of whom are parents and most of whom will be, are more likely to respond to assertive behavior in boys and to ignore it in girls (Fagot, Hagan, Leinbach, & Kronsberg, 1985); adult responses appeared to reinforce rather than punish boys while showing girls that assertive behavior is not the way to get attention. Kronsberg, Schmaling, and Fagot (1985) found that parents who had one boy indicated greater readiness to intervene when they saw a gender-ambiguous child doing something risky, followed by parents who had a boy and a girl, those with only a girl, and couples expecting their first child. Apparently, experience with little boys predisposes one to respond quickly to a child's risk taking; whereas parents of girls may expect children to be more cautious or less impulsive. We see that parents and others hold gender-specific expectations that color their perception of children's actions, and that experience with children of either sex helps shape the expectations adults hold. We might also consider how expectations color investigators' interpretations of their findings.

In looking at differential socialization by parents, it is important to determine what parents actually do as well as what they say, and probably believe, they do. Fagot (1974) found that fathers and mothers of toddlers differed in their views of sex-appropriate behavior, with fathers seeing more behaviors as sex-typed, but that parents of both sexes who were inclined to rate behaviors as sex-typed and parents who viewed the behaviors as equally appropriate for boys and girls differed very little in the treatment of their own children. A somewhat similar effect was shown in a recent study of maternal communication with daughters and sons by Weitzman, Birns, and Friend (1985). The Attitudes toward Women Scale (Spence, Helmreich, & Stapp, 1973) was used to classify mothers as traditional or nontraditional. Both groups showed significant sex-of-child differences in the ways mothers talked to their children, and nontraditional mothers were only slightly, and nonsignificantly, less likely to speak to boys and girls differently.

Despite controversy over the extent to which parents reinforce sex-typed behavior differentially (e.g., Block, 1983), differential reinforcement and punishment in sex typing are facts of life. There are sex-of-parent as well as sex-of-child effects, as Fagot (1978) found when she observed naturally-occurring behavior of toddlers and parents in their homes. The children were between 20 and 24 months of age, and already showed stereotypic sex differences in their actions, to which parents responded in stereotypic ways. Girls were given approval for doll play, dancing, "dressing up," watching television, helping a parent or asking for help, and following or staying close to a parent; they received negative reactions for running, jumping, climbing, and manipulating objects. Boys received more positive responses for block play, but more negative reactions when they played with dolls, or gave or asked for help. Fathers were more likely than mothers to encourage proximity in girls and discourage doll play in boys, while mothers were more encouraging toward girls' attempts to help. Langlois and Downs (1980), in a naturalistic laboratory study, found that girls were rewarded with approval by their mothers and peers for sex-typed play and punished by both for playing with cross-sex toys. Boys received both approval and disapproval from mothers and peers, no matter what they played with. Fathers rewarded children of both sexes for same-sex toy play, with this effect stronger for sons, and punished both sexes for cross-sex play. They also rewarded daughters more and punished sons more.

While many sex differences in the behaviors and attitudes of fathers and mothers toward boys and girls can be found, we must ask how these differences affect the child. Certainly, many treatment differences and later sex differences flow in the same direction. In the Weitzman et al. (1985) study, mothers consistently gave sons more stimulation on a number of language variables considered likely to facilitate cognitive development (teaching, action verbs, numbers, questioning, explicitness, directiveness). It is difficult to determine such effects, however, because many may not be evident in the immediate context, though they may surface in sex differences or sex-typical behavior later on, perhaps from the cumulative weight of behaviors that in themselves often seem inconsequential.

## DIFFERENTIAL SOCIALIZATION IN CHILDHOOD AND ADOLESCENCE

By the time children reach four years of age, we no longer find naturalistic observation studies of parent–child interaction in the home. Instead, we have laboratory analog studies and parent-report measures yielding results that are highly dependent on the different tasks and measures used. For example, Bellinger and Gleason (1982), using a construction task, found that fathers and mothers did not differ in the kinds of directives addressed to boys and girls, although fathers gave more direct, and mothers indirect, instructions. On the other hand, Frankel and Rollins (1983) used a task in which pictures were sorted into categories; here there were no sex-of-parent effects, but boys were given more direction and evaluation, while girls were dealt with in a more concrete, specific, and cooperative style. The studies differed in the nature of the task, the structure of their coding systems, the age of the children, and the area of the country in which they were conducted. Which of these variables, or other variables as yet unknown, accounted for the differences in findings? The literature is simply filled with examples of this kind, making it extremely difficult to confirm or disconfirm a theoretical position such as Block's. In general, however, studies with preschool and grade school children have shown either expected differences in the treatment of boys and girls or no difference at all. We were unable to find a single study in which boys were given less opportunity to explore, less encouragement of achievement, or more emotional support than girls. Thus, we have at least weak support for Block's position on parental differences in socialization, but much more work using comparable methodology with children of different ages and investigating families across a broader socioeconomic range is needed.

In later childhood and adolescence, another methodological change occurs. We now move from an emphasis on laboratory studies of parent–child interaction to studies where socialization is examined primarily via questionnaires given to children as well as parents. We find that adolescents and their parents believe that parents treat boys and girls differently (Block, 1978), but it is not clear whether parents are reacting to differences or creating them, or perhaps both. While the physiological changes of adolescence may bring heightened awareness of sex differences and sex-related expectations, the relationships between adolescents and their parents reflect long-practiced interactions, a heavy accumulation of attitudes, values, and behavior style that may simply lead to reenacting old scripts. Block (1983) found that parental socialization variables at age 4 predicted differently for boys and girls at age 15. While differences in adolescence are definitely present, we feel that to understand the family sex role socialization process we need to look at what parents are doing at a time when differences between boys and girls are minimal and parent–child interactions have not yet been structured by long practice.

## A SHORT-TERM LONGITUDINAL STUDY OF PARENT– CHILD INTERACTION

We have recently completed a short-term longitudinal project in which we followed the development of a group of children from the ages of 18 to 30 months. This study combined traditional macroanalytic measures of child behavior and parent attitudes with microsocial measures obtained via observation.

Fathers and mothers separately completed questionnaires and ratings of their own dyadic adjustment, stress, mood, and irritability, and for their child, temperament rating scales. Parent–child interaction was observed in the home when the children were 18 months old and again at 27 months, and the children were also observed in free play and natural interaction in our laboratory play groups over a period of at least six months. All observational data were collected using codes that allowed us to look at the effects of the behavior of one participant on the behavior of another. In addition, Ainsworth's Strange Situation (Ainsworth, Blehar, Waters, & Wall, 1978) was conducted with mother and child when the children were 18 months of age. At this point, we have analyzed data only for the entry period when children were 16–18 months old, which includes the Strange Situation, in-home observations, and parent-report measures.

We have begun to look at how the family variables derived from parent interviews and responses to questionnaires relate to parents' ongoing management of the child. We have concentrated on ways in which styles of reacting to misbehaviors—*punishment* (hitting, spanking, criticizing) and *positive instruction* (reasoning, diverting or stopping behavior, time out with reasoning or explanation)—are related to the parent-reported variables of mood, stress, and marital adjustment. We also looked at the interrelationships among these parent-reported variables, parents' reports of their own pleasure in child rearing, and the child's temperament.

There was a significant correlation between poor marital adjustment and the use of punishment by both mothers and fathers, but the correlation was much higher for boys than for girls, and boys were treated more harshly. When stressed, both mothers and fathers were more likely to punish boys and less likely to give them positive reinforcement, but this did not hold for girls. Mothers who reported high stress said they continued to give instructions, but fathers said they simply intervened less. The father's mood was related to use of punishment by both parents, but the mother's mood was not. Moreover, if the father said he had little pleasure in the child, both parents punished the child more. When a family used punishment as the major form of discipline, the child showed more resistance in the Strange Situation. These data suggest a very complex set of relationships among the parent-reported variables, parents' feelings about their children, use of discipline, and the child's sex, and for the variables we have studied, greater predictive value for fathers' characteristics than for those of mothers.

In the observation data from the homes of these families, we start to see a pattern emerging that doesn't totally support Block's idea on socialization differences, but that may help explain the finding that in early childhood parents and teachers rate girls more competent and less susceptible to emotional problems. We looked at four different sets of children's behavior: passive withdrawn behaviors, attempts to communicate, negative behaviors, and normative social play. There were no differences in any of these categories between boys and girls at the 16–18–month age.

We then looked at parents' reactions to these child behaviors. We looked at instructional comments such as directives, questions, or explanations, negatives such as physical punishment and criticisms, and positive responses such as smiling, hugging, and kissing. We did not find differences in parents' reactions to boys and girls. When girls engaged in attempts to communicate or normative social play, mothers were more likely to react to them with instructional comments than they were when boys engaged in similar behaviors. However, when boys engaged in negative behaviors, mothers were more likely to respond with negative reactions than they were when girls engaged in negative behaviors. Mothers did not differentiate in the amount of positive, loving responses they gave either sex. Fathers did not differ in the amount of instruction they gave to boys and girls, but they gave much less than mothers. Fathers also reacted negatively to boys' negative behavior more than they did to girls'. Fathers gave boys more warm, loving responses when they were passive and when they attempted to communicate than they did girls. More information and instruction was given to girls when they engaged in social interaction with their mothers. Boys got more negatives from both parents in response to their negative behaviors and more negatives from the father when they attempted to communicate than did girls. Boys received more loving responses from their fathers when they were being passive or engaged in social play than did girls.

We see here one confirmation of Block, that girls are being taught to conform to adult expectations while boys are not given nearly as much instructional feedback on their behaviors. We do not feel that Block was correct in thinking that boys receive more contingent responses. If anything, these data suggest that responses to boys are less contingent, and certainly less informative. At this stage, fathers are responding to their children primarily with emotional feedback, in that they are positive or negative in their responses, while the mothers' primary mode of response is instructional. Fathers do respond more to sons than daughters and mothers more to daughters, so that we see boys and girls receiving very different kinds of feedback in the family even at this early age and prior to the time when we see sex differences in the children's behavior.

When we look at the families reporting the highest levels of stress and marital difficulties, we find that both mothers and fathers increase negative reactions and decrease positives, but mothers continue to provide relatively high levels of instructional behaviors. In the high stress families, girls continue to receive instructions, boys receive more negatives, and the positives drop for both sexes. This has a particular effect for the boy, as much of his feedback has been positive feedback from the father. We reported earlier that boys appear to be more affected by stress and marital problems in the family. We would suggest that it is boys whose environments change more dramatically when parents are under stress. It is not surprising, then, that we see greater reactivity to family problems from boys than girls.

While we cannot rule out biological sex differences with this study, we can show that parents show differences in reactions to boys and girls prior to the time children are showing sex differences in behavior. Furthermore, the differences the parents show are consistent with the kinds of differences we see later in children. As we continue to follow this group of children, we expect to be able to make additional tests of Block's hypotheses. In particular, we will be able to look at emerging intellectual and problem solving abilities in boys and girls, as well as to continue to study the emergence of differences in social behaviors.

## REFERENCES

Ainsworth, M. D. S., Blehar, M. C., Waters, E., & Wall, S. (1978). *Patterns of attachment: A psychological study of the Strange Situation.* Hillsdale, NJ: Lawrence Erlbaum.

Bellinger, D. C. & Gleason, J. B. (1982). Sex differences in parental directives to young children. *Sex Roles, 8,* 1123–1139.

Block, J. H. (1976). Issues, problems, and pitfalls in assessing sex differences: A critical review of "The psychology of sex differences." *Merrill-Palmer Quarterly, 22,* 293–308.

Block, J. H. (1978). Another look at sex differentiation in the socialization behaviors of mothers and fathers. In J. Sherman & F. Denmark (Eds.), *Psychology of women: Future directions of research.* New York: Psychological Dimensions.

Block, J. H. (1983). Differential premises arising from differential socialization of the sexes: Some conjectures. *Child Development, 54,* 1335–1354.

Condry, J. & Condry, S. (1976). Sex differences: A study of the eye of the beholder. *Child Development, 47,* 812–819.

Condry, J. C. & Ross, D. F. (1985). Sex and aggression: The influence of gender label on the perception of aggression in children. *Child Development, 56,* 225–233.

Emery, R. E. & O'Leary, K. D. (1984). Marital discord and child behavior problems in a nonclinic sample. *Journal of Abnormal Child Psychology, 12,* 411–420.

Fagot, B. I. (1974). Sex differences in toddlers' behavior and parental reaction. *Developmental Psychology, 10,* 554–558.

Fagot, B. I. (1978). The influence of sex of child on parental reactions to toddler children. *Child Development, 49,* 459–465.

Fagot, B. I., Hagan, R., Leinbach, M. D., & Kronsberg, S. J. (1985). Differential reactions to assertive and communicative acts of toddler boys and girls. *Child Development, 56,* 1499–1505.

Frankel, M. T. & Rollins, H. A., Jr. (1983). Does mother know best? Mothers and fathers interacting with preschool sons and daughters. *Developmental Psychology, 19,* 694–702.

Frisch, H. L. (1977). Sex stereotypes in adult–infant play. *Child Development, 48,* 1671–1675.

Gunnar, M. R. & Donahue, M. (1980). Sex differences in social responsiveness between six months and twelve months. *Child Development, 51,* 262–265.

Haviland, J. M. (1977). Sex-related pragmatics in infants. *Journal of Communication, 27,* 80–84.

Haviland, J. M. & Malatesta, C. Z. (1981). The development of sex differences in nonverbal signals: Fallacies, facts, and fantasies. In C. Mayo & N. M. Henley (Eds.), *Gender and nonverbal behavior.* New York: Springer Verlag.

Hetherington, E. M., Cox, M., & Cox, R. (1982). Effects of divorce on parents and children. In M. E. Lamb (Ed.), *Nontraditional families: Parenting and child development*. Hillsdale, NJ: Erlbaum.

Hittleman, J. H. & Dickes, R. (1979). Sex differences in neonatal eye contact time. *Merrill-Palmer Quarterly, 25,* 171–184.

Huston, A. C. (1983). Sex-typing. In P. H. Mussen (Eds.), *Handbook of child psychology* (4th ed., Vol. 4). New York: Wiley.

Huston, A. C. (1985). The development of sex typing: Themes from recent research. *Developmental Review, 5,* 1–17.

Kronsberg, S., Schmaling, K., & Fagot, B. I. (1985). Risk in a parent's eyes: Effects of gender and parenting experience. *Sex Roles, 13,* 329–341.

Lamb, M. E. (Ed.). (1978). *Social and personality development.* New York: Holt, Rinehart, & Winston.

Langlois, J. H. & Downs, A. C. (1980). Mothers, fathers, and peers as socialization agents of sex-typed play behaviors in young children. *Child Development, 51,* 1237–1247.

Lewis, M. (1974). State as an infant–environment interaction: An analysis of mother–infant interactions as a function of sex. *Merrill-Palmer Quarterly, 20,* 195–204.

Maccoby, E. E. & Jacklin, C. N. (1974). *The psychology of sex differences.* Stanford, CA: Stanford University Press.

Moss, H. A. (1967). Sex, age, and state as determinants of mother–infant interaction. *Merrill-Palmer Quarterly, 13,* 19–36.

Osofsky, J. D. & O'Connell, E. J. (1977). Patterning of newborn behavior in an urban population. *Child Development, 48,* 532–536.

Parke, R. D. & Sawin, D. B. (1976). The father's role in infancy: A reevaluation. *The Family Coordinator, 25,* 265–371.

Rheingold, H. L. & Cook, K. V. (1975). The content of boys' and girls' rooms as an index of parents' behavior. *Child Development, 46,* 459–463.

Rubin, J. Z., Provenzano, F. J., & Luria, Z. (1974). The eye of the beholder: Parents' views on sex of newborns. *American Journal of Orthopsychiatry, 44,* 512–519.

Sameroff, A. J. & Seifer, R. (1983). Familial risk and child competence. *Child Development, 54,* 1254–1268.

Schau, C. G., Kahn, L., Diepold, J. H., & Cherry, F. (1980). The relationship of parental expectations and preschool children's verbal sex typing to their sex-typed toy play behavior. *Child Development, 51,* 607–609.

Shakin, M., Shakin, D., & Sternglanz, S. H. (1985). Infant clothing: Sex labeling for strangers. *Sex Roles, 12,* 955–963.

Smith, C. & Lloyd, B. (1978). Maternal behavior and perceived sex of infant: Revisited. *Child Development, 49,* 1263–1266.

Snow, M. E., Jacklin, C. N., & Maccoby, E. E. (1983). Sex-of-child differences in father–child interaction at one year of age. *Child Development, 54,* 227–232.

Spence, J. T., Helmreich, R., & Stapp, S. (1973). A short version of the Attitudes toward Women Scale. *Bulletin of Psychonomic Science, 2,* 219–220.

Weitzman, N., Birns, B., & Friend, R. (1985). Traditional and nontraditional mothers' communication with their daughters and sons. *Child Development, 56,* 894–898.

# 7

# The Roles of Peers in Sex Role Socialization

## D. Bruce Carter

## INTRODUCTION

Peers and peer interactions have long been thought to play important roles in the socialization process in general and in sex role socialization in particular (cf. Hartup, 1983). From the perspectives of the major theories of sex role socialization (e.g., Kohlberg, 1966; Mischel, 1970; Roopnarine & Mounts, this volume) peers provide information for children about sex role standards directly and indirectly. First, peers may provide information about sex-role norms through play activities and toys employed in play. Second, peers may provide information for children by their reactions to the behaviors of others, that is, through directly reinforcing certain behaviors while punishing other behaviors. Third, peers may influence children's adoption of sex-role norms through verbal endorsement of sex stereotypes and conventional sex-roles. Finally, children's conceptions of the gender-related attitudes and beliefs of their peers may lead to the adoption of sex-role standards that rely on beliefs about the behaviors and characteristics that the peer group is likely to tolerate among its members.

This chapter focuses on the influence of peer interaction on the sex-typing process from preschool through adolescence. Four major influences are outlined, the first two of which are experiential in nature while the remaining two are more cognitive. The first influence is that of the self-segregation of children into single-sex peer groups. This well documented segregation is discussed in terms of its occurrence both in nonhuman primate species and in human children. Second, the effects of direct reinforcement and punishment of sex-typed behaviors by peers on sex typing in children's behavior are discussed. Third, the influence of sex-stereotypes and the verbal and nonverbal endorsement of sex-stereotypical behavior by children are discussed. Fourth, the roles that children's conceptions of stereotypes and their beliefs about the responses of peers to sex-typical and sex-atypical behavior are discussed. Finally, the summary offers one means of integrating these sometimes diverging factors into a coherent pattern.

## EXPERIENTIAL FACTORS IN PEER INTERACTION: SEX SEGREGATION

Any discussion on the influence of peer groups on the socialization process must explicitly acknowledge the fact that boys and girls are socialized in two virtually nonoverlapping groups of peers: boys are socialized by their boy peers and girls by their girl peers. The pattern of sex-segregated interaction is so well documented in the developmental literature that a recent review noted that it did not "require extensive comment" (Hartup, 1983; p. 109). Indeed, sex segregation in play and peer interactions is evident both in Western and non-Western societies (e.g., D'Andrade, 1965; Mead, 1949/1977; Whiting & Child, 1953) and in many higher species of nonhuman primates (Mitchell, 1981). It is to these latter data that we now turn our attention.

### Sex Segregation in Nonhuman Primates.

Stable sex segregation patterns are seen in most species of both New World monkeys (e.g., spider monkeys), Old World monkeys (e.g., macaques and baboons), and apes (e.g., chimpanzees). In general such sex segregation occurs in the prepubescent period although in some species sex segregation does not appear until after puberty (Mitchell, 1981). In rhesus macaques, for example, sex segregation and preferences for interacting with same-sex individuals begin to emerge at around seven months of age and are maintained through puberty (around 3 years of age). Rhesus macaques show other-sex preferences for only a short period of time, however, shifting back to same-sex preferences at about three and a half years when adolescent males become peripheralized (i.e., move to the outer edges of the troop), join all-male groups, or join other troops. In general, across species of Old World monkeys, males are more likely to be solitary or to be on the periphery of a troop than are females while females are more likely to space themselves closer together than are males (Mitchell, 1981). In lesser apes (e.g., gibbons) sex differences in spacing are minimal and both males and females are peripheralized prior to puberty, i.e. at about 2 1/2 years of age. Among the great apes (chimpanzees, gorillas, and orangutans) males are also more likely to be peripheralized, to be more frequently solitary, and to sleep alone than are females of the same species (Mitchell, 1981). Because family units in both the lesser and greater ape species are smaller than the size of troops found among monkeys, fewer age-mates exist for prepubescent apes and little can be said about sex differences in patterns of peer interaction in these species (Jolly, 1972; van Lawick-Goodall, 1971). Nonetheless, it is clearly the case that the preadolescent segregation of males from their families and the existence of semipermanent, all-female troops of related individuals at least in some species (e.g., chimpanzees; van Lawick-Goodall, 1971) is indicative of sex segregation among our closest primate relatives.

The quality of play in sex-segregated nonhuman primate groups also exhibits sex differences. Suomi (1977), for example, notes that male–male pairings among rhesus macaques are more likely to result in reciprocal behaviors than are interactions among other pairings of juvenile monkeys. Moreover, both rough and tumble play and aggression are more likely to occur among male–male pairs of peers than among female–female pairs (Harlow & Lauersdorf, 1974). Similarly, Owens (1975) observes that play and aggression in *Papio anubis* (the olive baboon) serve different functions and differ between males and females. In this species, body contact is longer in play than in aggressive acts and chasing is longer in aggression than in play. Dominant and subordinant roles are often reversed in both male–male play and male–male aggression while such role reversals are uncommon in both female play and female aggression. Owens (1975) proposes that play in juvenile male baboons serves as practice for aggression while among females the more stable dominance hierarchies select against in-fighting that could damage a female's ability to reproduce or compromise her unborn fetus. Among the great apes, sex differences in quality of play emerge, with males engaging in more play overall and exhibiting greater levels of aggression than do females (Mitchell, 1981).

Sociobiological explanations of sex segregation in nonhuman primates rely largely on the importance attributed to the roles of within-sex dominance hierarchies in sexual reproduction (cf. Daly & Wilson, 1978). Dominance hierarchies for both males and females are established within sex-segregated groups. For males, early play experiences, especially rough and tumble or aggressive play, are thought to lay the groundwork both for acquiring social interactional skills and for these dominance hierarchies (Owens, 1975). Among females, in contrast, dominance is established with a minimum of overt aggression and, in some species, a female's place within the dominance hierarchy may be determined by her mother's position (Symons, 1979). In most species of nonhuman primates dominance is the crucial determinant of access to copulation (e.g., Symons, 1979). Less dominant males may be denied access to copulation by more dominant males and by the females themselves. Similarly, more dominant females may deny less dominant females access to males within the troop. Thus, sex segregation among nonhuman primates is a stable phenomenon that may serve the evolutionarily adaptive function of ensuring the mating of the most successful members of a species while simultaneously providing different social experiences for male and female members of a species (cf. Daly & Wilson, 1978).

The acknowledgment both of the existence of sex segregation across species of nonhuman primates and that it may serve particular roles for reproduction should not be taken as indicative that all such behavior is "merely instinctive" or that it may not also serve as a means of socialization. Nonhuman primate social behavior is, in many ways, as complex as much human social behavior and varies greatly across species (e.g., Lancaster, 1975). Indeed, recently certain primatologists have begun making "cross-cultural" comparisons between troops of primates living in geographically separate locales and have identified differences among the troops (e.g., McGrew, Tutin, & Baldwin, 1979). Thus, it would be misleading to trivialize a behavior or characteristic because it appears in related species of animals and thus may be "instinctive" in one sense of the word. Sex segregation in nonhuman primates does afford juvenile males and females of these species with experience in the behaviors that facilitate the roles they are most likely to play as adults in much the same way that sex segregation among human children facilitates their acquisition of sex-typical behaviors. Thus while it is important to avoid being anthropomorphic when describing social interaction patterns among nonhuman primates, it is equally important to avoid being "anthropocentric" when considering the importance such patterns play in the social life of these animals.

## Sex Segregation in Children

Sex segregation in human children is as commonplace as in our primate cousins. In general, boys are more likely to affiliate and play with other boys while girls are more likely to affiliate and play with other girls. Sex segregation in children's play groups is seen as early as three years of age (e.g., Charlesworth & Hartup, 1967; Serbin, Tonick, & Sternglanz, 1977) and children express definite preferences for affiliating with same-sex others from the preschool years through early adolescence (Carter & McCloskey, 1984; Serbin & Sprafkin, 1986). A variety of explanations have been advanced to explain this nearly universal phenomenon. Ethological explanations and explanations relying on notions of behavioral compatibility (e.g., Goodenough, 1934; Haskett, 1971; Mitchell, 1981) posit that the activities and behaviors of a child may attract members of the same sex while repelling members of the other sex. In contrast, cognitive developmental theories (e.g., Kohlberg, 1966) maintain that cognitive factors, especially gender constancy, contribute strongly to preferences for same-sex others and sex-typed behaviors. Finally, social learning theories (e.g., Mischel, 1970) rely on notions of both direct reinforcement provided by others to children playing with members of their own sex and the reinforcements for engaging in sex-typical behavior that are more likely to occur when children are playing with others who are similar in sex to themselves. Data pertinent to these three explanations are discussed below.

Several studies have investigated patterns of play among young boys and girls in an attempt to determine differences in young children's activity preferences and whether or not behavioral compatibility per se has a significant effect on patterns of play behavior. Crucial to the argument that behavioral compatibility is the crucial component of sex segregation are data from studies of play interactions and affiliation patterns among toddlers and preschoolers. Jacklin and Maccoby's (1978) study of social behavior in 45 same- and mixed-sex pairs of unacquainted toddlers provides such data. The 33–month-old participants in this study were observed in a laboratory play setting with a series of attractive toys and children's social behaviors directed towards their partners and their vocalizations served as the principal foci of the study. Overall, significant differences emerged in the behaviors of same- vs. mixed-sex pairs of children. Total social behavior was higher in same-sex pairs and lower in mixed-sex pairs, a difference especially marked in the behavior of girls in mixed sex pairs. Girls showed more passive behavior when paired with boys than did boys in mixed-sex pairs or for either sex in same-sex pairs. And while both boys and girls responded appropriately to verbal prohibitions by boy peers in same- and mixed-sex pairs, boys were less likely to respond to verbal prohibitions issued by girls in mixed-sex pairs than were girls in same-sex pairs. Finally, while the rates of social behavior in same-sex pairs were similar, boy–boy pairs were less likely to engage in the sustained social interaction found in girl–girl pairs. While Jacklin and Maccoby's data do not rule out the possibility that children's awareness of the others' sex relative to their own may influence the patterns of these play interactions, they are indicative of certain levels of behavioral compatibility in the play of toddlers that may lay the groundwork for the phenomenon of sex segregation in children.

Not surprisingly, significant differences also emerge among the play behaviors and patterns of social interaction exhibited by preschool-aged boys and girls. For example, Eisenberg, Tryon, and Cameron (1984) investigated relationships between toy preferences and affiliation patterns among 51 four-year-old girls and boys enrolled in a preschool. Children were videotaped during free-play and their use of sex-typed and sex-neutral toys as well as their interactions with other children were coded. As might be expected, children played more with stereotype-consistent (i.e., sex-appropriate) toys than with stereotype-inconsistent toys, although the greatest amount of play was observed with sex-neutral toys. Play with other sex peers was significantly and negatively correlated with preferences for stereotype-consistent toys for both boys and girls, although the correlation for same-sex peer preferences and play with stereotype-consistent toys approached significance. For all children, contact with others prior to beginning a play sequence with a toy was rare but both boys and girls were more likely to seek contact and begin playing with another same-sex peer than with an other-sex peer after securing a toy. Similar relationships in peer interaction patterns among kindergarteners have been found by a number of other researchers (e.g., Blomberg, 1983; Fagot & Leinbach, 1983; Lamb & Roopnarine, 1979; Langlois, Gottfried, & Seay, 1973; cf. Johnson & Roopnarine, 1983). Thus, it would appear to be the case that stable sex segregation patterns and sex differences in children's play with same- and other-sex peers are the norm among preschoolers and kindergarteners.

Sex segregation among preschool-aged children and kindergarteners would seem to be best explained by social learning treatments of this phenomenon. First, substantial evidence exists that children of these ages, as well as those younger than preschool age, are highly unlikely to have achieved the stable sense of gender constancy that is a prerequisite of the cognitive consistency postulated by the cognitive developmental model (cf., Carter & Taylor, 1987; Jacklin & Maccoby, 1978; Liss, 1983). In addition, some studies of relationships between stage of gender constancy and peer preferences among preschoolers and kindergarteners have indicated no significant relationships between children's awareness of gender constancy and either their peer or activity preferences (e.g., Carter & Taylor, 1987; Serbin & Sprafkin, 1986). Second, a number of research studies have indicated that children who violate sex role norms, including those for same-sex affiliation and play, are more likely to receive negative responses from their peers than are children who adhere to conventional norms for sex-typed behavior (e.g., Carter & McCloskey, 1984; Fagot, 1977; Lamb, Easterbrooks, & Holden, 1980). Moreover, intervention studies such as Serbin et al., (1977) indicate that preferences for same-sex others can be modified through changing the reinforcing contingencies that control such behavior. It should be noted, however, that the acceptance of social learning mechanisms as an explanation for the persistence of same sex affiliation and play preferences does not preclude the supposition that behavioral compatibility lies at the root of sex segregation.

Among school-aged children patterns of interaction similar to those found among preschoolers are found. For example, Stoneman, Brody and MacKinnon (1984) observed the play behaviors of school-aged children, their friends, and their younger siblings in same-sex pairs in naturalistic settings and identified several patterns of sex differences in both the settings and styles of play seen in young boys and girls. Girls were more likely to engage in indoor play and play with dolls than were boys and boys were more likely to engage in competitive physical activities than were girls. Interestingly, a pattern of lack of sustained social interaction among boys similar to that seen in the toddlers in Jacklin and Maccoby's data emerged in these data as well. Boys in this sample were significantly more likely to engage in solitary activities in the presence of a same-sex friend than were girls. Finally, girls and younger siblings of both sexes were more likely to accept direction from their play partners than were older boys. Similarly, Huston, Carpenter, Atwater, and Johnson's (1986) study of children's play interactions in a daycamp setting indicated that school-aged girls exhibited higher rates of social initiations than did their male peers while girls were more likely to be the recipients of direction from their peers than were boys. Thus it would appear that a certain degree of match between the behavior of boys and girls is present among preschoolers and that similar tendencies are maintained through social interaction among older children.

The patterns of play behavior and affiliation seen among school-aged children match predictions regarding these phenomena from both the social learning and cognitive development theories. The absence of any data on relationships between same-sex affiliation patterns, play preferences, and need to maintain cognitive consistency among children of these ages, however, makes it difficult to evaluate the predictions of the cognitive developmental theory. Nonetheless, certain data are available that offer some support for the hypotheses made by cognitive developmentalists regarding such relationships at these ages. Data from a number of studies offer evidence that it is during the early elementary school years that children begin to devalue reliably the other sex and its activities while placing increasing value on same-sex peers and the activities associated with their own sex (e.g., Carter & McCloskey, 1984; cf. Huston, 1983). Clearly, however, reinforcement for engaging in play with same-sex others remains a potent force during the elementary school years as well. Thus, while cognitive consistency may play a role in sex segregation in play and affiliation tendencies during the elementary school years, learning mechanisms continue to play an important role in these phenomena.

The nature of peer relationships among preadolescent and adolescent boys and girls shows a remarkable consistency with that seen at younger ages. As is the case with younger children, preadolescents and early adolescents are more likely to affiliate with same-sex than with other-sex peers (cf. Hartup, 1983). Pre- and early adolescent children, for example, tend to congregate in small groups of friends or cliques of around five persons that share common interests or attitudes. Such cliques are almost always unisexual in early adolescence, becoming heterosexual in middle adolescence (cf. Coleman, 1980). Moreover, relationships between individuals within a particular sex show differential patterns for boys and girls of these ages. For example, Eder and Hallinan (1978) performed a sociometric analysis of same-sex friendship patterns in preadolescents and found that girls were more likely than boys to be involved in exclusive friendships. As adolescence progresses, however, unisexual cliques begin to break down and heterosexual dating couples begin to emerge, signalling the end, or at least a truce, in the phenomenon of sex segregation.

## Summary

Despite differences in theoretical explanations of the origins and maintenance of sex segregation in play, a number of similarities emerge. First, it is clear that sex segregation in play groups and same sex affiliation preferences are present in both nonhuman primates and in human children from late infancy through early adolescence. Such findings are indicative of the strength of same-sex affiliative tendencies in these groups. Moreover, the pattern of findings offers support for the notion that sex segregation at institutional levels (such as play groups and schools) may serve further to support well-ingrained tendencies of children to associate with others of the same sex. Second, same-sex affiliation and play preferences appear to be malleable, but are fairly resistant to change in the absence of strong outside supports. While it is clear that external changes in the reinforcement and punishment contingencies can increase the amount of play with other-sex persons, indicating that such contingencies do exert some influence on same- and cross-sex play, the relatively rapid diminution of other-sex play when such contingencies return to their premanipulation rates indicate the robust nature of same-sex affiliations. Finally, it is clear that same-sex play and affiliation preferences limit children's exposure to alternative or cross-sex behaviors and strengthen their perceptions that behavior exhibited by same-sex peers is either the preferable or the only behavioral option open to them. While other factors clearly have an impact on the influence of peers on children's sex role socialization, it is undoubtedly the case that young children's socialization by peers occurs within the context of sex segregation. Thus, it is within this context that these remaining factors will be discussed.

## EXPERIENTIAL FACTORS IN PEER INTERACTION: TOY/ACTIVITY PREFERENCES

The fact that parents provide different toys for their sons and daughters (Rheingold & Cook, 1975), prefer same-sex peers for their toddlers' play companions (e.g., Lewis, Young, Brooks, & Michaelson, 1975), and encourage sex-typical behavior in their children (Fagot, 1978) especially their boys (Fagot, 1978; Fagot & Leinbach, this volume; Filing & Manosevitz, 1972), has been well established. Moreover, parental enactment of sex-typed roles in the home provides children with models for their own behavior and may encourage their adoption of traditional sex roles (cf. Fagot & Leinbach, this volume; Huston, 1983). Such behaviors on the part of parents lay the groundwork for the sex-typing processes that occur throughout childhood and adolescence. Yet the influence that parents have on children's preferences for sex-typed activities and sex-appropriate toys pales beside the powerful influences that peers exert on children's toy and activity preferences (e.g., Barry, 1980).

Peer influences on sex typing in toy and activity preferences are most readily viewed in the area of children's adherence to sex-stereotype consistent behaviors. As was the case with sex segregation, a variety of theoretical explanations for sex typing in children's toy and activity preferences have been advanced. Most compelling of the explanations are, however, those advanced by the cognitive development and the social learning theories. According to cognitive development theory (e.g., Kohlberg, 1966), children's adherence to sex role norms, much like their sex segregation tendencies in play, reflects their needs to maintain cognitive consistency between their positive evaluations of themselves and others of the same sex, and sex typing in their behavior. Crucial to this formulation is children's acquisition of gender constancy, an attainment which Kohlberg (1966) maintains is essential for adherence to sex typed behavioral norms. Social learning approaches to this phenomenon, in contrast, rely on children's direct and indirect (e.g., through modelling or instruction about stereotypes) experiences of reinforcement for stereotype-consistent behavior and punishment for stereotype-inconsistent behavior, as well as the expectancies for reward and punishment that emerge from these experiences. Data from studies of sex differences in children's toy and activity preferences are presented below with regard to these two theoretical formulations.

Sex differences in children's preferred play activities are well documented.

Boys, for example, are more likely than girls to play outdoors (e.g., Stoneman et al., 1984), to engage in rough and tumble play (DiPietro, 1981), and to behave aggressively in naturalistic settings (Maccoby & Jacklin, 1974). Indeed, a number of sex differences in the toy and activity preferences of children and adolescents have been established over the years. In particular, Fagot and her colleagues (e.g., Fagot & Leinbach, 1983; Fagot & Patterson, 1969) have conducted a series of studies over the past two decades that indicate remarkable stability in sex typing of behaviors and toys seen in young children from different age cohorts across this period of time. Fagot's method for determining sex differences in toy and activity preferences has involved the observation of preschool children in nursery school free play settings and the monitoring of the behavior and toy preferences that are reliably seen in each sex. Male typical behaviors that have been identified by this process include play with transportation toys (e.g., cars and trucks), and hammering and carpentry play, whereas female typical behaviors include participation in art activities, doll play, and dancing.

While Fagot's data address sex differences only in the behavior of preschoolers and kindergarteners, there is surprising consistency between the sex typed behaviors identified behaviorally by Fagot and the behaviors nominated as sex typical by kindergarteners through sixth graders in Carter and McCloskey's (1984) study of peer responses to cross-gender behavior (see Table 7.1). Overall, play with vehicles comprised the majority of nominations for "boys' toys" while dolls were reported to be the toy of choice for girls. Not surprisingly, both the behaviors identified through Fagot's behavioral observations and those nominated by children in Carter and McCloskey's study are consistent with the norms for sex-typed behavior present in American culture.

The factors that determine the influence of peers on children's adherence to sex-typed play and activity norms provide the crucial test of the explanatory power of the cognitive development and social learning theories to account for these phenomena. From a cognitive development perspective, children's knowledge of gender constancy should be the principal determinant of sex typing in their behavior and preferences while from a social learning perspective, behavior and preferences should be controlled by children's experiences with reward and punishment, modelling, and reinforcement expectancies. Data relevant to these hypothesized relationships are discussed below.

## Gender Constancy Effects on Preferences

A large number of studies have been conducted to assess relationships between sex typing in children's toy and activity preferences and their level of gender constancy (see Carter & Levy, 1987b and Huston, 1983, for reviews). In general, acquisition of gender constancy per se has been only weakly and tangentially related to sex typing in children's preferences and activities (e.g., Carter, Levy, & Cappabianca, 1985; Carter & Levy, 1987a; Carter & Taylor, 1987; Fagot et al., 1986; Serbin & Sprafkin, 1986). Contrary to theoretical predictions of cog-

**Table 7.1**
**Content of Child-Generated Sex Stereotypes and Percentages of Children Generating Traits in Each Grade by Stereotype Category**

| Category | Examples from Transcripts | Grade | | | |
|---|---|---|---|---|---|
| | | K | 2 | 4 | 6 |
| *Toys* | | | | | |
| Masculine | | | | | |
| Vehicles | Cars, skateboards, planes | 75 | 75 | 60 | 50 |
| Action games | Football, soccer, guns | 15 | 20 | 35 | 45 |
| Seated games | Chess, puzzles | 10 | 5 | 5 | 5 |
| Feminine | | | | | |
| Dolls | Baby Dolls, Barbie dolls | 90 | 95 | 95 | 90 |
| Other | Jump rope, jacks, puzzles | 10 | 5 | 5 | 10 |
| *Activities* | | | | | |
| Masculine | | | | | |
| Sports | Football, baseball | 40 | 35 | 65 | 60 |
| Rough play | Fighting, army games | 20 | 45 | 30 | 30 |
| Other | Teasing, tag | 30 | 15 | 5 | 10 |
| Not applicable | No response | 10 | 5 | — | — |
| Feminine | | | | | |
| School oriented | Reading, writing | — | 20 | 5 | 5 |
| Home-oriented | Cooking, sewing | 60 | 45 | 25 | 25 |
| Appearance | Makeup, wearing dresses, hair length | 20 | 15 | 25 | 25 |
| Physical | Dancing, jump-rope gymnastics | 15 | 20 | 45 | 45 |
| Not applicable | No response | 5 | — | — | — |

*Note:* K = kindergarteners;
     2 = second-graders;
     4 = fourth graders;
     6 = sixth-graders;
*Source:* From Carter & McCloskey (1984). Copyright Guilford Press. Reprinted with permission.

nitive development theory (Kohlberg, 1966), children's simple knowledge of their own and others' genders, and not degree of pure gender constancy, has been shown to be extremely predictive of sex typing in children's toy and activity preferences (e.g., Kuhn, Nash, & Brucken, 1977; Marcus & Overton, 1978; Smetana, 1986; Smetana & Letourneau, 1984; Weinraub, et al., 1984). Thus only minimal support can be offered for the hypothesis that gender constancy has a significant impact on sex typing in children's activities and preferences.

## Social Learning and Sex Typing in Preferences

The data on the effects of social learning variables (reinforcement, punishment, modelling, and expectancies) on sex typing in children's preferences and activities is strongly supportive of theoretical predictions about relationships between these variables. According to the social learning formulation, sex typing in children's activities and preferences should be strongly influenced by their experiences with and expectancies for reinforcement and punishment for engaging in sex typed behaviors. Moreover, children are expected to attend to and imitate more of the behavior of same-sex models and those whose behavior is consistent with norms for sex-typed behavior.

There are extensive data on the effects of peer reinforcement and punishment on sex-typing in children's behaviors and preferences (e.g., Fagot, 1977; Lamb, et al., 1980; Lamb & Roopnarine, 1979; Langlois & Downs, 1980; Roopnarine, 1984; Serbin, et al., 1977). Moreover, the patterns of relationships that emerge in these data are fully supportive of predictions made by social learning theory. Studies of preschoolers' responses toward cross-gender behavior in their peers indicate that they reliably punish children, especially boys, who engage in cross-gender behavior (e.g., Fagot, 1977; Fagot & Patterson, 1969; Langlois & Downs, 1980). Moreover, a number of investigators (e.g., Lamb, et al., 1980; Lamb & Roopnarine, 1979) have reported that kindergarteners actively reinforce children who engage in sex-appropriate behavior. Finally, research indicates that children adjust their behavior to conform to the norms for sex typing that their peers are enforcing (e.g., Lamb, et al., 1980; Lamb & Roopnarine, 1979). Sex-typed behavior in later childhood also has been linked to children's awareness of norms for sex-typed behavior and the ways in which peers may respond to violations of such norms (e.g., Carter & McCloskey, 1984). Thus, it appears to be the case that reinforcement and punishment by peers exert powerful influences on sex typing in children's behavior.

In many instances the mere presence of a peer may serve to influence sex typing in the play behavior of young children. For example, Serbin, Connor, Burchardt, and Citron (1979) examined the amount of time preschoolers spent playing with stereotype-consistent and -inconsistent toys in a free play setting. Children participated in each of three separate play sessions in which they either played alone, played in the presence of a same-sex peer, or played in the presence of an other-sex peer. The peer engaged in a coloring task while the target child played with toys and thus interaction between target child and peer was minimal. Overall, boys played with stereotype-inconsistent toys less than girls did and presence of a peer significantly affected children's play with stereotype-inconsistent toys. Interestingly, presence of an other-sex peer appeared to inhibit significantly children's play with stereotype-inconsistent toys relative to the amount of such play seen when children played alone. Amount of time spent playing with stereotype-inconsistent toys in the presence of a same-sex peer fell between the amounts of time spent playing with stereotype-inconsistent toys in both the solitary and other-sex peer conditions but was not significantly different from scores in these conditions. Thus, the mere presence of peers may exert an influence on sex typing in young children's play.

Stereotype-inconsistent behavior among older children and adolescents is com-

paratively rare, diminishing to nearly zero among children in middle childhood (cf. Carter & McCloskey, 1984). Yet both children's reports of responses toward their own cross-gender behavior and their beliefs about how
they would respond to hypothetical instances of cross-gender behavior in
peers indicate that reinforcement for sex-typical behavior and punishment for
sex-atypical behavior both exists for older children and adolescents and is
expected to occur when gender norms are violated. Friedman and Huling
(1982), for example, report that adolescent girls enrolled in predominately
male, sex-atypical vocational training programs in New York City are likely
to be the objects of harassment from both their male peers and from the
teachers and officials administrating the programs. Friedman and Huling
speculate that such treatment of adolescent girls enrolled in these programs
and the expectations of such treatment by girls not enrolled in the programs
account for the low rates of applications for admission to and graduation
from sex-atypical vocational training programs among adolescent girls. Similarly, Carter and McCloskey's (1984) data indicate that older children and
preadolescents are likely to respond very negatively to violations of conventional norms for sex-typed behavior. Clearly, both the overt behavior of
peers and children's expectations about how they would respond to sex-atypical behavior indicate strong support for the influence of peers on the maintenance of sex-typical behavior beyond the preschool.

Modelling of sex-typical behavior by peers is the final influence of interest
from a social learning perspective. According to this theoretical formulation,
children are more likely to exhibit behaviors modelled by same-sex peers than
that exhibited by other-sex peers, especially if the behavior is perceived to be
consistent with gender norms. Studies of the roles of modelling on the acquisition
of sex-typed behavior in young children have consistently indicated that stereotype-consistent behaviors modelled by same-sex peers or adults are more likely
to be imitated than those exhibited by other-sex peers or adults (cf. Huston,
1983). Two recent studies by Bussey and Perry (Perry & Bussey, 1979; Bussey
& Perry, 1982) indicate, however, that children's attention to both the gender
of a model and the degree to which the model's behavior is representative of
members of the same sex are important determinants of imitation of the model.

In both the Bussey and Perry (1982) and Perry and Bussey (1979) studies
children viewed videotapes of a panel of eight peer models (four boys, four girls)
who indicated preferences for sex neutral objects in a manner that gave the
impression that the objects were either masculine-typed (i.e., the majority of
male peer models showed a preference for the items), feminine-typed (i.e., the
majority of female peer models showed a preference for the items), or sex neutral
(i.e., male and female peer models showed equal preferences for the items). In
both studies children were asked to indicate their preferences for items for which
they had previously seen one or more models indicate their preferences. Not
surprisingly, in both studies children were more likely to indicate preferences
for items that had been rendered sex-typical by the choice patterns of the models.

Interestingly, in the Perry and Bussey (1979) study, consistency of the model's behavior with other same-sex models had a significant impact on children's imitation of the modelled preferences. When a model's behavior was consistent with the behavior of other same-sex models, children were more likely to imitate the model's behavior along gender lines (i.e., boys would imitate the behavior of a boy model whose behavior was consistent with that of other boy models and avoid the behavior of consistent cross-sex models) and avoided imitation of same-sex peer models whose behavior was not consistent with other same-sex models. Thus the imitation of behavior modelled by same- and other-sex peers would appear to be influenced by both the gender of the model and the consistency with sex typed behavioral norms.

### Summary

It is clearly the case that the social learning processes of reinforcement, punishment, modelling, and expectancies have a significant impact on sex typing in the behavior of young children and that peers are an important source of these processes. Peers have been shown to react positively to stereotype-consistent behavior and negatively to stereotype-inconsistent behavior in children and the behavior of children in response to such reactions has been shown to be modified. It is also apparent that young children do not imitate blindly the behaviors of same-sex peers but rather they appear to engage in a process in which they compare the sex typicality of a peer's behavior to the behavior of other same-sex individuals in deciding whether or not they should imitate the behavior. The ability to make such comparisons is clearly a function of a child's level of cognitive development and it might be expected that such abilities would change across the preschool and elementary school years. Thus, it might be expected that the roles that sex-typicality of behavior would play in children's imitation of same- and other-sex models would vary as a function of level of cognitive development. Nonetheless, it remains the case that the relative influence of peer enforcement of gender related norms and modelling of sex-typed behavior have a significant impact on children's adherence to such norms.

## COGNITIVE FACTORS IN PEER INTERACTION: STEREOTYPING

Sex stereotypes and children's knowledge of norms for gender relevant behavior are considered by the major theoretical treatments of sex role socialization as a primary source of information regarding the acceptability of sex-typed behavior (cf. Roopnarine & Mounts, this volume). Clearly, several sources of stereotypes for gender relevant behavior exist, including parental values, images presented by the media, information contained in books and classroom materials, and the behavior of peers (e.g., Huston, 1983). Moreover, the stereotypical information contained in these sources traditionally is thought to have a significant impact on adherence to sex role norms across the lifespan (cf. Carter & Taylor, 1987). Thus, children's knowledge and understanding of sex role stereotypes, especially those espoused by peers, should have a significant impact on children's adoption of sex-typed behavior.

The majority of studies of stereotype acquisition and the development of children's understanding of gender norms show a consistent pattern (cf. Huston, 1983). Both children's knowledge of cultural stereotypes for gender relevant behavior and their recognition of flexibility in these behavioral norms show significant linear increases across the elementary school years, approximating adult knowledge and understanding of these norms by around 10 years of age (e.g., Carter & Patterson, 1982; Tremaine, Schau, & Busch, 1982). Despite such increases in children's understanding that gender norms are subject to exception, however, children show a concurrent development of intolerance for peers who violate norms for sex typed behavior (e.g., Carter & McCloskey, 1984). Interestingly, while children's knowledge of sex stereotypes, their intolerance for cross gender behavior, and their adherence to sex-typed norms show similar patterns of development, little evidence exists that links knowledge of stereotypes to sex typing in behavior (Carter & Taylor, 1987; Huston, 1983). In large part, however, the absence of such relationships between stereotype knowledge and adherence to sex typing in behavior probably reflects the fairly high levels of stereotype knowledge and low levels of cross gender play evinced by children in the majority of studies conducted (e.g., Carter & Taylor, 1987).

Unfortunately, the roles that peers directly play in children's acquisition of knowledge about sex stereotype norms has not been an area that has received much attention in the empirical literature. In part this problem may reflect the fact that stereotypes for sex typing in behavior have multitudinous sources, only one of which is the peer group, and may be taught either directly or indirectly. Direct teaching of sex role norms by peers is a well known "fact" based on anecdotal evidence, but empirical evidence on this phenomenon is rather sparse. In contrast, indirect teaching, such as that provided by modelling of behavior (e.g., Bussey & Perry, 1982), children's responses to sex-typical and sex-atypical behavior (e.g., Carter & McCloskey, 1984; Fagot, 1978), and the fact that children may limit behavioral choices open to others to sex-typical choices (e.g., Blomberg, 1983), is well documented in the empirical literature and provides yet another means by which children may acquire information about sex stereotypes from their peers. These latter data can only partially address the issue of the roles that peers may play in the stereotyping process.

The absence of reliable data on the influence of peers on children's knowledge of and adherence to sex stereotype norms is a distressing shortcoming in the empirical literature on peer influences on sex role socialization. This lack of evidence is surprising given the fact that peers may provide a source for new sex stereotypes for children, especially those children entering a new situation or setting. For example, prior to the sixth grade the author attended a small private elementary school where the game of jacks was one that both boys and girls played and at which I became quite proficient. Imagine my chagrin when, upon moving to a larger public elementary school in the sixth grade, I discovered that I was a potential champion for a "girls' game"! The source of my information, and shame, was my male peer group, who let me know right off the bat that such behavior was unacceptable among boys—especially the new kid. Clearly other children have found themselves in comparable situations and such transitions may provide valuable insight into the roles of peers in teaching stereotypes to other children.

## Summary

The roles that peers play in the acquisition of sex stereotypes represents an area of empirical investigation that is ripe for study and should provide valuable insight into the process of sex role socialization in the peer group. A number of strategies are possible for such study. For example, clinical interview studies, in the Piagetian mode, could be conducted to assess either children's conceptions of sources of their sex stereotupes, children's conceptions of ways in which they might impart sex role norms to new or existing peers, or both. From a more behavioral perspective, classrooms or schools that varied along the dimension of how sex-typed behavior in the classroom was, could be identified and compared with children's knowledge of sex stereotypes and responses to violations of sex role norms. Similarly, naturalistic or experimental observations of children teaching other children about sex role norms would provide valuable information on the influence of peers on the sex stereotyping process. Clearly further attention can and should be devoted to the influence of peers on this phenomenon.

## COGNITIVE FACTORS IN PEER INTERACTION: CONCEPTIONS ABOUT PEERS AND GENDER

Children's conceptions of peers and the roles that peers play in their lives is the fourth context in which the influence of peers on sex role socialization may be investigated. Children's understanding of the roles they play in the community of peers and their knowledge or expectations about how peers may respond to sex typing in their behavior theoretically should serve as an important cognitive factor in their decisions about adhering to or failing to follow conventional norms for sex typed behavior (e.g., Kohlberg, 1966; Mischel, 1970; cf. Roopnarine & Mounts, this volume). From a cognitive development perspective (e.g., Kohlberg, 1966), the development of children's understanding of peer relationships and children's interactions with other children are especially important. Unfortunately, as was the case with peer influences on the development of stereotype knowledge and understanding, very little research has been conducted that assesses children's conceptions of peers and peer influences on sex-typing norms.

Carter and McCloskey's (1984) study of the development of children's conceptions of cross-gender behavior in their peers comes closest to assessing relationships that might emerge between children's conceptions of sex role norms and their beliefs about peers and their responses to cross gender behavior. In this study, children were asked to indicate how they and their peers would respond to violations of four kinds of gender norms (viz., toy preferences, activity preferences, friendship preferences, and personality characteristics) in hypothetical peers. As might be expected, children's reports of how they would respond to violations of gender norms were negative and became increasingly negative across the kindergarten through sixth grade years. Interestingly, children's reports of how peers would respond to gender norm violations indicated that they believed that their peers would respond more negatively to such violations than they would. Unfortunately, while Carter and McCloskey (1984) allude to the importance of peers in the development of such expectancies and the changing roles that peers may play in this process across the elementary school years, they provide no evidence supporting their speculations.

## Summary

Theoretical treatments of the sex role socialization process attribute importance to the roles that children's conceptions of peers may play in the acquisition of and adherence to gender norms. It might be expected that children's developing understanding of their relationships with peers and the roles that they and their peers play in the formation and enforcement of gender norms would change with age. There is, however, virtually no empirical research that has assessed relationships between children's conceptions of peers and gender norms. Thus, it is difficult to assess the validity of theoretical predictions in this area. Clearly, research on this topic should provide significant information about the sex role socialization process and represents a major gap in what is known about the influence of peers on this process.

## CONCLUSIONS

The roles that peers play in sex role socialization are considered to be among the most important influences on children's acquisition and adherence to sex-typed behavior. From the major theoretical perspectives, peers provide information for children through their endorsement of sex stereotypes, their modelling and enforcement of norms for sex-typed behavior, and through the patterns of play and verbal interaction in which they engage. Moreover, children's developing conceptions of peers and their understanding of social rules in general are thought both to be influenced by peer interaction and to play a significant role in children's adherence to sex-typed behavior.

Research on the behavioral components of the sex typing process indicates uniformly that peers exert a significant influence on sex typing in children's behavior. Evidence indicates that peers differentially reinforce and punish children who engage in sex-typed and those who engage in cross gender behavior, that children are more likely to model behavior exhibited by same-sex peers who are engaging in sex-typical behavior, and that boys' and girls' patterns of play behaviors and toy preferences are significantly influenced by the peers with whom they play. Not surprisingly, children respond appropriately to the positive reinforcements they receive for sex-typical behavior and the punishments they receive for cross gender behavior. Thus, at a behavioral level, the evidence overwhelmingly indicates that peers play among the most significant roles of any reference group in the formation of and adherence to sex-typed norms.

The evidence for the roles of peers in the cognitive components of the sex typing process, while indicative of the potential importance of peers, is simply not well developed enough to allow for any precise conclusions about peer influences on the development of children's understanding of gender and gender norms. Such evidence as exists does support theoretical predictions that peers should influence these cognitive aspects of sex role socialization, but research in this area is minimal and often fails to address specific intersecting issues about peer influences on children's understanding of gender and gender norms and the ways in which such understanding is manifested in behavior. In many ways this gap is similar to gaps in the other literatures on relationships between a cognitive characteristic and its behavioral manifestation. Clearly the interaction of peer influences, cognitive factors in sex typing, and behavioral manifestations of the sex typing process is an important issue for study. The absence of empirical evidence on this process suggests that researchers could profitably turn their attention to this aspect of sex role socialization and make a significant contribution to the field.

The fact that preadolescent children tend to play with and show preferences for same-sex peers provides the context in which sex role socialization by peers occurs. Given the overwhelming tendency for children to associate primarily, if not exclusively, with same-sex others, the potential for reinforcing indirectly children's conceptions that acceptable behavior is divided along gender lines is clear. Children are likely to view their playmates' behavior as desirable or acceptable and to limit their activity choices to match those in which their peers are engaging. Moreover, the fact that peers respond negatively to violations of gender norms means that those intrepid few who attempt to expand their behavioral repertoire to include cross gender behaviors are likely to be punished severely for their efforts or to be ostracized from the company of their peers. Thus, conservatism in adherence to sex role norms can be seen as a direct outgrowth of the fact that children associate with same sex others who consistently and persistently enforce traditional gender role norms. The fact that interaction with other-sex peers and cross gender behavior can be enhanced through adult intervention but return to baseline levels once the intervention ceases (e.g., Serbin, et al., 1977) indicates the difficult task facing those who wish to encourage the development of "androgynous" behaviors and attitudes among children. Given the structure, composition, and nature of children's peer groups and affiliation tendencies such a task, however admirable, becomes a formidable one.

It is apparent that a number of promising areas of research on the influence of peers in sex role socialization remain open. Primary among these areas is research on the influence of peers and children's understanding of peer relationships on the development of conceptions of gender role norms and the stereotyping process. For example, despite the volume of research on the development of children's knowledge of sex stereotypes, the roles of peers in enforcing stereotypical behavior, and the incidence of sex-typical and sex-atypical behavior in young children, it remains unclear how these areas intersect. Obviously children's expectations about how peers may respond to violations of gender norms should have an impact on their adherence to such norms, but no research project of which I am aware has provided the empirical data that would support such an assumption. In my opinion, a focus on relationships between conceptual understanding of gender norms and the enactment of such norms has the greatest potential for advancing our understanding of sex role socialization in general.

## REFERENCES

Barry, R. J. (1980). Stereotyping of sex role in preschoolers in relation to age, family structure, and parental sexism. *Sex Roles, 6,* 795–806.

Blomberg, J. F. (April 1983). Sex-typed toy choices by preschoolers in same-sex and cross-sex play dyads. Paper presented at the biennial meetings of the Society for Research in Child Development, Detroit.

Bussey, K. & Perry, D. G. (1982). Same-sex imitation: The avoidance of cross-sex behavior or the acceptance of same-sex models. *Sex Roles, 8,* 773–784.

Carter, D. B. & Levy, G. D. (1987a). Cognitive aspects of early sex role development: The influence of gender schematization on preschoolers' memories and preferences for sex-typed toys and activities. *Child Development,* (in press).

Carter, D. B. & Levy, G. D. (1987b). Gender constancy and early sex role development: A conceptual and empirical critique. Unpublished manuscript, Syracuse University.

Carter, D. B., Levy, G. D., & Cappabianca, J. M. (April 1985). Stereotype knowledge, flexibility, and gender constancy: Applications of Gender Schema Theory to sex-typing by preschoolers. Paper presented at the biennial meetings of the Society for Research in Child Development; Toronto, Canada.

Carter, D. B. & McCloskey, L. A. (1984). Peers and the maintenance of sex-typed behavior: The development of children's conceptions of cross-gender behavior in their peers. *Social Cognition, 2,* 294–314.

Carter, D. B. & Patterson, C. J. (1982). Sex roles as social conventions: The development of children's conceptions of sex-role stereotypes. *Developmental Psychology, 18,* 812–824.

Carter, D. B. & Taylor, R. D. (1987). The development of children's awareness and understanding of flexibility in sex-role stereotypes: Implications for preferences, attitudes, and behavior. *Sex Roles,* (in press).

Charlesworth, R. & Hartup, W. W. (1967). Positive social reinforcement in the nursery school peer group. *Child Development, 38,* 993–1002.

Coleman, J. C. (1980). Friendship and the peer group in adolescence. In J. Adelson (Ed.), *Handbook of adolescent psychology* (pp. 408–431). New York: Wiley.

Daly, M. & Wilson, M. (1978). *Sex, evolution and behavior.* North Scituate, MA: Duxbury Press.

D'Andrade, R. G. (1965). Sex differences and cultural institutions. In E. E. Maccoby (Ed.), *The development of sex differences* (pp. 174–204). Stanford, CA: Stanford University Press.

DiPietro, J. A. (1981). Rough and tumble play: A function of gender. *Developmental Psychology, 17,* 50–58.

Eder, D. & Hallinan, M. T. (1978). Sex differences in children's friendships. *American Sociological Review, 43,* 237–250.

Eisenberg, N., Tryon, K., & Cameron, E. (1984). The relation of preschoolers' peer interaction to their sex-typed choices. *Child Development, 55,* 1044–1050.

Fagot, B. I. (1977). Consequences of moderate cross-gender behavior in preschool children. *Child Development, 48,* 902–907.

Fagot, B. I. (1978). The effects of sex of child on parental reactions to toddler children. *Child Development, 49,* 459–465.

Fagot, B. I. & Leinbach, M. D. (1983). Play styles in early childhood: Social consequences for boys and girls. In M. B. Liss (Ed.), *Social and cognitive skills: Sex roles and children's play* (pp. 93–116). New York: Academic Press.

Fagot, B. I., Leinbach, M. D., & Hagan, R. (1986). Gender labeling and the adoption of sex-typed behaviors. *Developmental Psychology, 22,* 440–443.

Fagot, B. I. & Patterson, G. R. (1969). An *in vivo* analysis of reinforcing contingencies for sex-role behaviors in preschool children. *Developmental Psychology, 1,* 563–568.

Fling, S. & Manosevitz, M. (1972). Sex typing in nursery school children's play interests. *Developmental Psychology, 2,* 146–152.

Friedman, R. & Huling, T. (1982). *Their "proper" place: A report on sex discrimination in New York City's vocational high schools.* New York: Center for Public Advocacy Research, Inc.

Goodenough, F. (1934). *Developmental psychology: An introduction to the study of human behavior.* New York: Appleton-Century-Crofts.

Harlow, H. F. & Lauersdorf, H. E. (1974). Sex differences in passion and play. *Perspectives in Biology and Medicine, 17,* 348–360.

Hartup, W. W. (1983). Peer relations, In P. H. Mussen & E. M. Hetherington (Eds.), *Handbook of child psychology* (4th Ed., Vol. IV). *Socialization, personality, and social development* (pp. 103–196). New York: Wiley.

Haskett, G. J. (1971). Modification of peer preferences of first-grade children. *Developmental Psychology, 4,* 429–433.

Huston, A. C. (1983). Sex-typing. In P. H. Mussen & E. M. Hetherington (Eds.), *Handbook of child psychology* (4th Ed., Vol. IV). *Socialization, personality, and social development* (pp. 387–468). New York: Wiley.

Huston, A. C., Carpenter, C. J., Atwater, J. B., & Johnson, L. M. (1986). Gender, adult structuring of activities, and social behavior in middle childhood. *Child Development, 57,* 1200–1209.

Jacklin, C. N. & Maccoby, E. E. (1978). Social behavior at thirty-three months in same-sex and mixed-sex dyads. *Child Development, 49,* 557–569.

Johnson, J. E. & Roopnarine, J. L. (1983). The preschool classroom and sex differences in children's play. In M. B. Liss (Ed.), *Social and cognitive skills: Sex roles and children's play* (pp. 193–218). New York: Academic Press.

Jolly, A. (1972). *The evolution of primate behavior.* New York: MacMillan.

Kohlberg, L. A. (1966). A cognitive-developmental analysis of children's sex-role concepts and attitudes. In E. E. Maccoby (Ed.), *The development of sex differences* (pp. 82–172). Stanford, CA: Stanford University Press.

Kuhn, D., Nash, S. C., & Brucken, L. (1977). Sex role concepts of two- and three-year olds. *Child Development, 49,* 445–451.

Lamb, M. E., Easterbrooks, M. A., & Holden, G. (1980). Reinforcement and punishment among preschoolers: Characteristics, effects, and correlates. *Child Development, 51,* 1230–1236.

Lamb, M. E. & Roopnarine, J. L. (1979). Peer influences on sex-role development in preschoolers. *Child Development, 50,* 1219–1222.

Lancaster, J. B. (1975). *Primate behavior and the emergence of human culture.* New York: Holt, Rinehart, & Winston.

Langlois, J. H. & Downs, A. C. (1980). Mothers, fathers, and peers as socialization agents of sex-typed play behaviors in young children. *Child Development, 51,* 1237–1247.

Langlois, J. H., Gottfried, N. W., & Seay, B. (1973). The influence of sex of peer on the social behavior of preschool children. *Developmental Psychology, 8,* 93–98.

Lewis, M., Young, G., Brooks, J., & Michaelson, L. (1975). The beginning of friendship. In M. Lewis & L. A. Rosenblum (Eds.), *Friendship and peer relations.* New York: Wiley.

Liss, M. B. (1983). Learning gender-related skills through play. In M. B. Liss (Ed.), *Social and cognitive skills: Sex roles and children's play* (pp. 147–167). New York: Academic Press.

Maccoby, E. E. & Jacklin, C. N. (1974). *The psychology of sex differences.* Stanford, CA: Stanford University Press.

Marcus, D. E. & Overton, W. F. (1978). The development of cognitive gender constancy and sex-role preferences. *Child Development, 49,* 434–444.

McGrew, W. C., Tutin, C. E., & Baldwin, P. J. (1979). Chimpanzees, tools, and termites: Cross-cultural comparisons of Senegal, Tanzania, and Rio Muni. *Man, 14,* 185–214.

Mead, M. (1949/1977). *Male and female: A study of the sexes in a changing world.* New York: Morrow Quill Paperbacks.

Mischel, W. (1970). Sex-typing and socialization. In P. H. Mussen (Ed.), *Carmichael's Manual of Child Psychology* (3rd Ed., Vol. II), (pp. 3–72). New York: Wiley.

Mitchell, G. (1981). *Human sex differences: A primatologist's perspective.* New York: Van Nostrand Rheinhold.

Owens, N. W. (1975). A comparison of aggressive play and aggression in free-living baboons, *Papio anubis. Animal Behavior, 23,* 757–765.

Perry, D. G. & Bussey, K. (1979). The social learning theory of sex differences: Imitation is alive and well. *Journal of Personality and Social Psychology, 37,* 1699–1712.

Rheingold, H. L. & Cook, K. V. (1975). The content of boys' and girls' rooms as an index of parents' behavior. *Child Development, 46,* 459–463.

Roopnarine, J. L. (1984). Sex-typed socialization in mixed-age preschool classrooms. *Child Development, 55,* 1078–1084.

Serbin, L. A., Connor, J. M., Burchardt, C. J., & Citron, C. C. (1979). Effects of peer presence on sex-typing of children's play. *Journal of Experimental Child Psychology, 27,* 303–309.

Serbin, L. A. & Sprafkin, C. (1986). The salience of gender and the process of sex-typing in three- to seven-year-old children. *Child Development, 57,* 1188–1199.

Serbin, L. A., Tonick, I. J., & Sternglanz, S. H. (1977). Shaping cooperative cross-sex play. *Child Development, 48,* 924–929.

Slaby, R. G. & Frey, K. S. (1975). Development of gender constancy and selective attention to same sex models. *Child Development, 46,* 849–856.

Smetana, J. G. (1986). Preschool children's conceptions of sex-role transgressions. *Child Development, 57,* 862–871.

Smetana, J. G. & Letourneau, K. J. (1984). Development of gender constancy and children's sex-typed free play behavior. *Developmental Psychology, 20,* 691–696.

Stoneman, Z., Brody, G. H., & MacKinnon, C. (1984). Naturalistic observations of children's activities and roles while playing with their siblings and friends. *Child Development, 55,* 617–627.

Suomi, S. J. (1977). Social behaviors in rhesus monkeys. In T. Alloway, P. Pliner, & L. Krames (Eds.), *Attachment behavior.* New York: Plenum Press.

Symons, D. (1979). *The evolution of human sexuality.* New York: Oxford University Press.

Tremaine, L. S., Schau, C. G., & Busch, J. W. (1982). Children's occupational sex-typing. *Sex Roles, 8,* 691–710.

van Lawick-Goodall, J. (1971). *In the shadow of man.* Boston: Houghton-Mifflin.

Weinraub, M., Clemens, L. P., Sockloff, A., Ethridge, T., Gracely, E., & Myers, B. (1984). The development of sex role stereotypes in the third year: Relationships to gender labeling, gender identity, sex-typed toy preferences, and family characteristics. *Child Development, 55,* 1493–1503.

Whiting, J. W. & Child, I. L. (1953). *Child training and personality: A cross-cultural study.* New Haven: Yale University Press.

# 8
# The Roles of Cognition in Sex Role Acquisition
## Carol Lynn Martin
## Charles F. Halverson

One day a preschool class went to the university track to compete in running competitions. The children raced against the clock and each child's score was recorded. The fastest child in the class was a girl. After the competition, a boy from the class was running around the track with his preschool teacher. As they jogged along, a female university student ran past them. The young boy exclaimed to the teacher, "What's she doing? Girls don't run" (L. Serbin, personal communication).

This example demonstrates that children's expectations about the sexes are often not susceptible to information in their social environments. It is this lack of susceptibility to new information that is one of the major concerns of cognitive theories of sex typing and stereotyping.

Interest in the cognitive processes underlying stereotypes can be noted in some of the earliest writings about stereotypes. Walter Lippman (1922), considered stereotypes to be mental images or pictures in the head. Allport (1954) and other early theorists (e.g., Vinacke, 1957) also focused their interest on the cognitive aspects of stereotypes. Specific applications of cognitive interpretations to the area of sex role development began with Kohlberg's chapter in Maccoby's (1966) influential book on sex role development. Using Piaget's ideas about cognitive development, Kohlberg elaborated a conceptual approach where children play an active role in their own sex role socialization. Interest in the cognitive processes involved in sex roles and stereotypes have continued to develop since then, with many excellent papers and books devoted to the topic (e.g., Ashmore & DelBoca, 1979, 1981; Constantinople, 1979; Hamilton, 1981; Miller, 1982). More recently, cognitive approaches exemplified by gender schema theories have been providing more explicit notions about the ways cognitive processes can influence individuals' beliefs and behavior.

## COGNITIVE APPROACHES

The assumption underlying cognitive approaches is that individuals take an active role in perceiving and interpreting information from their environments. Rather than being shaped passively by environmental forces, scientists using cognitive approaches assume that persons use "theories" to interpret environmental information and that in so doing they create environments supportive of their theories. Because an active organism is assumed, the research based on cognitive approaches has focused on "top down" processing where concern is on what "theories" persons hold and how those "theories" influence the information individuals attend to, perceive, and remember. Schematic processing theories about gender represent one direction cognitive approaches have taken.

Three gender schema theories have been proposed in recent years (Bem, 1981; Markus, Crane, Bernstein, & Siladi, 1982; Martin & Halverson, 1981). These models are similar in that they share the assumption that gender schemas have specific effects on memory and behavior. They differ mainly in emphasis. The Martin and Halverson (1981) schematic processing theory emphasizes developmental changes in schemas and their functions and resulting biases. This model also differentiates among several different gender schemas. The models proposed by Bem (1981) and Markus et al. (1982) emphasize individual differences in sex-typing gender schemas. These models differ mainly in their views of what it means for an individual to be androgynous.

Cognitive approaches in general, and gender schema theories in particular, have highlighted new and interesting areas in the study of sex roles. There has been much research in the last few years suggesting that gender schema models are useful for describing the processes involved in learning, maintaining, and changing cognitions and behavior. In this chapter, we will focus on the cognitive bases of sex role development in children and, therefore, we will tend to rely most heavily on our schematic processing model as a conceptual framework.

## GENDER SCHEMAS

In 1981 we proposed a model of sex typing and stereotyping that was intended to integrate ideas about information processing with developmental research on sex role acquisition. The basic unit of the model is the schema. Although the exact nature of gender schemas has not yet been determined, the working assumption is that individuals have clearly defined theories about the sexes and these theories, or "schemas", directly influence behavior and thinking. In our 1981 paper, we described many of the different ways that gender schemas can function. Research conducted in recent years has generally supported our original contentions. Below we will briefly highlight some of the functions of gender schemas.

*Regulating behavior.* Gender schemas regulate behavior in several ways, by providing a basis for anticipating future events, setting goals, making plans, and developing the behavioral routines or scripts necessary to carry out plans. Even when we first published our model, there were many studies suggesting that gender schemas regulate children's behavior. Very young children tend to play with traditionally sex-appropriate toys while avoiding sex-inappropriate toys (e.g., Connor & Serbin, 1978; Fagot, 1974; Hartup, Moore, & Sager, 1963). Children also chose to play with same-sex peers at a young age (e.g., Jacklin & Maccoby, 1978). The most obvious demonstrations of the influence of gender schemas, however, have involved cases where children were given novel or unfamiliar objects with experimenter-supplied, sex-typed labels ("for boys," "for girls," "for both boys and girls," etc.). This novel object methodology has been particularly effective in demonstrating the effects of gender schemas because it minimizes the problems related to prior experience or differential exposure when real toys are used. Using the novel object methodology, Bradbard and Endsley (1983) found that children explored more and later better remembered the names of toys labeled for their own sex than toys labeled for the opposite sex. Two new studies by Brinson and Bradbard (1984) and Bradbard, Martin, Endsley, and Halverson (1986) have replicated and extended the results of the first study.

These studies suggest that gender schemas influence the kinds of interests and activities in which children engage. Prior experience cannot completely account for differential interest in traditionally sex-appropriate objects and activities. Instead, the mere labeling of objects and activities seems to make gender schemas salient so that they are used to regulate behavior.

*Organizing and attending to information.* Gender schemas also influence information processing by drawing attention to specific kinds of information and by providing a structure for learning and remembering. In our 1981 paper we argued that information organization varied depending on the type of gender schema. Specifically, the superordinate schema (which contains general information about the activities, roles, etc. associated with each gender group) was expected to influence learning about behaviors appropriate for both sexes. That is, children learn about the kinds of activities, behaviors, and so on associated with both sexes. Also, we predicted that children would selectively remember information appropriate for both sexes while forgetting information inappropriate for both sexes. Empirical evidence supports this prediction (Carter & Levy, 1987; Koblinsky, Cruse, & Sugawara, 1978; Levy & Carter 1987). In contrast, the application of the own-sex schema (which contains detailed plans of action or scripts for sex-appropriate behavior) was expected to produce a different kind of selectivity in learning. We have argued that childrens' in-depth knowledge would be selective in that children would learn more about carrying out sex-appropriate activities than sex-inappropriate activities (Bradbard et al., 1986; Martin & Halverson, 1981). Evidence for this kind of selectivity for in-depth information has been found when we assessed children's knowledge of real toys (Halverson & Martin, 1985) and novel objects (Bradbard, et al., 1986). For instance, we presented children with detailed information about the functions of novel objects assigned sex-typed labels. Children's recall of this in-depth information was found to be selective; that is, they remembered more details about the objects labeled for their own sex than for objects labeled for the opposite sex.

From a cognitive perspective, what a child remembers is expected to influence how a child behaves. How does a gender schema exert this kind of influence on behavior? Social learning theorists (e.g., Mischel, 1966) argue that sex roles limit the performance of behaviors, that is, children perform sex-appropriate behaviors because they are rewarded for them and they avoid sex-inappropriate behaviors because they are punished. In contrast, we have argued that one way schemas produce behavior conformity is by limiting the acquisition and/or retention of the in-depth information about performing sex-inappropriate behaviors (see Martin & Halverson, 1981; Bradbard et al., 1986). If attention is not paid to sex-inappropriate behaviors and if information about sex-inappropriate behaviors is not retained, then the child's competence concerning these behaviors would be limited. The Bradbard et al. (1986) study was done to assess competence limitations. One week after presenting in-depth information about novel toys given sex-typed labels, children's recall was assessed. Incentives to recall information were varied to ensure that children were not selectively reporting (rather than selectively learning). The incentives had no effect, thereby suggesting that sex-typed labels influenced children's competence rather than their performance. It appears then that children learn more in-depth information about sex-appropriate objects than about sex-inappropriate objects. By knowing more about the details of carrying out sex-appropriate activities, children should be more comfortable engaging in sex-appropriate activities.

*Structuring inferences and interpretations.* Since perceivers cannot and do not attend to all available information, schemas are used to guide us in making inferences about our social worlds. Schemas are also used in information-deficient situations. Recent research on both children and adults provide one confirmation of the inferential/interpretative functions of gender schemas. In 1980, Haugh, Hoffman, & Cowan demonstrated that children infer masculine and feminine characteristics in infants when the infants are labeled as male or female. More recently, Gelman, Collman, and Maccoby (1986) assessed children's tendency to make inferences about new gender-related information. After training children in novel characteristics associated with gender, they found that children were extremely likely to draw inferences about new instances. Three recent studies have demonstrated that children make sex-related inferences and predictions about unknown others (Berndt & Heller, 1986; Martin, 1985; Zucker, Wilson, & Stern, 1985).

## Development of Gender Schemas

Quite a few studies have been done to investigate how children learn different aspects of sex role information (e.g., stereotypes, preferences, gender understanding) (e.g., Carter & Patterson, 1982; Edelbrock & Sugawara, 1978; Kuhn, Nash, & Brucken, 1978; Levy & Carter, 1987.) Most of the research on gender schemas has involved the demonstration of how schemas influence behavior, thinking, or memory once they have been acquired. Very little empirical work, however, has been done on the development of any type of schema, much less on the development of gender schemas. Nonetheless, there has been some speculation on how and why gender schemas are acquired (Bem, 1981; Martin & Halverson, 1981, 1983; Martin, 1985).

To understand the development of gender schemas we must consider how children learn to identify and discriminate the sexes and how they associate visible and abstract attributes with the sexes. We also need to explore how and why children develop the evaluations associated with gender groups. Although these are just a few of the different kinds of gender-related learning that occur (cf. Huston, 1983), they appear to be the most central to the development of sex roles.

How and why do children group people according to gender? The development of gender groupings is believed to be influenced by both the characteristics of the environment and the characteristics of the perceiver. The perceiver is assumed to have some predisposition to categorize events in the world in order to simplify the extremely complex social and physical environment (Martin & Halverson, 1981). And indeed, research on infants' abilities to categorize strongly suggests a readiness to categorize (Cohen & Strauss, 1979). A tendency to categorize information is not sufficient, however, to result in the formation of gender categories. A second condition that is necessary for the formation of gender categories is that such categories must be salient for the perceiver. Salience is partly determined by the predictiveness or functionality of the category; in other words; gender must be perceived to be correlated with other attributes (Bem, 1981; Martin & Halverson, 1981). Because our society strongly emphasizes the links among behavioral, social, physical, and psychological characteristics and gender, gender takes on functional significance for the child.

When children are learning to make gender discriminations, they tend to use physical appearance cues such as hairstyle, clothing, and body build/size (e.g., Thompson & Bentler, 1971). They cannot use genitals as a basis for discrimination until they are older (McConaghy, 1979). Although adults tend to think of gender as being defined by a genital rule, genital information is seldom available and, in fact, can be wrong. It is likely then, that both children and adults use physical appearance cues to discriminate the sexes. However, it is still not fully understood how this is accomplished.

In an attempt to discover more about how members of groups are discriminated, Martin and Bullock (1986) created new, complex categories and investigated how the ability to identify category members changed over five trials. Adults were presented with examples of two types of creatures from a mythical planet. The creatures had some characteristics in common (called nondiagnostic features) and had some characteristics that occurred only in one group or the other (called diagnostic features). Not surprisingly, the ability to distinguish group members improved over trials. What was surprising was that people tended to rely on only the few diagnostic features that occurred frequently to distinguish group members. The other diagnostic features that occurred less frequently added little to the ability to identify category exemplars. The results of this study suggest that children may first use a limited number of physical appearance characteristics to distinguish the sexes rather than using a large constellation of features. These features would tend to be those that occur at a high level of frequency in one group and at a very low level in the other.

In addition to the perceptual discrimination that naturally occurs when a dimension is salient and predictive, there is a social component to discrimination that has often been neglected. Children certainly do not live in a vacuum where they must use only visual cues to discriminate gender groups. Instead, parents, teachers, and peers in the child's environment conveniently provide additional information about groups by labeling group members (i.e., ``Look at that little girl'') (Katz, 1983).

As well as learning to identify the sexes by their appearance, children also learn to associate selectively a variety of characteristics with each sex. One aspect of this process is children noticing gender related attributes in the environment, and abstracting rules (Perry & Bussey, 1979) and drawing inferences on the basis of these correlations. The categorical nature of the gender groups may also contribute to the process by providing an expectation that there are other differences between gender groups (McArthur, 1982; Martin, 1985). This type of priming may lead to attributions of sex differences for characteristics on which the sexes do not differ.

Another critical component in the development of gender schemas is the child's recognition of group membership—that he/she belongs to one gender category and not to the other (Martin & Halverson, 1981). Group membership is one aspect of stereotypes that differentiates them from other types of categories. By knowing the relationship between the self and the gender groups, children have a basis for making decisions and this also provides motivation for acting consistently with the ``norms'' for one's gender group. Children's recognition of group membership, therefore, should relate to their sex-typed preferences although many other factors, such as activity level, type of environment, and reward contingencies also may influence toy and peer preferences. On the positive side, membership in a gender group probably provides information relevant to self definition. For example, the child can identify others who are similar and others who are dissimilar. On the negative side, the in-group/out-group nature of gender categories lays the foundation for associating evaluation of each group. We know that placing individuals in even relatively arbitrary groups leads to positive evaluations of the in-group members and negative evaluations of out-group members (Tajfel, 1981).

It is not yet clear how the various types of gender-relevant learning are related. For instance, research has demonstrated little relation between children's stereotypes of the sexes and their sex-related preferences (Carter & Taylor, in press;

Perry, White, & Perry, 1984). It may be that sophisticated gender knowledge (e.g., gender constancy, trait stereotypes) is relatively unimportant for influencing behavior and, instead, only a rudimentary understanding of gender is critical (Constantinople, 1979). For instance, the ability to label the sexes accurately is related to children's play behavior (Fagot, 1985), and basic gender understanding (labeling, discriminating groups, and group membership) is related to sex stereotypic knowledge and children's toy and peer preferences (Levy & Carter, 1987; Martin & Little, 1986). Further research is needed to explore the relations among the various gender components.

### The Maintenance of Gender Schemas

Why are stereotypes held so rigidly, even in the face of disconfirming evidence? We think that cognitive approaches have been relatively more effective in resolving this question than any other approach.

One consistent finding in the literature on sex roles is that behavior, memory and attention tend to be internally consistent (and therefore, presumably schema consistent). Children attend to and explore sex-appropriate toys, and they remember details of sex-appropriate behaviors. Gender schemas seem to work by bringing behavior and thinking in line with the schema. One result of schematic consistency is that children's potential environment is constrained. What they notice, do, and remember is generally supportive of their gender schemas. This tendency toward schematic consistency probably facilitates the maintenance of gender schemas (Martin & Halverson, 1981).

There are other types of schematic consistency effects, however, that may be even more powerful in maintaining gender schemas. Specifically, these are the kinds of biases and distortions that result from schematic processing. One type of bias is the misperception of covariation, often called "illusory correlations" (Chapman & Chapman, 1967; Hamilton, 1981). Illusory correlations concerning occupational stereotypes have been demonstrated many times in adults. Adults tend to overestimate the number of times they think they have seen information consistent with their beliefs about the traits associated with occupations relative to information inconsistent with their beliefs. For instance, even when both descriptions are presented equally often, individuals will say they heard "salesmen are talkative" more often than "librarians like loud music." Recently, illusory correlations about the sexes have been demonstrated in adults (Hepburn, 1985). To date, no research has been done to examine illusory correlations in children. Children may be even more prone to making these illusory correlations about the sexes if they tend to process information in a more rigid way than do adults. Because illusory correlations suggest that individuals are construing their environments to support rather than to disconfirm their gender schemas, we would expect that this process greatly contributes to the maintenance of gender schemas.

Another kind of process contributing to the maintenance of gender schemas is information distortion and change. These "type 1" errors (Taylor & Crocker, 1979) occur when the perceiver incorrectly remembers information in a way that makes it fit their expectations. Many studies have been done to demonstrate type 1 errors related to sex roles in children (e.g., Cann & Newbern, 1984; Carter & Levy, 1987; Cordua, McGraw, & Drabman, 1979; Liben & Signorella, 1980; Martin & Halverson, 1983). In most cases, children tend to distort information that does not fit their gender schemas into information that does fit their schemas. For example, children shown a picture of a boy cooking later recall and are quite confident they saw a picture of a girl cooking (Martin & Halverson, 1983). These types of distortions are powerful in maintaining gender schemas because they effectively change examples of disconfirming evidence into instances that confirm and perpetuate the schema.

## Changes in Gender Schemas

In our schematic processing model, we discussed several different kinds of changes that occur in gender schemas. It is now clear that there are two distinct classes of changes that can be investigated (Martin, 1985, 1986). The first class we have called "intra-schema" changes and the second class we have called "inter-schema" changes.

Intra-schema changes refer to those changes that occur within the gender schemas. One example of this kind of change is the different domains of information that become associated with gender. Some information—for example, activities (Nadelman, 1974) and roles (Edelbrock & Sugawara, 1978)—is associated with gender before other kinds of information, such as personality traits (Williams, Bennett, & Best, 1975), is. As children tune in to specific information domains, these domains seem to become associated with gender. Thus, children's gender schemas change as more information is added and as the domains of information gradually change. A second type of intra-schema change concerns the differentiation of the gender schema. After exposure to many exemplars from gender groups, children probably begin to recognize that although boys and girls are in different categories, members *within* a category vary considerably. In other words, not all boys are alike and not all girls are alike. In gender schemas, the first type of differentiations would probably be based on gender-related activities and interests. For example, the category of boys may subdivide into "boys who act like boys" and "boys who act like girls." By around the age of seven, children begin to recognize "reverse stereotypes"; that is, that some children do not fit neatly into stereotypic categories (Martin & Halverson, 1985). Differentiation may become increasingly complex as the child grows older.

The second class of changes in stereotypes are inter-schema changes. Whereas intra-schema changes influence how schemas are applied, inter-schema changes refer to general changes in children's structures of knowledge that influence when schemas are used. For example, one kind of inter-schema change would be when children learn about other dimensions useful for classifying people. To the extent that these new classification dimensions are unrelated to gender, we would expect to see a change in the use of gender schemas (Martin & Halverson, 1981). The more methods the child has of classifying information and the better these are for predicting, the less salient the gender schema may become. More empirical and theoretical work needs to be done on how stereotypes change and differentiate during development. For example, we need to investigate more fully the qualitative changes in the kinds of information associated with gender, such as activities versus personality traits. Also, we need to assess quantitative changes in how strongly or rigidly information is associated with gender.

## Salience of Gender Schemas

In our culture, gender tends to be a central theme as is reflected in styles of dress, literature, music, and language (Katz, 1983). No one is completely a-schematic for gender in that everyone can describe the cultural stereotypes of the sexes. We can conclude, therefore, that for most people gender is a dominant dimension for processing information. It is still interesting, however, to consider individual and situational differences in the tendency to use gender as a processing dimension.

Schema salience has been described as the "top of the bin" (Wyer & Srull, 1981) or the "top of the head" phenomenon (Taylor & Fiske, 1978). That is, those schemas that are often found to be useful for processing information tend to move to the top of the bin of dimensions likely to be chosen for information processing. Certain situations may move gender schemas to the top of the bin. For example, if the only information one has about another person is their biological sex, gender is likely to become a salient processing dimension. Also, certain individuals may have more of a tendency to use gender for information processing than others. As Markus (1977) has demonstrated, individuals differ in their salient processing dimensions. Individual differences in the salience of gender may produce some of the variations seen in sex-typed behavior and preferences.

When investigating gender-related issues, we often ignore the fact that our experimental instructions or manipulations may in fact cause gender to become salient. For example, telling children that certain toys are "for boys" or "for girls" probably makes sex stereotypes salient even for those children who may not spontaneously invoke sex stereotypes. A study by Kropp (1983) highlights the various ways schemas can be salient. Four- and five-year-old children were tested in two situations: a standard toy preference test (children select preferred toys) and a standard play behavior test (children's actual play with the same toys). When gender was made salient (by asking children which toys were for boys or for girls), both girls and boys played with own-sex toys. When gender was not made salient, boys but not girls showed sex-typed play. Our interpretation is that for boys gender tends to be more salient so that they think of gender even in relatively ambiguous situations. In contrast, gender appears less salient for girls and they have to have external reminders to make gender salient.

We need to know much more about the conditions, both situational and interpersonal, that lead to gender schemas being used. Many of the inconsistencies in the findings of sex role research may be due to problems of differential salience. If gender schemas are invoked frequently in interpersonal situations, we tend to see schematic behavior; if they are invoked infrequently, we tend to see aschematic behavior.

Despite the importance of understanding when and how gender schemas become salient, little empirical evidence exists concerning the salience of gender as compared to other classification dimensions. In the developmental area, Lisa Serbin and her colleagues (e.g., Serbin & Sprafkin, 1983) have been conducting an extensive investigation of gender salience in children. Such studies are critical if we are to understand not just what kinds of gender knowledge children have but also when those knowledge structures are used as information processing guides.

## ISSUES IN GENDER SCHEMA RESEARCH

Although gender schema approaches have been developed in both the social psychological literature (Bem, 1981; Markus, et al., 1982) and in the developmental literature (Martin & Halverson, 1981) the content and applications of the approach vary considerably depending on the target population. Both the Bem and Markus et al. applications of gender schema theory have emphasized individual differences; that is, how and why do adults vary in their degree of gender schematicity. In the majority of adult studies, "sex typing" is used as a method of classifying individuals on the basis of gender schematicity. Individuals who attribute one type of trait to themselves (masculine or feminine) are considered sex-typed or gender schematic. Identifying gender aschematics has been more controversial. Bem argues that people with both masculine and feminine characteristics are androgynous and therefore are not gender schematic. In contrast, Markus implies that androgynous people are not aschematic; instead, they have incorporated into their self images schemas for *both* masculinity and femininity. Although the controversy about who is gender aschematic continues, most adult studies using gender schema theory have involved comparisons of masculine, feminine, and androgynous individuals on some outcome measure.

The Martin and Halverson approach in the developmental literature discussed individual differences in gender schemas but mainly emphasized how gender schemas function and lead to biases in thinking and behavior. Our belief was that most children have well-developed gender schemas and that it is only later in development that individual differences in gender schemas would account for much variance in an outcome measure. This idea is supported in that generally even young children show high levels of knowledge about sex stereotypes, most children prefer same-sex playmates, and many children show strong sex-typed toy/activity preferences. Most of the gender schema research on children has included some measure of individual differences, but often they do not predict differences in outcome measures. The majority of developmental studies, then, have demonstrated the effects of gender schemas on children rather than focusing on predicting individual differences.

Comparisons between adult and child studies of gender schemas are also complicated by measurement methods. Currently the most popular method of assessing gender schematicity in adults is by using endorsement of masculine and feminine personality characteristics. Because young children do not think of themselves or others in terms of traits, measures directly comparable to adult measures are seldom used. In studies of children, a wide variety of measures are used, including toy preferences, peer preferences, gender constancy, gender discrimination, gender labeling, and sex stereotyping and reaction times. Directly comparing the performance of children who have well-developed sex stereotypes with the performance of adults who have endorsed a high number of sex-appropriate traits is difficult and most likely also misleading.

## SOCIAL SCHEMAS AND SOCIAL CONTEXTS

In some ways, the term schema has been interpreted in a very broad sense and in other ways the term has taken on a relatively narrow meaning. By the broad interpretation, we mean that many different types of constructs and many different operational definitions of schemas have been employed. In the sex role area, this broad perspective has had the advantage of allowing work on sex types, sex roles, and sex stereotypes to be integrated with the more inclusive work on prediction, concept acquisition, category formation, and information processing strategies. This broad perspective has also led, however, to a disregard for differences among these areas and, most importantly, to a failure to distinguish among various constructs and measures related to sex roles. To rectify this problem, researchers using gender schema approaches need to begin speculating and formulating ideas about how one particular area of sex roles relates to other areas and how various sex role measures and constructs are similar or different from one another (Huston, 1983).

The term schema has also come to acquire a relatively narrow meaning. By this we mean that much more attention has been given to the idea of schemas as static asocial knowledge structures than to the idea of a schema that is a richly elaborated structure sensitive to the social context. Cognitive theorists need to begin thinking about the social and contextual factors associated with schemas. One approach is to begin to expand cognitive processing ideas about individuals to the realms of dyadic interaction, parent–child and family relations, and cultural variations. We could also begin to consider "match/mismatch" models to explain sex role development. For example, some children may be more strongly predisposed to categorize along gender lines while others tend to rely on other classification dimensions or some children may be more predisposed than others to act in stereotypic ways (e.g., aggressive boys). Some children may find that they are in an environment that is conducive to using gender (e.g., gender distinctions and "appropriate" behavior are important to parents, teachers) and that they are responded to on the basis of gender more so than other children. What would then happen when considering each child in each type of environment? Even this simple interactive case is probably not adequate to capture the complexity of sex role development. To fully understand sex role development, we need to consider the context of situations and children's ability to vary their behavior to suit situational demands. Changes over time also need to be considered. The resulting model is a transactional one where the child, the family, and the society influence each other and those influence patterns change over time. Such models are difficult to conceptualize and yet may be very heuristic. For example, if we adopt this perspective we might ask questions such as, "At what time(s) or situations in a child's life will cognitive factors drive the system?" "When and why will contextual factors drive the system?" Theories that can explain how and why changes in the predominant influence occur will be critical in our acquiring a complete picture of the process of sex role acquisition.

## REFERENCES

Allport, G. W. (1954). *The nature of prejudice,* (p. 161–173). Cambridge, Ma: Addison-Wesley Publishing.

Ashmore, R.D. & Del Boca, F.K. (1979). Sex stereotypes and implicit personality theory: Toward a cognitive–social psychological conceptualization. *Sex Roles, 5,* 219–248.

Ashmore, R.D. & Del Boca, F.K. (1981). Conceptual approaches to stereotypes and stereotyping. In D.L. Hamilton (Ed.), *Cognitive processes in stereotyping and intergroup behavior.* Hillsdale, NJ: Lawrence Erlbaum Associates.

Bem, S.L. (1981). Gender schema theory: A cognitive account of sex typing. *Psychological Review, 88,* 354–364.

Berndt, T. & Heller, K.A. (1986). Gender stereotypes and social influences: A developmental study. *Journal of Personality and Social Psychology, 50,* 889–898.

Bradbard, M.R. & Endsley, R.C. (1983). The effects of sex-typed labeling on preschool children's information seeking and retention. *Sex Roles, 9,* 247–260.

Bradbard, M.R., Martin, C.L., Endsley, R.C., & Halverson, C.F. (1986). Influence of sex stereotypes on children's exploration and memory: A competence versus performance distinction. *Developmental Psychology, 22,* 481–486.

Brinson, P.S. & Bradbard, M.R. (April 1984). *Sex-typed labeling, parent-presence, and age as determinants of parents' curiosity-orienting behaviors.* Presented at the Biennial Meeting of the Southeastern Conference on Human Development. Athens, GA.

Cann, A. & Newbern, S.R. (1984). Sex stereotype effects in children's picture recognition. *Child Development, 55,* 1085–1090.

Carter, D.B. & Patterson, C.J. (1982). Sex-roles as social conventions: The development of children's conceptions of sex-role stereotypes. *Developmental Psychology, 18,* 812–824.

Carter, D. B. & Levy, G. D. (1987). Cognitive aspects of early sex-role development: The influence of gender schematization on preschoolers' memories and preferences for sex-typed toys and activities. *Child Development*.

Carter, D. B. & Taylor, R. D. (in press). The development of children's awareness and understanding of flexibility in sex-role stereotypes: Implications for preferences, attitudes, and behavior. *Sex Roles*, in press.

Chapman, L.J. & Chapman, J.P. (1967). Genesis of popular but erroneous psychodiagnostic observations. *Journal of Abnormal Psychology, 72*, 193–204.

Cohen, L.B. & Strauss, M.S. (1979). Concept acquisition in the human infant. *Child Development, 50*, 419–424.

Connor, J.M. & Serbin, L.A. (1978). Behaviorally based masculine- and feminine-activity-preference scales for preschoolers: Correlates with other classroom behaviors and cognitive tests. *Child Development, 48*,1411–1416.

Constantinople, A. (1979). Sex-role acquisition: In search of the elephant. *Sex Roles, 5*, 121–132.

Cordua, G.D., McGraw, K.O., & Drabman, R.S. (1979). Doctor or nurse: Children's perception of sex-typed occupations. *Child Development, 50*, 590–593.

Edelbrock, C. & Sugawara, A.I. (1978). Acquisition of sex-typed preferences in preschool children. *Developmental Psychology, 14*, 614–623.

Fagot, B.I. (1974). Sex differences in toddlers' behavior and parental reaction. *Developmental Psychology, 10*, 554–558.

Fagot, B.I. (1985). Changes in thinking about early sex role development. *Developmental Review, 5*, 83–98.

Gelman, S.A., Collman, P., & Maccoby, E.E. (1986). Inferring properties from categories versus inferring categories from properties: The case of gender. *Child Development, 57*, 396–404.

Halverson, C.F. & Martin, C.L. (1985). *Sex-typed knowledge: Who remembers what?* Unpublished manuscript.

Hamilton, D.L. (1981). Illusory correlation as a basis for stereotyping. In D.L. Hamilton (Ed.), *Cognitive processes in stereotyping and intergroup behavior*. Hillsdale, NJ: Lawrence Erlbaum Associates.

Hamilton, D.L. (Ed.) (1981). *Cognitive processes in stereotyping and intergroup behavior*. Hillsdale, NJ: Lawrence Erlbaum Associates.

Hartup, W.W., Moore, S.G., & Sager, G. (1963). Avoidance of inappropriate sex-typing by young children. *Journal of Consulting Psychology, 27*, 467–473.

Haugh, S.S., Hoffman, C.D., & Cowan, G. (1980). The eye of the very young beholder: Sex typing of infants by young children. *Child Development, 51*, 598–600.

Hepburn, C. (1985). Memory for the frequency of sex-typed versus neutral behaviors: Implications for the maintenance of sex stereotypes. *Sex Roles, 12*, 771–776.

Huston, A.C. (1983). Sex-typing. In E.M. Hetherington (Ed.) *Handbook of Child Psychology (4th ed., Vol. 4). Socialization, personality, and social development*. New York: Wiley.

Jacklin, C.N. & Maccoby, E.E. (1978). Social behavior at 33 months in same-sex and mixed-sex dyads. *Child Development, 49*, 557–569.

Katz, P.A. (1983). Developmental foundations of gender and racial attitudes. In R.L. Leahy (Ed.), *The child's construction of social inequality*. New York: Academic Press.

Koblinsky, S., Cruse, D.F., & Sugawara, A.I. (1978). Sex-role stereotypes and children's memory for story content. *Child Development, 49,* 452–458.

Kohlberg, L.A. (1966). A cognitive-developmental analysis of children's sex role concepts and attitudes. In E.E. Maccoby (Ed.), *The development of sex differences.* Stanford, CA: Stanford University Press.

Kropp, J.J. (1983). *Measuring gender related attitudes and behaviors in preschool children.* Paper presented at the meetings of Society for Research in Child Development, Detroit.

Kuhn, D., Nash, S.C., & Brucken, L. (1978). Sex role concepts of two- and three-year-old children. *Child Development, 49,* 445–451.

Levy, G. D. & Carter, D.B. (April, 1987). Gender schema, gender constancy, and sex-stereotype knowledge: The roles of cognitive factors in sex-stereotype attributions. Paper presented at the biennial meetings of the Society for Research in Child Development, Baltimore, MD.

Liben, L.S. & Signorella, M.L. (1980). Gender-related schemata and constructive memory in children. *Child Development, 51,* 11–18.

Lippman, W. (1922). *Public Opinion.* New York: Harcourt Brace.

Markus, H. (1977). Self-schemata and processing information about the self. *Journal of Personality and Social Psychology, 35,* 63–78.

Markus, H., Crane, M., Bernstein, S., & Siladi, M. (1982). Self-schemas and gender. *Journal of Personality and Social Psychology, 42,* 38–50.

Martin, C.L. (1985). *The development of gender roles.* Paper presented at the meetings of the International Society for the Study of Behavioral Development, France, July.

Martin, C.L. (1986). *The influence of gender schemas on children's impression formation.* Manuscript submitted for publication.

Martin, C.L. & Bullock, M. (1986). *Learning stereotypes: Biases in judging characteristics.* Paper presented at the meeting of the American Psychological Association, Washington, D.C.

Martin, C.L. & Halverson, C.F. (1981). A schematic processing model of sex typing and stereotyping in children. *Child Development, 52,* 1119–1134.

Martin, C.L. & Halverson, C.F. (1983). The effects of sex-typing schemas on young children's memory. *Child Development, 54,* 563–574.

Martin, C.L. & Halverson, C.F. (1985). *Children's understanding of reverse stereotypes: A case of affect preceding cognition.* Unpublished manuscript.

Martin, C.L. & Little, J.K. (1986). *The cognitive basis of sex role knowledge and preferences.* Unpublished manuscript.

McArthur, L.Z. (1982). Judging a book by its cover: A cognitive analysis of the relationship between physical appearance and stereotyping. In A.H. Hastorf & A.M. Isen (Eds.), *Cognitive social psychology.* New York: Elsevier.

McConaghy, M.J. (1979). Gender permanence and the genital basis of gender: Stages in the development of constancy of gender identity. *Child Development, 50,* 1223–1226.

Miller, A.G. (1982). *In the eye of the beholder.* New York: Praeger.

Mischel, W. (1966). A social learning view of sex differences in behavior. In E.E. Maccoby (Ed.), *The development of sex differences.* Stanford, Ca: Stanford University Press.

Nadelman, L. (1974). Sex identity in American children: Memory, knowledge, and preference tests. *Developmental Psychology, 10,* 413–417.

Perry, D.G. & Bussey, K. (1979) The social learning theory of sex differences: Imitation is alive and well. *Journal of Personality and Social Psychology, 37,* 1699–1712.

Perry, D.G., White, A.J., & Perry, L.C. (1984). Does early sex typing result from children's attempts to match their behavior to sex role stereotypes? *Child Development, 55,* 2114–2121.

Serbin, L.A. & Sprafkin, C. (1983). *The development of gender salience and affiliation patterns from three to seven.* Presented at the meeting of the Society for Research in Child Development, Detroit.

Tajfel, H. (1981). *Human groups and social categories.* Cambridge: Cambridge University Press.

Taylor, S.E. & Crocker, J. (1979). Schematic bases of social information processing. In E.T. Higgins, P. Herman, & M.P. Zanna (Eds.), *The Ontario symposium in personality and social psychology* (Vol. 1). Hillsdale, NJ: Lawrence Erlbaum Associates.

Taylor, S.E. & Fiske, S.T. (1978). Salience, attention, and attribution: Top of the head phenomena. In L. Berkowitz (Ed.), *Advances in experimental social psychology,* (Vol. 10). New York: Academic Press.

Thompson, S.K. & Bentler, P.M. (1971). The priority of cues in sex discrimination by children and adults. *Developmental Psychology, 5,* 181–185.

Vinacke, W.E. (1957). Stereotypes as social concepts. *Journal of Social Psychology, 46,* 339–347.

Williams, J.E., Bennett, S.M., & Best, D.L. (1975). Awareness and expression of sex stereotypes in young children. *Developmental Psychology, 11,* 635–642.

Wyer, R.S. & Srull, T.K. (1981). Category accessibility: Some theoretical and empirical issues concerning the processing of social stimulus information. In E.T. Higgins, C.P. Herman, & M.P. Zanna (Eds.), *Social cognition: The Ontario symposium on personality and social psychology.* Hillsdale, NJ: Lawrence Erlbaum Associates.

Zucker, J.K., Wilson, D.N., & Stern, A. (April 1985). *Children's appraisals of sex-typed behavior in their peers.* Paper presented at the meeting of the Society for Research in Child Development, Toronto.

# 9
# Gender and Conversation: Mixing and Matching Styles
## Laura A. McCloskey

"Words are a form of action, capable of influencing change. Their articulation represents a complete, lived experience."

Ingrid Bengis

There are many ways children and adults express gender identity and attitudes surrounding gender in our society. A major avenue for such expression is language in conversation. Conversations provide a forum for the presentation of self (Goffman, 1959) and the negotiation of social relationships. Since conversation is such a pervasive medium for our identity, we would expect gender, perhaps the most salient of social categories (Bem, 1984), to have an impact on conversational style. Indeed males and females do adopt different styles, and the ways in which they communicate reflect underlying differences in their social roles. Thus, the study of how men and women communicate illuminates the study of sex roles and stereotypes in general.

While language serves to reflect our social identity, it also acts as a powerful socializing agent. We express attitudes, expectations, and stereotypes by the conscious and unconscious choices we make in our conversations. For example, Shatz and Gelman (1973) found that even four-year olds adjust their speech when addressing younger children, talking in what is commonly referred to as the "baby talk register" (DePaulo & Coleman, 1981; Ferguson, 1977). Coleman (1980) found that college students invoked this baby talk register when addressing mentally retarded adults and foreigners. These speech adjustments reveal underlying attitudes towards the listener.

It is unknown what effect baby talk has on the adult addressee, although at the very least it assaults one's self-perception and dignity (Schneider, Hastorf, & Ellsworth, 1979). For example, an acquaintance of mine who is a highly educated

Japanese woman, fluent in English, complained of how demoralized she felt when storekeepers and other strangers talked to her as though she were a child. She had lived in northern California, where there are many Asians, without encountering such overt condescension. One also is reminded of Nora, from Ibsen's *Doll House,* whose psychological imprisonment by her husband is perpetuated through the mutual exchange of baby talk that infantalizes Nora while empowering her husband. Conversation, and how one chooses to convey one's messages, can become a device for reaffirming negative stereotypes and maintaining rigid social hierarchies.

## EVIDENCE FOR GENDER DIFFERENCES IN SPEECH

During the past decade there has been burgeoning interest in the area of gender differences in language: in describing such differences, in probing what gender differences signify socially and psychologically, and in understanding how such differences reflect and maintain the social roles designated by gender. Although Lakoff (1975) was hardly the first linguist to call attention to sex differences in speech (e.g., Jesperson, 1922), her monograph was among the first to frame the discussion of such differences within both a social psychological and apparently feminist context. She argued for a one to one mapping between the speech selections of men and women and their ascribed social roles. Thus, according to Lakoff (1975), men's speech conveys power and assertiveness, while uncertainty and subordination mark that of women. Among the variables Lakoff attributed to female speech were tag questions, hedges such as ''I think,'' qualifying phrases such as ''you know,'' and other lexical and syntactic forms that serve to qualify or obscure the speaker's intentions.

Subsequent research, however, has failed to find gender differences in the use of the linguistic features that Lakoff described. For instance, Dubois and Crouch (1975) found that in a professional conference men used tag questions exclusively, and women not at all. Similarly, Holmes (1986) also failed to find significant differences in the number of times men and women used hedges in their speech. These authors recommend that before consulting our intuitions about what features of language are sex-typed, we should examine the actual distribution of such variables in men's and women's speech.

Null findings are reported far less often in the literature than are positive findings, and there are undoubtedly many more similarities in communication than there are differences between the sexes. Since no feature of speech ascribed to males or females is exclusively under the demesne of either, we should expect that considerable overlap in speech style occurs between the sexes. Men and women express both uncertainty and assertiveness in their conversations and may use similar devices to convey attitudes and affect. Thus, we are more likely, even when focusing on multiple discourse features, to unearth a trend rather than a sharp delineation between male and female speech style and strategies.

What we refer to as conversational ''style'' encompasses a matrix of discourse features, with any single variable present or not at the time of observation, but not uniquely crucial to identifying the speech as male or female. Focusing on only one variable, especially if it is not widely distributed in speech, is unlikely to yield significant differences. For example, tag questions and hedges are uncommon in the speech of both males and females. In contrast, the identification of a matrix of relevant variables can corroborate a specific interpretation. Setting forth features that seem likely candidates for such a matrix has been the work of a number of researchers.

One way to think of sex differences in speech is within the framework of a politeness continuum (Brown & Levinson, 1978). The more polite a speaker, the more subordinate; the less polite, the more superior in social status. While this rule is neither global nor inflexible, it does seem to characterize at least some language differences between different-status interlocutors. Linguistic status or politeness markers can be morphological, as in the use of politeness particles among Mayans speaking Tzeltal (Brown, 1980), or can be more discourse based, as in the use of interruptions by men in mixed-sex dyads (Zimmerman & West, 1975; West & Zimmerman, 1983). Thus, much research has focused on sex differences in markers of politeness.

A number of researchers have provided data on sex-differentiated use of linguistic politeness markers. For example, Goodwin's (1980) report on boys' and girls' use of direct or indirect requests indicates that boys tend to use direct requests more often when talking with peers. Girls use more indirect requests, employing modals ("We could do . . . ") with the third person plural. Similarly, Fishman (1983) describes a variety of features that indicate differences in style between spouses. For example, wives prompt their husbands more often with questions and encourage the men to speak while simultaneously they must struggle to capture their husbands' attention. Men talk more and successfully initiate topics more often, than than do women. McConnell-Ginet (1983) reports gender differences in the use of intonation. She describes the female intonational register as consisting of more pitch variation, while males are more monotonic. She suggests that females develop a more varied prosodic communicative style in order to capture the attention of otherwise inattentive males.

This research indicates that males and females do exhibit differences in style. However, the task of untangling these disparate findings to arrive at a global perspective on gender-differentiated speech remains formidable. Studies reporting gender markers in speech are conducted in a wide variety of contexts, with same- or opposite-sex conversational partners, some intimate and some strangers. Researchers apply different methods of data collection and select disparate variables in their investigations. For example, in one study interruptions between opposite sex interlocutors may comprise the main variable (e.g., West and Zimmerman, 1983), whereas in another, the researcher examines the use of politeness particles between same-sex acquaintances in Guatemala (Brown, 1980). The heterogeneity of methods and sociolinguistic variables, while enriching the field, also fosters confusion, since often findings are not directly comparable. The many dimensions of context, the relationship between speaker and listener, the ways in which researchers attribute meaning to differences, and the researchers' biases are all factors to consider in evaluating reports of gender differences or similarities in communication.

## WOMEN'S TALK, MEN'S TALK AND CROSS SEX DIALOGUE

Interpersonal context is crucial in determining meaning. That is, who the speakers and listeners are, whether their relationship is intimate or unfamiliar, and under what circumstances they are talking with each other are among the many contextual variables that may constrain self-expression. The research described above includes both men and women talking to a range of discourse partners in a variety of social contexts. In some studies participants only addressed opposite-sex partners while in others they communicated with same-sex peers. In some studies, conversational partners were strangers, while in others, they were husband and wife. These factors are bound to affect language choices.

Social context influences what choices a speaker makes in conversation as well as how listeners interpret such choices. Exchanges appropriate to casual acquaintances at the local swimming pool, for example, would be at the very least bizarre at a State Department dinner. We code-switch to accommodate these different situations and relationships. Thus, gender differences that might appear between intimates (e.g., Fishman, 1983) may not occur between men and women in the workplace or other contexts. For example, Brouwer, Gerritsen, and De Haan (1979) failed to find differences between male and female Dutch travellers requesting a ticket in a train station, while Fishman reports sex differences between husbands and wives. However, the context in which Brouwer et al.'s recordings were collected might not have been sufficiently sensitive to detect gender differences. In formal and brief interactions, sex differences, as well as markers of social identity, may be mitigated since the interaction is fairly routinized and scripted. Differences may not be as prominent in heavily scripted situations as they might be in more flexible, less predictable social settings. It is unknown in what ways context interacts with gender to produce different effects. This area is clearly one needing further exploration.

Social class, race, ethnicity, and even political orientation also contribute to the ways in which people express gender in speech. For example, Adams (1980) found that black females were more dominant in their speech than white females or black males. She points out that sex and race interact, and thus research on one population cannot be generalized to other populations. Similarly, Giles, Smith, Browne, Whiteman, and Williams (1980) found that speech samples from British women who viewed themselves as feminists were rated as more "lucid, confident, intelligent, and sincere" than was the speech of non-feminists. Therefore, many factors influence how we construct individual style, although gender is among the most prominent.

How we interpret the dissimilarities in cross-sex situations will differ from how we explain stylistic distinctions between men conversing with men and women with women. Researchers often frame differences in cross-sex conversations within the broader arena of sexual politics. As a result, divergent styles are attributed to the asymmetries in social power that so often characterize male–female relations. The view frequently adopted is that social structure and sex roles constrain an individual's self-expression, ultimately dictating communicative strategies. For example, Susan Harding (1975) describes women in a Spanish village who, because they are excluded from the (private) male world, engage their husbands with obtuse, partly formed questions. Harding contends that women devise these subversive discourse strategies to gain access to the man's world, its gossip, its politics. The question/answer episodes she describes are like discreet "foot-in-the-door" techniques to break, gradually and temporarily, through distrust, closely resembling the exchanges described by Fishman (1983). Dale Spender (1980) taped the following dialogue at a social occasion that exemplifies women's prompting strategies:

*Female:* Did he have the papers ready for you?

*Male:* Mmm.

*Female:* And were they all right . . . was anything missing?

*Male:* Not that I could see.

*Female:* Well that must have been a relief anyway. I suppose everything went well after that?

*Male:* Almost.

*Female:* Oh. Was there something else?

*Male:* Yes, actually.

*Female:* It wasn't X . . . was it? He didn't let you down again?

*Male:* I'd say he did.

*Female:* He really is irresponsible you know, you should get . . .

*Male:* . . . I'm going to do something about it. It was just the last straw today. How many times do you think that makes this week? . . . (Spender, 1980, p. 48)

In the above dialogue, the woman makes great effort to draw the man out. He finally responds fully by interrupting her and then proceeding with his complaint.

While women facilitate, men appropriate conversational space in the form of interruptions and extended turn-taking (Edelsky, 1981; Zimmerman & West, 1975; West & Zimmerman, 1983). Zimmerman and West (1975) found that in cross-sex dyads in which the participants know each other, as well as in unfamiliar dyads (West and Zimmerman, 1983), men accounted for approximately ninety percent of the interruptions. Men intrude upon the women's conversational boundaries both verbally and nonverbally (Henley, 1977; Thorne, 1986). The authors contend that men express their dominance with such discourse devices, although these studies do not show whether men frequently interrupt men as well. Since the studies do not include comparison groups of same-sex peers, the authors are not fully justified in concluding that the use of interruptions is exclusively a result of power displays of males over females. That is, rather than depicting men as dominating and women as submissive conversationally, it may be that there are gender-differentiated speech styles used with same sex peers that do not converge with the discourse strategies of opposite sex peers. Consequently, we may be witnessing in these studies a case of miscommunication rather than of oppression. There is clear evidence that women do not elicit these interruptions, and, on the contrary, struggle to maintain their floor even when interrupted.

Conversations between men and women may reflect the "sex game" (Bernard, 1972), but the differences observed between conversations with same-sex participants suggest an alternative mechanism. Sexual politics, while relevant, does not clearly account for the emergence of sex-differentiated speech styles in same-sex relationships. Explanations of gender differences in this context should focus on identifying the nature of female and male worlds to the extent that they are segregated. Thus, by probing gender determined experiences and socialization, we can uncover the social psychological reality engendering divergent styles in communication.

## THE SOCIAL AND CONVERSATIONAL WORLDS OF MEN AND WOMEN

A number of authors and researchers have noted the importance of sex differentiation in socialization experiences on the language of males and females. For example, Maltz and Borker (1983) have suggested that because of the different social worlds constructed by males and females, children develop different interpretive rules in conversation that may lead to misunderstanding and conflict in adult communicative attempts. As a result, males and females may invoke different conversational "schemas" arising from different social structures and experiences. In some communities, such forms of talk are autonomous, as in the lives of Bedouin women (Abu-Lughod, 1985). Abu-Lughod quotes a Bedouin woman describing the boundary between men's and women's talk: "We have lived together for seventeen years and never has any woman brought women's talk to the men! In our community we have one way. Women don't tell the men what goes on between women" (p. 645).

Sentiments similar to those expressed by contemporary Bedouin women were shared by upperclass Edwardian women in England, as noted by Virginia Woolf in her novel *Night and Day*. Woolf (1920/1948) writes that when the ladies took leave of the gentlemen after dinner, both sexes, but especially the women, were able to relax from the burden of accommodating their styles. Woolf (1920/1948) states that "these short, but clearly marked, periods of separation between the sexes were always used for an intimate postscript to what had been said at dinner, the sense of being women together coming out most strongly when the male sex was, as if by some religious rite, secluded from the female'' (p. 101). Thus, the act of keeping women's talk separate and limiting the range of domestic topics shared between husband and wife offered a way for otherwise disenfranchised women to maintain some control over both their own lives and those of their husbands (Abu-Lughod, 1985; Harding, 1975).

Gender differences in language and language usage need not, however, emerge from or in sex-segregated conversational settings. Rather, gender differences may be reflected in day-to-day conversations between women and men as well as in conversations among women. For example, Brown (1980) reports that Mayan women in Guatemala, speaking Tzeltal, use more politeness markers, represented in their use of particles, when talking to other women than men do when speaking with their male peers. Brown suggests that the use of politeness markers in women's speech springs from their powerless position with respect to the men in this patriarchal society. However, the gender differences do not appear between men and women, which is what one would expect if such markers originated from deference to males. This finding suggests that politeness strategies develop between women independently of cross-sex relations.

One explanation for why these Mayan women appear excessively polite with each other is that while their interrelationships are crucial to social survival in the village, such relationships are often fragile since they are maintained without the support of biological family ties. As is the case in many other societies, Mayans in Guatemala practice patriarchal exogamy in which a new bride leaves her natal village to live in the village of her husband's family. As a result, these women must be especially careful not to offend their in-laws. Women in this culture are very important to each other, providing the social contact and emotional support their husbands generally neglect to give. Thus we must further examine women's mutual relationships as well as their relationships with men in order to identify the origins of sex-differentiated speech.

## EVALUATING GENDER DIFFERENCES AND INTERPRETING STYLE

> In truth women have never set up female values in opposition to male values; it is man who, desirous of maintaining masculine perogatives, has invited that divergence.
>
> Simone de Beauvoir (1952/1972)

Simone de Beauvoir's comment is relevant to the issue of how we value or devalue sex differences in social behavior and language. It is common among cultures to devalue women's work, and to identify women with nature and entropy while associating men with culture and achievement (Ortner, 1974). Indeed, data from a number of studies indicate that knowledge or assumption of an individual's gender affects a perceiver's interpretation of his/her behavior. For example, Condry and Condry (1976) demonstrated such sex biases in a study in which adults viewed the same infant exhibiting the same behavior. Half of the subjects in the study were told the infant was a boy, and the other half were told the infant was a girl. Adults judged the alleged female as being more fearful than the male, and the male infant as more angry.

Macauley (1978) argues that researchers' biases, rather than positive evidence, gave rise to claims that girls are superior in language ability. Macauley inspected the data reported by several researchers who maintained that females learned language earlier than males and used it more effectively. Upon reexamination of the reported findings, however, he found no statistically significant sex differences. Nonetheless, the authors cited by Macauley offer elaborate and biased explanations for a phenomenon that is nonexistent. In the following passage, he cites Moore's (1967) confounded assessment of female communication:

The little girl, showing in her domestic play the overriding absorption in personal relationships through which she will later fulfill her role of wife, mother and 'expressive leader' of the family, learns language early in order to communicate. The kind of communication in which she is chiefly interested at this stage concerns the nurturant routines which are the stuff of family life.

This view of female precocity in language, though false, is widely accepted since it is consonant with other female stereotyped traits such as "nurturance" and "expressiveness."

Stereotypes intrude on our judgments of male and female speech, whether we are engaged in conversational exchange or research. Lakoff's early work testifies to the power of stereotypes even when the researcher holds the best intentions. One problem in the approach Lakoff and others take is their implicit assumption of a one to one mapping between discourse features (e.g., tag questions) and social meaning (e.g., insecurity and inferior status). Consistent with this assumption is the notion that discourse markers and speech acts are inherently meaningful in the sociopolitical ways these authors conceive of them.

These assumptions deserve further scrutiny. For example, tag questions or other forms in speech are not inherently significant regarding the status, the attitudes, or the personality of the speaker. Tag questions may signify uncertainty in one context, and express aggression in another. In London, working class schoolboys use first-person tag questions to challenge authority, as in, "I didn't have time to do my homework last night, now *did I*?" by a secondary school student to his instructor. The tag question, like most speech act phenomena, serves multiple discourse functions. Holmes (1986) points out that hedges ("I think") have several communicative functions, either tentative (expressing uncertainty) or deliberative (expressing self-confidence). She finds, contrary to Lakoff's predictions, that men tend to use "I think" in its tentative function and women in its deliberative function. Thus women express self-assurance rather than insecurity with their use of hedges.

Dualistic functions attend other features of speech as well. For instance, Edelsky (1981) points out that men and women take turns differently and make different use of "floor." Fishman (1983) in her analysis of married couples, observed gender differences in how partners used minimal responses (e.g., "uh huh" or "hmm"). Men tended to use minimal responses when women addressed them with questions or topic initiations thus straining the dialogue (much like the example cited by Spender above). Women, on the other hand, used these same responses as prompts and signs of encouragement when listening to men. The same features meet different social purposes.

What determines the meaning of a given speech act in much of this research is often unspecified, although Lakoff and others presume that the sex distribution of features of speech is sufficient evidence for a sex-typed interpretation; if certain forms are more prevalent in female speech they must spring from "feminine" traits of insecurity or excessive sociability. With this logic, any distinction between men's and women's speech is regarded as further evidence for women's inferiority and men's supremacy. One wonders whether Lakoff would have described the same variable list as signifying masculine rather than feminine sex-typed qualities, had she believed them to be more common in men's speech. To argue that any feature of speech expresses uncertainty because it is common to females is not only tautological, but pernicious. Such arguments devalue women's talk, while erecting men's talk as a model by which all other discourse styles should be judged.

McConnell-Ginet's (1983) work on intonation provides an example of how women's speech is compared unfavorably with the male model. She remarks that women vary their pitch in speaking, while men are "monotonic." She argues that this pitch variation may serve as an attention-getting device for women. Feminine tone of voice is devalued and frequently mocked in our society, simply because of its association with females (Brend, 1975; McConnell-Ginet, 1983).

Since many researchers believe that gender differences reflect power differences between the sexes, it is remarkable that so few studies have attempted to link power and language directly. Eakins and Eakins (1976) reported that in a faculty meeting, untenured professors, regardless of sex, were interrupted more often and spoke less; those with tenure spoke more. However, there was an interaction between gender and power, with untenured women speaking less than untenured men. O'Barr and Atkins (1980) reported findings from a study of three men and three women testifying in a law court. They found that expert witnesses, who had both status and experience in testifying, spoke with similar assurance. However, those witnesses with little status and experience, regardless of gender, exhibited many of the features cited by Lakoff as characterizing women's language. O'Barr and Atkins conclude that what is commonly regarded as female speech is actually the language of the powerless. These studies are limited to a small number of subjects and therefore, while suggestive, they require further substantiation. The study reported below involves the comparison between male and female speech styles with the styles employed by those in powerful or subordinate positions as bestowed by age. We wanted to examine the link between the speech of children who had status and boys and girls speaking with each other.

## A STUDY OF CONVERSATIONAL STYLE AMONG CHILDREN

Lerita Coleman and I completed an investigation of gender differences in conversations among elementary school children (McCloskey and Coleman, 1982). We were interested in examining the role of dominance in social interaction. We tape recorded dyads of third grade girls and boys with same- and opposite-sex peers, and third grade boys with first grade boys, playing a game of checkers together. Our hypothesis was that if power explained gender differences, then boys' speech with girls' should resemble their speech with younger boys, since age is a determinant of status among elementary school children.

Twelve dyads were tape recorded for each of the four conditions, resulting in 48 transcripts: third grade boys with male peers; third grade girls with female peers; third grade girls with boys; third grade boys with first grade boys. After tapes were transcribed, we coded conversations for a number of variables. We derived our coding scheme from the work by Brown and Levinson (1978), who divided speech acts into two major categories: face-threatening and face-saving acts. Face, as they use the term, refers to the social countenance we project, and we depend on others in part to support through their behavior toward us. Face-saving acts, then, would involve politeness strategies and raising the image of the other during interaction. Face-threatening acts, on the other hand, would involve direct assertions of power, consecrating one's own position at the expense of another's. Brown and Levinson postulate that face-saving acts characterize the speech of the underclass, while the socially empowered can use face-threatening acts without recrimination.

Among the speech acts incorporated within the face-saving category were indirect requests, questions, compliments to the other, and self-abnegating statements (such as "I'm no good at this game."). Face-threatening acts were captured by direct requests, insults, and self-aggrandizing statements. We found that boys exhibited more face-threatening acts than girls, and girls exhibited more face-saving acts than boys when talking with same-sex peers. Boys when addressing either boys or girls of the same age used more direct than indirect requests, and were more likely to use insults or to challenge the other directly than were girls in either the same-sex or mixed-sex dyads. Girls, on the other hand, used more indirect requests than boys in either dyadic condition and also asked twice as many questions in either condition than boys in either condition. There were no differences on the number of compliments or self-aggrandizing statements exhibited by either group.

While boys and girls sustained stylistic differences regardless of sex of partner, and did not differ significantly in their use of speech acts in different dyadic conditions, there was an independent finding suggesting that perhaps girls make more adjustments when talking with opposite-sex peers. Girls used somewhat more face-threatening acts with males than with females (p <.12). Although not a statistically significant difference, this finding becomes more meaningful when regarded within the context of male–female dynamics. Although neither males nor females were successful social proprietors of the conversation, different dynamics appeared in opposite-sex than in either of the same-sex groups. Boys and girls engaged more in verbal altercations than either boys or girls did in same-sex dyads. Two examples of this verbal repartee follow:

*Boy (1)*

I'm moving here.

I don't care. (moves piece)

*Boy (2)*

No, you gotta be there and you go.

No you won't.

*Girl (1)*

No you can't.

*Girl (2)*

No! You gotta be right here and you go like that.

If you jump I'll jump you.

Although usually brief, these exchanges were more common in mixed-sex than in same-sex dyads and generally involved rule violations or challenges to the other's prowess. These findings suggest that tension exists between boys and girls; not male dominance or female subordination, but the clash of free and opposing wills. Goodwin (1980) reported similar findings among black children. She found that while girls were more "polite" and indirect with other girls, and boys more assertive and face-threatening in their speech with boys, in cross-sex situations girls were as skillful and adamant in conversational combat as were boys.

What appears to happen in these exchanges is that females adopt the males' more aggressive style when it becomes necessary to maintain their position. They have the skills, though apparently not the inclination to engage in verbal combat, since they do not use these discourse strategies in talking with same sex peers. Males and females sustain different rhetorical styles, but masculine appropriates feminine in mixed-sex discourse. It is the little girl in these arguments, and the woman in science and industry, who abdicates their gender, not the male. As Harding (1986) has observed: "Women exchange major aspects of their gender identity for the masculine version—without prescribing a similar degendering process for men" (p. 53). Unfortunately, women may have little choice, since males repudiate those traits and styles associated with the feminine. As Simone de Beauvoir has pointed out, masculine identity depends on viewing the female as "other," and subsequently as inferior.

The subtle alterations of style observed among the girls in our study, and in the work by Goodwin, indicate that the female's appropriation of male forms may begin early in both conversation and the socialization process. Those girls who recoil from adopting such strategies may suffer in their adult lives, when they find they cannot generate a "voice" that will be heard, that will be attended to by those socialized in masculine rhetoric (Belenky, Clinchy, Goldberger, and Tarule, 1986). There have been feminist proposals urging women to advance their own rhetorical style (Belenky et al. 1986; Daly, 1978; D.N. McCloskey, 1985), and these are laudable in their promotion of female autonomy. However, exactly how females avoid sexist devaluation in conversation, in the office, in the laboratory, in history, while expressing an independent female identity, remains unspecified, and it is perhaps the most serious question facing feminist theory today (Harding, 1986).

Of particular interest were comparisons of the different-age dyads with same-age dyads. Boys talking with younger boys used significantly fewer face-threatening acts, and significantly more indirect requests than boys talking with same-age peers (of either sex). First grade boys, on the other hand, used more face-threatening acts than third graders in any dyadic condition. This finding, contrary to the predictions of Brown and Levinson, suggests that it is the subordinate class rather than the ruling class that is most likely to adopt a bellicose style. Those who have to struggle to assert status are more likely to rely on aggressive discourse strategies than those already assured of a dominant position in the hierarchy.

How then should we interpret signs of conversational dominance when it is observed in male speech with females? It seems more valid to regard such speech as a struggle for power rather than an assertion of indisputable dominance. The problem the enfranchised classes face is protecting their position and privileges from the encroaching underclass. If they are not secure in their position, they will appear anxious to defend it.

## IMPLICATIONS FOR FUTURE RESEARCH

There are several issues raised in this chapter bearing on how properly to investigate gender and its linguistic manifestations. Probably the most crucial point is that researchers and those evaluating research should attend carefully to their own biases and those of their culture. We should not be so ready to attribute sex differences to simple stereotypes. Behavior common to one sex or the other is not necessarily a reflection of a given stereotyped trait. The research reviewed in this chapter highlights how our expectations prime the interpretation of sex differences. These biases often serve to perpetuate a view of female as victim, male as powerful, and do not advance the position of men or women in our as yet inegalitarian society. Researchers must analyze meaning in behavior independently of gender, whether it be running in playgrounds or using polite forms in requests. By developing an analytical framework by which to examine sociolinguistic behavior, we can proceed with the serious work of discovering an interface between such behavior and gender identity.

It is common in the social sciences to compare all human behavior against male models. However, while a great deal is shared by the sexes, there are also many experiences unique to the female or male worlds that must be fully acknowledged and understood before we can explain perceived differences. Jessie Bernard (1982) argues that a single social phenomenon, such as marriage, is experienced utterly differently by male and female participants. Researchers frequently overlook the gender differentiation of unitary experiences or variables. In the same way marriage is different for men and women, so is language; the same variables (e.g., minimal responses, tag questions, avoidant eye gaze) have different socioemotional significance. Understanding the socialization experiences of males and females and linking such experiences to communication is a primary step in explaining sex differences in conversation.

While research begins to present fuller descriptions of sex differences in communication, the answers to many basic questions, like a mirage, appear farther away as we move toward them. To understand the multi-functional nature of language and how it interfaces with our social identity and psyche should not be a simple matter. Nor is it, as the study of gender and speech attests. Uncovering gender differences in conversation is difficult, but interpreting those differences once excavated is an even more arduous task. It is a task well worth pursuing.

## REFERENCES

Abu-Lughod, L. (1985). A community of secrets: The separate world of Bedouin women. *Signs, 10*, 637–657.

Adams, K. A. (1980). Who has the final word? Sex, race and dominance behavior. *Journal of Personality and Social Psychology, 38*, 1–8.

Belenky, M.F., Clinchy, B.M., Goldberger, N.R., & Tarule, J.M. (1986). *Women's ways of knowing: The development of self, voice and mind.* New York: Basic Books.

Bem, S. L. (1984). Gender schema theory: A conceptual and empirical integration. *Nebraska Symposium on Motivation: Psychology and gender.* 1–71.

Bernard, J. (1972). *The sex game.* Englewood Cliffs, NJ: Prentice-Hall.

Bernard, J. (1982). *The future of marriage* (2nd Ed.). New Haven: Yale University Press.

Brend, R. (1975). Male–female intonation patterns in American English. In B. Thorne & N. Henley (Eds.), *Language and sex: Difference and dominance.* Rowley, MA: Newbury House.

Brouwer, D., Gerritsen, M., & De Haan, D. (1979). Speech differences between women and men: on the wrong track? *Language in Society, 8*, 33–50.

Brown, P. (1980). How and why are women more polite: some evidence from a Mayan community. In S. McConnell-Ginet, R. Borker, & N. Furman (Eds.), *Women and language in literature and society.* New York: Praeger.

Brown, P. & Levinson, S. (1978). Universals in language usage: Politeness phenomena. In E. Goody (Ed.)., *Questions and politeness: Strategies in social interaction.* Cambridge: Cambridge University Press.

Coleman, L. (1980). Characteristics of the speech addressed to children, foreigners and mentally retarded adults. Unpublished doctoral dissertation, Harvard University.

Condry, J. & Condry, S. (1976). Sex differences: A study of the eye of the beholder. *Child Development, 47,* 812–819.

Daly, M. (1978). *Gyn/Ecology: The metaethics of radical feminism.* Boston: Beacon Press.

de Beauvoir, S. (1952/1972). *The second-sex.* New York: Penguin.

DePaulo, B. & Coleman, L. (1981). Evidence for the specialness of a "baby talk" register. *Language and Speech, 24,* 223–231.

Dubois, L. & Crouch, I. (1975). The question of tag questions in women's speech. They don't really use more of them, do they? *Language in Society, 4,* 289–294.

Eakins, B. & Eakins, G. (1976), Verbal turn-taking and exchanges in faculty dialogue. In B. Dubois & I. Crouch (Eds.), *The sociology of the language of American women.* San Antonio: Trinity Press.

Edelsky, C. (1981). Who's got the floor? *Language in Society, 10,* 383–421.

Ferguson, C.A. (1977). Baby talk as a simplified register. In C.E. Snow & C.A. Ferguson (Eds.), *Talking to children.* Cambridge: Cambridge University Press.

Fishman, P. (1983). Interaction: The work women do. In B. Thorne, C. Kramarae, & N. Henley (Eds.), *Language, gender and society.* Rowley, MA: Newbury House.

Giles, H., Smith, P., Browne, C., Whiteman, S., & Williams, J. (1980). Women's speech: the voice of feminism. In S. McConnell-Ginet, R. Borker, & N. Furman (Eds.), *Women and language in literature and society.* New York: Praeger.

Goffman, E. (1959). *The presentation of self in everyday life.* New York: Doubleday & Co.

Goodwin, M.H. (1980) Directive-response speech sequences in girls' and boys' task activities. In S. McConnell-Ginet, R. Borker, & N. Furman (Eds.), *Women and language in literature and society.* New York: Praeger.

Harding, S. (1986). *The science question in feminism.* Ithaca: Cornell University Press.

Harding, S. (1975). Women and words in a Spanish village. In R. Reiter (Ed.), *Toward an anthropology of women.* New York: Monthly Review Press.

Henley, N. (1977). *Body politics: Power, sex, and nonverbal communication.* Englewood Cliffs, NJ: Prentice-Hall.

Holmes, J. (1986). Functions of "you know" in women's and men's speech. *Language in Society, 22,* 1–21.

Jesperson, O. (1922). *Language: Its nature, development and origin.* London: Allen & Unwin.

Lakoff, R. (1975). *Language and woman's place.* New York: Harper & Row.

Macauley, R. K. S. (1978). The myth of female superiority in language. *Journal of Child Language, 5,* 353–363.

Maltz, D.N. & Borker, R.A. (1983). A cultural approach to male–female miscommunication. In J.J. Gumperz (Ed.), *Language and social identity.* New York: Cambridge University Press.

McCloskey, D.N. (1985). Some consequences of a feminine economics. Paper presented at the annual meetings of the American Economic Association, New York.

McCloskey, L.A. & Coleman, L. (1982). Combat and compliance among children: establishing dominance through gender-differentiated speech. Paper presented at the annual meetings of the American Psychological Association, Washington, D.C.

McConnell-Ginet, S. (1983). Intonation in a man's world. In B. Thorne, C. Kramarae, & N. Henley (Eds.), *Language, gender and society*. Rowley, MA: Newbury House.

Moore, T. (1967). Language and intelligence: A longitudinal study of the first eight years. Part I. Patterns of development in boys and girls. *Human Development, 10,* 88–106.

O'Barr, W. & Atkins, B. (1980). "Women's language" or "powerless language"? In S. McConnell-Ginet, R. Borker, & N. Furman (Eds.), *Women and language in literature and society*. New York: Praeger.

Ortner, S. (1974). Is female to male as nature is to culture? In M.Z. Rosaldo & L. Lamphere (Eds.), *Woman, Culture and Society*. Stanford, CA: Stanford University Press.

Schneider, D.J., Hastorf, A.H., & Ellsworth, P. (1979). *Person perception*. Reading, MA: Addison-Wesley.

Shatz, M. & Gelman, R. (1973). The development of communication skills: Modifications in the speech of young children as a function of listener. *Monographs of the Society for Research in Child Development, 152* (38, Whole No. 5).

Spender, D. (1980). *Man made language*. London: Routledge & Kegan Paul.

Thorne, B. (1986). Girls and boys together . . . but mostly apart: Gender arrangements in elementary schools. In W. Hartup & Z. Rubin (Eds.), *Relationships and development*. Hillsdale, NJ: Lawrence Erlbaum Associates.

West, C. & Zimmerman, D. (1977). Women's place in everyday talk: Reflections on parent–child interaction. *Social Problems, 24,* 521–529.

West, C. & Zimmerman, D. (1983). Small insults: A study of interruptions in cross-sex conversations between unacquainted persons. In B. Thorne, C. Kramarae, & N. Henley (Eds.), *Language, gender and society*. Rowley, MA: Newbury House.

Woolf, V. (1920/1948). *Night and day*. New York: Harcourt, Brace, Jovanovich.

Zimmerman, D. & West, C. (1975). Sex roles, interruptions and silences in conversations. In B. Thorne & N. Henley (Eds.), *Language and sex: Difference and dominance*. Rowley, MA: Newbury House.

# 10
# Sex Roles in Adulthood and Old Age
## Jan D. Sinnott

Several important issues will be examined in this chapter: why we look at sex roles and aging at all; what theoretical advances might be linked to those topics; and what is known about sex roles in later years from current research. The chapter will conclude with recommendations for the field in general. The reader is encouraged to see Sinnott (1986) for a more complete treatment of this topic.

In the period of time since the topics of sex roles and of aging became important to psychologists, to researchers, and to the general public, considerable work on theory, measurement, and data collection has been performed. The major purpose of this chapter is to consolidate material on sex roles and aging, and to attempt to interpret what has been done. A further purpose is to suggest ways in which advances in other fields—fields as divergent as sociobiology, systems theory, cognitive psychology, and the so-called "new" physics—can assist in the understanding of sex role development in later life. This chapter, then, represents an attempt to bridge disciplines and areas within psychology in order to make sense of currently available information and to suggest new directions in which we might proceed.

The lifespan approach to sex role development has been a relatively recent phenomenon. Neugarten (1964), Gutmann (1975), and Block (1973) explored changes in male and female role expectations during adulthood that were based on social expectation and major developmental tasks. Block (1973) and Riegel (1973) viewed the manifestation of cultural sex roles as a function not only of biological demands and past learning experiences, but of the nature of the economic system, the historical moment, and the philosophical system within which they are defined. Thus sex roles in this perspective imply dynamic change based on the individual and the social and cultural climate.

Loevinger's (1977) concept of the milestones of ego development and their extrapolations to sex role development form the basis of Block's (1973) approach. In the earliest period, the main developmental concerns of the child are genderless, and identity constitutes a mere naming of gender: "I am a boy/girl." Later, conformity to learned patterns becomes the main task; this is reflected in the development of sex role stereotypes and sex role bifurcation. The conformist stage is followed by one of self-criticism based on comparison with an abstract ideal, thereby moderating the stereotypical role. With the advent of autonomy, individualization results as conflicts, aroused during the conformity and conscientious stages, are resolved. At this point, differentiation of sex role is said to occur. The highest, most integrated level of functioning finds the individual evolving a complex identity that combines aspiration, experience, and previously polarized traits. In sex role terms, this period is one of androgyny.

Hefner, Rebecca, and Oleshansky (1975) have proposed a lifespan approach to the development of sex role identity. Their hierarchical stages include: (1) global, undifferentiated sex roles; (2) polarized, or traditional masculine/feminine roles; and (3) transcendent roles that combine both masculinity and femininity. While the young child most likely has not defined a sex role, and the adolescent most likely has overdefined it, the adult synthesizes roles into more complex wholes. For individuals who have "transcended" masculinity and femininity, psychological adjustment is no longer tied to these dichotomous sets of traits. Unfortunately, the measurement of "transcendence" as distinct from androgyny has not yet been fully operationalized.

Garnets and Pleck (1979) have approached this task with their concept of sex role salience, which is currently under empirical scrutiny, and have presented the most recent conceptual analysis on the basic of sex role strain analysis. Their viewpoint combines social learning and lifespan development. They feel that the ultimate harm of traditional sex roles is the devaluation that an individual may experience if he/she does not conform to the traditional standards of the sex role norms. Thus, strain results from discrepancy between the individual's self-perception and his/her perceptions of social expectations. Garnets and Pleck also measure the degree of salience of sex role characteristics for the individual. The dichotomy of "masculine" versus "feminine" may not be an equally important distinction to everyone. Thus the salience or importance of sex role characteristics as a filter through which the individual views his/her behavior is measured. By combining measures of the individual's "real" self-concept, same-sex "ideal", and degree of sex role salience, Garnets and Pleck derive two variables of real versus ideal discrepancy and sex role strain outcome. As in Bem's (1979) conception, the long-run developmental trend is toward reduced sex role salience.

## THEORETICAL ADVANCES THAT SPEAK TO LIFESPAN SEX ROLE THEORY

Ideas about sex roles and sex role development have been linked to ideas and advances in other aspects of science. In this chapter, two new approaches to conceptualizing lifespan sex role development are presented. They involve an examination of the *context* in which roles serve individuals, and an analysis of the ways in which the social system and the individual system *interact* to their mutual benefit. The first new approach is a consideration of how adult cognitive development (Piagetian formal and postformal operations, relativistic thought, awareness of necessary but subjective belief systems) might cause mature adults to know roles differently and therefore behave differently. The second new approach is an application of systems theory to role development, considering roles as the intersections of two living systems, that of the organism and that of society.

## Piagetian Formal and Postformal Thinking: Adult Cognitive Development and Sex Role Concepts

A number of investigators have recently addressed the topic of "postformal" operations, that is, those structures of thought that are a stage more complex in organization than Piaget's formal operations (see Richards & Commons, 1984; Kramer, 1983, for summaries and critiques of the various postformal positions). More work on postformal, mature adult thought is being done—in part, perhaps—because the idea of cognitive development beyond adolescence is appealing. The question of interest is: how might formal and postformal operations be related to a lifespan model of sex role development? To address this question it is necessary to examine some aspects of postformal operations and the argument itself more closely.

What kind of case is being made for a relation between cognitive development, especially formal and postformal operations, and sex roles? To oversimplify, it is the same type of case that Kohlberg (1966) makes about cognitive development and early sex role development and about cognitive and moral development. Social relations, of which sex-roles and moral development are examples (Carter & Patterson, 1982), may be seen as based upon cognitive skills. As cognitive skills develop, social relations become both understood and more complex. At those times, when the world can be known in a more complex manner than purely abstract and formal, roles may also be known in a way that is more complex. Having thought of the role in a complex way, one could then live it in a complex way.

How would roles be known in postformal terms? To answer this question, one must look at theories of postformal operations. According to Kramer (1983), postformal operations theorists all state that postformal thought (1) is a distinct stage; (2) subsumes formal operations; and (3) incorporates a relativistic view of truth. Generally, then, a postformal cognitive stage could underlie a view in which sex roles are not absolute but are created relative to the actor, that is, with a subjective component. Some given, formal structure of roles would be consciously chosen based on some belief system that is a subjective view of "truth", from among a number of formal role structures. Further, what constitutes a given role (e.g., "masculinity") would be known to be somewhat arbitrary and based partly on the perceiver's own experiences and resultant ideas of truth. Things are what they are only within a particular system (von Bertalanffy, 1968). The postformal concept of sex roles, then, includes a necessary subjectivity and operates by laws like those of the "new physics" (Sinnott, 1981, 1983, 1985a).

In a personal context, the role taken, or the role that one perceives another to take, becomes what it is agreed to be by the persons in the interaction. The "truth" of what the role is is therefore determined by a system of beliefs held by the persons in the interaction. And those persons in the interaction may even be aware that all roles are potentially available to them and that they are the ones to call the shots and decide what a given set of behaviors means in role terms. The individual is not in a role-less, undefined state, nor in possession of an absolute unchanging role that is a permanent descriptor of one's identity, but rather is constantly—perhaps even consciously—creating a flexible role defined in relation to individuals and circumstances in one's context (see Sinnott, 1977). This last—the context—is a shared but also dually created perception of reality. In the framework of George Kelly's theory of personality (1955), persons are always moving to new "places" where they must construct a new social meaning for the self in the context of evolving social structure within a given society's institutions. From the standpoint of sociobiological theory (Lumsden & Wilson, 1981), human social behaviors that have evolutionary use are possible because a cognitive filter permits them. Genes, in turn, control the type of cognitive filter that occurs. If potentially postformal cognitive filters are adaptive, then, we would see more and more societies where adult sex roles are relativistic and flexible. This, indeed, seems to be the case.

Role behaviors also may be seen as attempts to solve everyday life problems. Individuals learn to act in ways that help them to meet their goals. In the context of problem solving, roles based on postformal thinking might permit greater creativity in using strategies to solve problems where the goal is unclear. Most everyday problems fall into that category (Wood, 1983). The individual has the cognitive freedom to jump out of the system (Hofstadter, 1979) to some meta-level, make a decision about the rules of the game (i.e., which roles constitute his/her goals today and, therefore, which goals are appropriate) and then to jump back into the processing system to continue the work of solving the particular problem. For the postformal problem solver the solution to a problem may be in reaching a meta-goal, namely the creation of a *process,* which then usually works in many systems despite widely varying sets of rules or belief systems. The adult postformal-operations problem solver who is attempting to solve the problem of how to act in a sex role-related situation in which the goal is unclear can (1) jump out of the system to a higher level; (2) decide which belief/rule system (related to sex roles) to use; (3) jump back in and operate within that system of "masculinity"/"femininity"; (4) test the results of that problem-solving attempt; (5) reinforce the use of the "good process" (which is in step

2); and (6) continue living using this sort of meta-solution to problems of this type (Sinnott, 1985a).

These possibilities may be put into more concrete terms. Consider this scenario. A 40–year-old woman, who lost her husband to cancer some months prior, notices that her house needs an exterior paint job. She knows from her childhood training and her neighbors' behavior that it is not considered feminine to paint the house herself, although her gentle, feminine mother once did so for the sake of the family. She knows that the money for that job would be better spent for herself and the children's needs. She dislikes the immensity of the task, but she likes working outside with her hands for a change since her usual job requires only mental activity. If she does the paint job, will she be taking over her late husband's masculine role? Should she do the job?

Thinking about the scenario in a personal framework, we notice that the woman and her husband and the woman and her neighbors had apparently agreed together that painting the house was "masculine", while she and her mother defined the same behavior as nurturing and "feminine." Thinking of her own needs and likes, and the needs of her children, she realized that it is not clear whether what she has thought about doing is more instrumental or more nurturant, more "masculine" or more "feminine". It seems to be both. She decides that if she is ever to do anything she must step back from the situation (use postformal logical operations), choose a behavior based on a chosen belief system about truth (belief system: "be pragmatic"); call it acceptably "feminine" in terms of her own ("feminine") self-image; and act. She has faced the fact that this knowledge is partly subjective, chosen to know in a certain way, and let that influence her behavior.

Thinking about the scenario in problem solving terms, the woman seems to have a clear sub-goal—getting the house painted—but a fuzzy larger goal—keeping a coherent self-image. She therefore "jumps out" of the system to a higher meta-level, decides that the most important thing is to do *something*. That means dealing with the potential relativity of the self-image by making a decision as to what is "feminine," to her, in relation to this situation and in view of her past history. The next step was to jump back into the problem solving system and decide that she would still be "feminine" in this situation if she painted the house, since it was also nurturant behavior and felt a little like a hobby. She tested the workability of this solution on several neighbors and one of her children, and they did not respond in a way that threatened her self-image. Pleased at the results, she filed the *process* away as a "good process" to be used again later.

Thinking about the scenario in terms of the evolution of society, decisions such as that of this woman, multiplied over many individuals and occasions, could change the nature of concepts of "femininity" and "masculinity". Simple awareness that sex roles are relative would also have that effect. The current phenomenon, in which society considers questions of equity between the sexes, attests to the fact that when individuals are aware that roles are not fixed by some natural law, individuals permit themselves role flexibility.

### Systems Theory and Lifespan Roles

Systems theory is a theory of interacting processes and the way they influence each other over time to permit the continuity of some larger whole. Systems act so as to continue and change because their own balances are not optimal or because they are influenced by other systems. Some authors who provide descriptions of these general ideas are von Bertalanffy (1968), Buckley (1968), Hofstadter (1979), Miller (1978), and Sinnott (1985b). Miller's discussion of living systems is especially useful to consider for a discussion of roles. Individuals, societies, and cells all appear to use similar processes to create boundaries, to take in stimulation, to process information, to act, and to change. For example, information is handled by cells, persons, and societies. For cells, information may be chemical and may be filtered by cell walls. For persons, information may be conceptual and may be filtered by perceptions. For societies, information may be news, filtered by censors. Cells, persons, and societies all exist in relation to each other. For example, a liver cell could not have formed into a liver cell without the feedback of the body and an English-speaking child could not be such without the feedback of a culture. The liver cell exposed to carcinogens by the person system hosting it (and indirectly by the social system producing those substances) is influenced. The production of the carcinogen may keep the social living system healthy, but kill the cell system and the person system. Within systems theory, roles are structures of the social system that are equivalent to organs in the physical/person system. Roles are organized ways of ensuring that some vital function is performed.

As all living systems develop and age they appear to proceed through a regular set of stages. They begin in disorder, that is, with few parts concrete and defined. They become more orderly, defined and bounded over time. They become over-ordered, over-bounded, and mechanical or rigid before they disintegrate into disorder/new order. For example, early embryonic tissue is largely potential, able to be changed into a number of different cell/organ types. This flexibility without structure is gradually transformed into a state of some structure (e.g., organs) and some flexibility (e.g., ability to repair and regenerate tissue). Later in development some organs cannot regenerate any longer since tissues are too differentiated. In senescence all flexibility has been lost and any damage leads to deterioration and disintegration/death. When we move to the psychological realm we see series of these "deaths" as persons' transitions from one state to another, suffering disorder in between, then reordering at a more complex level. Notice that the manner of change described here so briefly is similar in form to the ideas of Prigogene (1980; Prigogene & Stengers, 1984) and the principles of entropy articulated in the so-called "new physics."

Living systems that survive for any period of time contain many potential orders of complexity. The late orders are contained as "seeds" in the earlier orders. An example is the more complex order of adolescence contained implicitly in the earlier forms of childhood. Systems that survive also contain a process by which the new can replace the old. Resistance to the emerging change means eventual massive harm—or death—to the system. Systems set up for change are said to be in a ready state. Systems that survive monitor their change processes to ensure continuity while change is permitted. They also are flexible enough, therefore, to adapt to many contexts. They can interface with many other systems without being engulfed or walling off valuable information from the other systems. The degree of order necessary to a system to keep it going is idiosyncratic for that system.

How does this relate to sex role development over the lifespan? Consider the person and society as living systems, each seeking continuity and fulfillment of survival needs. These needs include control of information and energy flow. Sex roles are ways person and social systems can regulate the flow of information and energy (effort) while taking care of survival needs. The early stages of these systems are disordered in regard to roles—no roles are apparent. For example, the newborn is sex role-less, and a group of strangers is role-less. Later stages are associated with more concrete roles; in the person and in the group, masculinity and femininity may emerge. Final stages find the roles rigid and inflexible, so they may fail to respond to the pull of new needs. This failure of response leads to disorder and a search for a new, more complex order. Systems theory suggests that this may be the transition we are seeing now in society and after the reproductive period and "parental imperative" in each developing person. Rigid roles in the presence of new demands may lead to more complex integrations of role-related behaviors.

Systems theory leads to suggestions for the conceptualization of aging in general, and therefore for the understanding of sex role development in older adults. The lifespan in systems terms might be thought of as three phases: (Youth) personal expansion and definition; (Mature adulthood) interactions with other systems while improving existing structure; and (Decline) imposition of personal order irrespective of fit. In youth, data gathering is a major activity, cognition grows to the level of abstraction, energy is plentiful, breaking away and learning about the world are main developmental demands, and the system is driven less by preconception and more by events of the moment, which often include social learning. This would be a period of rigid roles. In maturity, energy and memory are less available and partly commited to already existing structures. Thought is practical and contextual as well as abstract and is determined by both past structures of thought and present incoming data. Demands are for interface with other systems, which increases differentiation. This would be an age for complex roles. In decline (notice, not "old age" but "decline") energy is lacking and the easiest way to orient the system is "top down." That is, using the structures already available, whether they fit or not, to make sense of everything. Roles at this point would be idiosyncratic representations of the last stage of role development of the organism, before energy diminished so much that flexibility was lost. Interface with other systems would be avoided at this time and boundaries hardened defensively.

This general summary may give a flavor for the multifaceted causes, effects, and processes—all related to roles—stemming from need for system continuity and intersystem interfaces. The reader is urged to look at the "new physics" literature and systems literature mentioned earlier (e.g., Wolf, 1981) for more detailed and technical information.

## WHAT IS KNOWN FROM CURRENT RESEARCH

A summary of recent studies is given in Table 10.1. In general, recent theoretical work has pointed to the complexities of reaching meaningful measurements of masculinity, femininity, androgyny, adjustment, or self-concept. Few investigators can hope to address all the issues raised, but more can be conscious of them in interpreting data. Together, all of the authors seem to be urging use of a complex model for change and for any role-related behavior. The perceptions of the respondent—about the meaning of items, about social sanctions, about situational salience—stand out as factors to which attention should be paid in future work as soon as means can be found to measure them. The authors in the table deal with: the nature of adaptivity in a social setting; social approval and disapproval of role-related behaviors; the utility of stereotype based scales, especially in predicting everyday behavior; developmental stage needs; social–cognitive aspects; theoretical approaches; and ideographic considerations. All these topics lead to greater awareness of the difficulty of knowing a social reality that is co-created by all participants and changing over time. The biological, the cognitive, the identity, the social, and the historical aspects of the situation must be addressed in sex role development research.

Successful adaptation to the environment becomes increasingly important with aging but the ability to adapt may depend upon already having certain traits, skills, and attributes, many of which are communal in nature (Rabin, 1986). The valuing of communal traits by our culture must increase if people are to transit old age successfully. Then we can all share David Bakan's (1966) vision that the "proper way of dying is from fatigue after a life of trying to mitigate agency with communion" (p. 236).

## RECOMMENDATIONS FOR FUTURE RESEARCH AND THEORY

Several conclusions can be drawn from the early and the recent literature on lifespan sex role development.

*We must not jump to conclusions that responses on a scale will be predictive of behavior.* Individuals may say that they are "masculine" by their scale responses, but may mean they are masculine in regard to stereotyping concepts.

**Table 10.1**
**Summary of Some Major Recent Theoretical and Empirical Studies of Sex Roles and Aging**

| Author(s) & Date | Topic | Age of Subjects'/ Focal age | Major Findings |
|---|---|---|---|
| *I. Theoretical Work* | | | |
| Bernard (1976) | Models of role change | Lifespan | Change may be incremental; may come from elimination of maladaptive behavior; may come suddenly due to a state of developmental readiness |
| Braden (1982) | Humanistic study of sex roles | Middle-aged | Roles are associated with current life but not anticipated future; sex differences disappear when future is described |
| Breytspraak (1984) | Self-concept | Lifespan | Multiple perspectives on roles and their lifespan development stimulated by the diverse theories of the "self" |
| Datan & Rodenheaver (1983) | Love, sexuality | Lifespan | Learning to love over time demands unlearning old sex roles |
| Lenney (1979) | Sex role development based on individual change | Lifespan | Roles depend on global self-description, beliefs, emotional responsiveness, motivation |
| Livson (1976) | Roles and confict | Lifespan | Androgynous are more conflicted in youth and less conflicted in later years |

**Table 10.1—***Continued*

| Author(s) & Date | Topic | Age of Subjects'/ Focal age | Major Findings |
|---|---|---|---|
| McGee & Wells (1982) | Gutmann's role reversal theory compared with Sinnott's theory | Later adulthood | Authors advocate a multidimensional concept of gender typing and phenomenologically oriented studies |
| Mooreland, et al. (1979) | Roles and decision making | NA | Females could endorse male or female decision styles; sex role expression was occurring |
| Rabin (1986) | Adaptive roles in old age | Old age | Feminine traits may be most adaptive in later life |
| Sinnott (1977) | Dialectical model of adaptive sex roles in older age | Lifespan | The dialectical model of Riegel is useful in conceptualizing old age roles |
| Weg (1983) | Changing roles allow us to deal with life stage changes in sexuality | Lifespan | Complex role description can be associated with complex enjoyment of multiple forms of sexual expression |
| *II. Empirical Work*<br>Alpaugh & Birren (1975) | Creativity | Lifespan | Creativity was not related to role |
| Ames et al. (1954) | Roles, organic brain damage diagnosis, and Rorschach responses—longitudinal data | Older | Profiles with sex stereotyping characteristics were associated with clinical diagnoses |

Table 10.1—*Continued*

| Author(s) & Date | Topic | Age of Subjects'/ Focal age | Major Findings |
|---|---|---|---|
| Barrows & Zuckerman (1976) | Men adopt F traits | Older males | Males showed an increase in F interests as they aged |
| Cameron (1976) | Rate M and F of cohorts | Lifespan | Perceived M and F varied by generation rated, with old considered least M or F |
| Cherry & Zarit (1973) | Life satisfaction | Young and aged females | Life satisfaction was associated with M |
| Costa & McCrae (1977) | Personality-organizing power of M/F factors | Lifespan males | Personality was less likely to be organized by M or F as time goes on; with age, contrast between M & F values was less distinct |
| Douglas & Arenberg (1978) | Male decline in M | Lifespan males | In Guilford-Zimmerman Temperament Survey men declined in M as they aged |
| Foley & Murphy (1977) | Androgyny | Older | As cohort age increased, each sex incorporated characteristics of the other, especially for their ideal selves |
| Gillett et al. (1977) | Social competence | Lifespan females | The middle aged were most androgynous |
| Gutmann (1975) | Parental demands influence roles | Lifespan | Roles shifted in response to ebb and flow of "parental imperative" |

**Table 10.1**—*Continued*

| Author(s) & Date | Topic | Age of Subjects'/ Focal age | Major Findings |
|---|---|---|---|
| Gutmann et al. (1979) plus Bell (1978), Gross (1978), Wells (1979) | Pathology | Middle-aged | Submerged aspects of personality (e.g., M to women) arose and caused defensive responses; role change indicated redefinitions of self |
| Hoffman & Fidell (1979) | Correlates of BSRI | Young and middle-aged females | Demographic, attitudinal, time-use and personality differences were consistent with BSRI descriptors |
| Hubbard et al. (1979) | Role change in dyads | Middle-aged & older married couples | Role diffusion occurred; older adults, especially, saw themselves changing |
| Jewett (1973) | Longevity and roles | Older | Long-lived persons appeared androgynous |
| Livson (1976) | Life crises and roles | Middle-aged females | There may be more than one role-related "successful" style of functioning |
| Lowenthal et al. (1975) | Androgyny | Older | All sex role behaviors did not converge but expressiveness behaviors did |
| Murphy (1976) | Real and ideal self | Young and older | Older females and males had similar real ratings and ideal ratings; some age differences were found |
| Neugarten et al. (1964) | Roles and satisfaction | Older | Those with integrated roles were most satisfied |

166

**Table 10.1—***Continued*

| Author(s) & Date | Topic | Age of Subjects'/ Focal age | Major Findings |
|---|---|---|---|
| Neugarten & Gutmann (1968) | Role reversal; traits expected in older persons | Middle-aged and older | Women and men reversed roles as they aged; older females and males were expected to increase their opposite-sex traits |
| Neugarten et al. (1968) | Life satisfaction | Older | Those integrating M and F were most satisfied |
| O'Sullivan (1980) plus Wish (1976) | Complex self-concepts and age | Lifespan | Compared with younger counterparts, older women have greater acceptance of M self-descriptions and older men had greater acceptance of F self-descriptions (for Wish, women's results were the reverse) |
| Puglisi & Jackson (1980–81) | Self-esteem, role change | Lifespan | M was the best predictor of self-esteem and peaked in middle years; F did not change |
| Reichard et al. (1962) | Roles and adjustment to aging | Older men | Androgynous roles were associated with more successful aging |
| Sedney (1977) | Coping responses and roles | Middle-aged females | M characteristics added to F |
| Silverman (1977) | Perceived M in men | Lifespan men | College students perceived older males as less masculine |

**Table 10.1—***Continued*

| Author(s) & Date | Topic | Age of Subjects'/ Focal age | Major Findings |
|---|---|---|---|
| Sinnott (1982) | Correlates of older adults' sex roles | Older | Demographic, ability, attitudinal and other descriptions were consistent with BSRI categorizations |
| Sinnott (1984) | Older adults' perceptions of roles expected of them | Older | Older adults saw others as expecting them to use dual roles |
| Sinnott (1984–85) | Role conflict and mental health | Older | Conflict between actual sex role and sex role expected of them not associated with symptoms, but conflict over one's M relative to one's F was |
| Skinner (1979) | Roles and health | Older females | Androgynous women were more likely to rate their health "good" than the feminine were; androgynous and feminine women were more likely than others to worry about health |
| Smith (1981) | Effect of environment on role change | Older | Environment and social support had more influence than age or role change |
| Spence & Helmreich (1979) | Role changes over time | Adolescents and middle-aged | Complex life circumstances changed trait balance |

**Table 10.1**—*Continued*

| Author(s) & Date | Topic | Age of Subjects'/ Focal age | Major Findings |
|---|---|---|---|
| Suzuki (1979) | Self-esteem & role | Younger and older | Self-esteem was related to M for all groups; role identity was related both to age and developmental stage |
| Turner (1977) | Androgyny | Older | Older men expressed more tenderness and dependency; older women expressed more autonomy |
| Urberg (1979) | Stereotyping | Lifespan | Both sexes described themselves in the same terms but described an ideal member of the opposite sex in stereotypical terms |
| Williams & Wirth (1965) | Roles and successful aging | Older | Dual roles were related to successful aging |
| Windle (1984) | Cognitive flexibility and life satisfaction | Older | Sex role was not predictive of flexibility or life satisfaction |
| Windle & Sinnott (1985) | Validity of BSRI for old | Older | Longitudinal studies were needed to answer this question, but BSRI may have three factors for old |
| Zaks et al. (1979) | Life events and roles | Adult | Events triggered role shifts |

*Source*: Compiled by the author.

They may rate themselves differently in other situations, may act other than their ratings, and their behavior may vary from situation to situation. They may do what is most rewarding and that may happen to be masculine. They may score themselves masculine due to development of an identity labeled masculine. They may do so since masculine behavior is socially desirable. They may change in self definition due to life stage demands, or when their own concept of masculinity is no longer like their behavior, even if to everyone else they are still "masculine" by some other definition. And they may label themselves or act as they perceive society expects them to do. Since all these factors may underlie their responses to the scale, it is hard to predict behavior.

*Responses to sex role instruments do mean something.* What is meant may be tempered by each person's perception of unspoken situational constraints and other factors mentioned alone. If individuals respond appropriately they are matching themselves to global standards designed to reflect the clearest opposition between gender-assigned roles.

*Masculinity, femininity, and androgyny have been shown to be adaptive.* Depending upon the situational demands, subject to the constraints above, any of the roles might be adaptive. The real question is, what is the most useful role in a certain setting: masculine, feminine, both, or neither? Useful may mean "liable to be rewarded" or "consistent", or "workable by some external criterion." Androgyny may be the most adaptive response in terms of the last criterion; masculinity may be the most adaptive in terms of the first.

*Sex roles are meaningful in terms of social expectations.* The concept of global, oppositional, gender-linked roles is present for all members of society, and society imposes these role expectations on individuals so long as the real characteristics of those individuals are not known. So whatever complex designation of role and behavior one adopts, the general "other" is still seen as conforming to the global stereotypes. Individuals also read role expectations projected by others, and, to the degree they are conformists, attempt to conform to them.

*Sex roles are meaningful ways to order one's sense of self as socially efficacious, to create a sense of personal conformity, and to order self-concept.* The creation of the self-concept is partially accomplished by acting and noticing that the self is the center of effective acts. Roles permit structured action likely to work in a society. They also are labels that live on beyond the individual and can be generalized to many situations. Knowing one's sex role without knowing the meaning of that role to the person is to take only half a step toward knowledge.

*The meaning of sex roles depends on age and developmental stage.* Meanings are related to modes of cognition and social demands at each period. They are also related to the previous history and experience of the person and the historical period in which the society finds itself. Infants can know roles in direct physical forms, but cannot know them abstractly. The concrete operational person can know roles in the abstract, and the formal operational person can build logical systems of roles. The postformal person can see roles relativistically, as co-created by persons in them.

*Models of sex role changes over time can be of many types.* Change can be more complex than increase or decrease in global qualities. Change might occur on one dimension but not on another, or global role traits but not on behavior, or visa versa. Change might be triggered by specific events or might represent an accretion over time. It may be reversible. Change might result from diffusion of a self concept until its meaning is so muddy that it can become something new. Change might depend on past rates of change. It is useful for investigators to be clear about their underlying model of change as they discuss sex role development.

*Sex role complexity and later-life sex role development may be linked to cognitive abilities like postformal thought or problem solving skills.* Roles have been linked to cognitive processes such as concept formation. As cognitive operations become more complex, their associated roles might be seen as multifaceted rather than undimensional. They might also be seen as relativistic, that is conceptualizable only in relation to a certain set of beliefs or a certain situation. In adulthood a person discovers that roles do not exist "out there" as givens but instead depend partly on one's own thinking processes and moment to moment cognitive creations. At that point the person is thinking in a complex way that some (e.g., Commons et al., 1984; Sinnott, 1984) would say is beyond Piaget's formal operations. Postformal thinkers might be more capable of androgynous concepts, or sex role transcendence.

Sex role development related questions (e.g. "Am I being feminine?" "What is the masculine thing to do at my age?") may be conceptualized in decision theory or problem solving theory terms as ill-structured problems. This means among other things that they have an unclear goal. Decisions must be made about the nature of the goal as a part of solving the problem. Problem solving literature can be a guide to dimensions we need to test to understand the process of solving sex role behavior/self-concept problems. This application of cognitive theory has not yet been attempted.

*Sex role developmental theories suggest "new physics" concepts and might make use of them.* The development of sex roles over time is the development of two interfacing systems in motion. It involves the kinds of dynamics described in relativistic and quantum physics (see Sinnott, 1981, 1985b). From the literature reviewed above it is clear that a multivariate approach needs to be taken in sex role studies, and that adjacent centers of causality—other persons, the social order—cause changes in an individual's sex roles. The person, in turn, causes changes in the social order by his/her perception of roles and by action on that perception. It is clear that one's vantage point in measuring sex roles is very important in drawing conclusions about the results. These ideas have companion ideas in the physical sciences that could be used in studies of change, both in a person and among systems.

The most useful laws of lifespan development may be those that apply analyses and models of the new physics. This approach can take into account the conceptual distance between two individuals or more, the developmental rate of one relative to the other(s), and the effects of other changing persons or events in that same interpersonal space. This may be what individuals do when they solve the problems of which sex role to identify with or to act out.

*Sex role development theory can make use of ideas in systems theory.* Personal and social systems are connected by many roles, among them sex roles. Theories of living systems (see Miller, 1978) give us an outline of the processes within and between those two systems. The flow of information can be studied within and between systems and roles are part of that information flow. A study of system boundaries can be conceptualized as a study of rigid or flexible roles and the capability of society or person to perceive or enact them. Future studies can take this model of living systems into account.

### Roles as "Possibilities"

Emerging ideas suggest that in the future roles will be orchestrated consciously by the person, rather than being imposed consciously or unconsciously by society, or being left to the mercy of unexamined forces. Each child may grow up aware that she/he has a spectrum of role possibilities within, a cast of characters and a library of dramas that can be acted out. The child will see that at some times in life one character or one drama is more useful than the others and can be invited into life. The child will be aware that using only one character or drama gets to be habit forming, and that alternatives should be practiced so that they are ready for use as desired. This child will remember, even before old age, that these characters and dramas are only roles, not his/her entire self, and that each person has much greater potential than can ever be confined within a role framework. After all, we are either an emerging species or a dying species. That child will see that change is expected, and as good a representation of life as is continuity. She/He will be aware that maleness and femaleness are only what we decide they are.

If peers communicate expectations, those expectations can be consciously and calmly met, or not, with choice. This child of the future can then remind others that they too can be more; that they are potentially all the characters; that they can act in all the dramas. So the author predicts that roles will soon come to be seen as a reflection of personal problem-solving styles. This will create a more flexible social organism, in turn, after transitional upheaval and reaction to that upheaval are finished.

### Fourteen Suggestions

This author suggests that future work address some of the following questions and issues:

1. Role stereotypes (positive and negative), role-related behavior, and gender-linked expectations all must be considered as potentially different phenomena in sex role research. The nature of test questions themselves is important. The scope, nature, variability, and contextual factors in each must be explored.

2. Roles must not be assumed to be linked to actual behavior or predictive of behavior, without evidence.

3. Role strength must be considered; one can be considered masculine, feminine, or androgynous *only* relative to some standard.

4. Perceptions, intentions, belief systems, and meanings are important neglected variables in sex role research.

5. Sex role lifespan research can be integrated with Piagetian approaches, cognitive work in general, problem solving research—and should be.

6. Sex role development research should use models of change over time from new physics, systems theory, and so forth, to broaden the repertoire of multivariate approaches at its disposal and better reflect the reality of these complex multi-system changes.

7. The impact of roles on society and the species and the utility of roles for society and species need to be considered.

8. Learning and developmental effects need to be considered jointly in future research.

9. What is adaptive depends on situation, developmental stage, reward and punishment contingencies, past history, and the energy-available state of the person-system at that time.

10. People have different styles of achieving the same goal or enacting the same intention, or reporting the same attitude.

11. Self-concept, personal continuity, and personal effectiveness are seldom examined but enter into the picture of sex role development.

12. Methodological issues need to be clarified, especially including longitudinal research on factor changes. But current approaches still give useful information with careful interpretation.

13. Tighter theory is needed, preferably from a systems perspective.

14. Longitudinal studies and studies with behavioral validation need to be performed.

These modest proposed investigations would be beginning steps in the understanding of later stages of sex role development, an important co-created dimension of social-self-in-action.

## REFERENCES

Alpaugh, P.K. & Birren, J.E. (1975). Are there sex differences in creativity across the lifespan? *Human Development, 18,* 461–465.

Ames L.B., Learned J., Metraux. R., & Walter, R. (1954). *Rorschach responses in old age.* New York: Hoeber.

Bakan, D. (1966). *The duality of human existence.* Chicago: Rand-McNally.

Barrows, G.W. & Zuckerman, M. (1976). Construct validity of three masculinity–femininity tests. *Journal of Counseling and Clinical Psychology, 34,* 1–7.

Bell, J.Z. (1978). Disengagement versus engagement—a need for greater expectations. *Journal of the American Geriatrics Society, 26,* 89–95.

Bem, S.L. (1979). Theory and measurement of androgyny: A reply to the Pedhazur-Tetenbaum and Locksley-Colten critiques. *Journal of Personality & Social Psychology, 37,* 1047–1054.

Bernard, J. (1976). Change and stability in sex-role norms and behavior. *Journal of Social Issues, 32,* 207–223.

Block, J.H. (1973). Conceptions of sex role. *American Psychologist, 28,* 512–526.

Braden, B.B. (1982). Dreams for development: Midlife perspectives on relational vs. individualistic goals. Unpublished dissertation, Adelphi University.

Breytspraak, L.M. (1984). *The development of self in later life.* Boston: Little, Brown.

Buckley, W. (1968). *Modern systems research for the behavioral scientist.* Chicago: Aldine.

Cameron, P. (1976). Masculinity/femininity of the generations: As self reported and stereotypically appraised. *International Journal of Aging and Human Development, 7,* 143–151.

Carter, D. B. & Patterson, C. J. (1982). Sex roles as social conventions: The development of children's conceptions of sex-role stereotypes. *Developmental Psychology, 18.* 812–824.

Cherry, D.L. & Zarit W.H. (1973). Sex-role and age differences in competency, flexibility, and affective status of women. Received with personal communication from author.

Commons, M., Richards, F.A., & Armon, C. (Eds.) (1984). *Beyond formal operations: Late adolescent and adult cognitive development.* New York: Praeger.

Costa, P. & McCrae, R. (1977). Cross-sectional differences in masculinity and femininity in adult men. Meeting of the Gerontological Society, San Francisco.

Datan, N. & Rodenheaver, D. (1983). Beyond generativity: Toward a sensuality of later life. In R. Weg, (Ed.), *Sexuality in the later years.* New York: Academic Press.

Douglas, K. & Arenberg, D. (1978). Age changes, cohort differences and cultural change on the Guilford-Zimmerman Temperament Survey. *Journal of Gerontology, 33,* 737–747.

Foley, J.M. & Murphy, D.M. (1977). Sex role identity in the aged. Meeting of the Gerontological Society, San Francisco.

Garnets, L. & Pleck, J.H. (1979). Sex role identity, androgyny, and sex role transcendence: A sex role strain analysis. *Psychology of Women Quarterly, 3,* 270–283.

Gillett, N., Levitt, M., & Antonucci, T. (1977). The relationship between masculinity, femininity, and social competence in three generations of women. Meeting of the Gerontological Society, San Francisco.

Gross, A.E. (1978). The male role and heterosexual behavior. *Journal of Social Issues, 34,* 87–107.

Gutmann, D. (1975). Parenthood: a key to the comparative study of the life cycle. In N. Datan & L. Ginsberg, (Eds.), *Life-span developmental psychology: Normative crises.* New York: Academic Press.

Gutmann, D., Grunes, J., & Griffin, B. (1979). The clinical psychology of later life: Developmental paradigms. Meeting of the Gerontological Society, Washington, D.C.

Hefner, R., Rebecca, M., & Oleshansky, B. (1975). Development of sex-role transcendence. *Human Development, 18,* 143–158.

Hoffman, D.M. & Fidell, L.S. (1979). Characteristics of androgynous, undifferentiated, masculine and feminine middle-class women. *Sex Roles, 5,* 765–781.

Hofstadter, D.R. (1979). *Gödel, Esher, and Bach: An eternal golden braid.* New York: Vintage.

Hubbard, R.W., Santos, J.F., & Farrow, B.J. (1979). Age differences in sex role diffusion: A study of middle-aged and older adult married couples. Meeting of the Gerontological Society, Washington, D.C.

Jewett, S. (1973). Longevity and the longevity syndrome. *Gerontologist, 13,* 91–99.

Kelly, G.A. (1955). *The psychology of personal constructs.* New York: Norton.

Kohlberg, L. A. (1966). A cognitive-developmental analysis of children's sex-role concepts and attitudes. In E. E. Maccoby (Ed.). *The psychology of sex differences.* Stanford, CA: Stanford University Press.

Kramer, D. (1983). Postformal operations? A need for further conceptualization. *Human Development, 26,* 91–105.

Lenny E. (1979). Concluding comments on androgyny: Some limitations of its mature development. *Sex Roles, 5,* 829.

Livson, F.B. (1976). Patterns of personality development in middle-aged women: A longitudinal study. *International Journal of Aging and Human Development, 7,* 107–115.

Loevinger, J. (1977). *Ego development.* San Francisco: Jossey-Bass.

Lowenthal, M.F., Thurnher, M., & Chiriboga, D. (1975). *Four stages of life: A comparative study of women and men facing transition.* San Francisco: Jossey-Bass.

Lumsden, C.J. & Wilson, E.O. (1981). *Genes, mind, and culture: A coevolutionary process.* Cambridge: Harvard University Press.

McGee, J. & Wells, K. (1982). Gender typing and androgyny in later life: New directions for theory and research. *Human Development, 25,* 116–139.

Miller, J. (1978). *Living systems.* New York: McGraw-Hill.

Mooreland, J.R., Harren, V.A., Krimsky-Montague. E., & Tuisley, E.A. (1979). Sex role self concept and career decision making. *Journal of Counseling Psychology, 26,* 329–336.

Murphy, D.M. (1976). Sex role identity in the aged. Doctoral dissertation, Loyola University of Chicago.

Neugarten, B. (1964). *Personality in middle and late life.* New York: Prentice-Hall.

Neugarten, B., Crotty, G., & Tobin, S. (1964). Personality types in an aging population. In B. Neugarten, *Personality in middle and late life.* New York: Prentice-Hall.

Neugarten, B. & Gutmann, D. (1968). Age–sex roles and personality in middle age: A TAT study. In B. Neugarten, *Middle age and aging.* Chicago: University of Chicago Press.

Neugarten, B., Havighurst, R., & Tobin, S. (1968). Personality and patterns of aging. In B. Neugarten, *Middle age and aging.* Chicago: University of Chicago Press.

O'Sullivan, W.M. (1980). A study of the relationship between life satisfaction of the aged and perceptions they hold concerning their own masculinity and femininity. Doctoral dissertation, New York University.

Prigogene, I. (1980). *From being to becoming.* San Francisco: Freeman.

Prigogene, I. & Stengers, I. (1984). *Order out of chaos, man's new dialogue with nature.* New York: Bantam.

Puglisi, J.T. & Jackson, D.W. (1980–81). Sex role identity and self esteem in adulthood. *International Journal of Aging and Human Development, 12,* 129–138.

Rabin, J. (1986). Adaptation across the lifespan: Evaluation, future shock, and sex roles. In J. Sinnott (Ed.), *Sex roles and aging: Theory and research from a systems perspective.* New York: S. Karger.

Reichard, S., Livson, F., & Peterson, P. (1962). *Aging and personality.* New York: Wiley.

Richards, F. A. & Commons, M. L. (1984). Systematic, metasystematic, and cross-paradigmatic reasoning: A case for stages of reasoning beyond formal operations. In M. L. Commons, F. A. Richards, & C. Armon (Eds.), *Beyond formal operations: Late adolescent and adult cognitive development* (pp. 92–119). New York: Praeger.

Riegel, K.F. (1973). Dialectical operations: The final period of human development. *Human Development, 16,* 346–370.

Sedney, M.A. (1977). Process of sex-role development during life crises of middle-aged women. Meeting of the Gerontological Society, San Francisco.

Silverman, M. (1977). The old man as woman: Detecting stereotypes of aged men with a femininity scale. *Perceptual and Motor Skills, 44,* 336–338.

Sinnott, J.D. (1977). Sex-role inconstancy, biology, and successful aging: A dialectical model. *The Gerontologist, 17,* 459–463.

Sinnott, J.D. (1981). The theory of relativity: A metatheory for development? *Human Development, 24,* 293–311.

Sinnott, J.D. (1982). Correlates of sex roles in older adults. *Journal of Gerontology, 37,* 587–594.

Sinnott, J.D. (1983). A model for solutions of illstructured problems: Implications for everyday and abstract problem solving. Meeting of the Gerontological Society, San Francisco.

Sinnott, J.D. (1984). Older men, older women: Are their perceived sex roles similar? *Sex Roles, 10,* 847–856.

Sinnott, J.D. (1984–85). Sex, health, and mental health of older women and men. *International Journal of Aging and Human Development, 20,* 123–132.

Sinnott, J.D. (1985a). Lifespan relativistic postformal thought: Methodology and data from everyday problem solving studies. In M. Commons, C. Armon, L. Kohlberg, J. Sinnott, F. Richards (Eds.), *Beyond formal operations III.* New York: Praeger.

Sinnott, J.D. (1985b). General systems theory: A rationale for the study of everyday memory. In L. Poon, D. Rubin, & B. Wilson (Eds.), *Cognition in everyday life.* Hillsdale, NJ: Lawrence Erlbaum Associates.

Sinnott, J.D. (1986). *Sex roles and aging: Theory and research from a systems perspective.* New York: S. Karger.

Skinner, R.J. (1979). Relationship between sex role identity and perceived health in elderly females. Doctoral dissertation, University of Texas at Austin.

Smith, M.Y. (1981). Impact of age and environment on gender roles among S.R. 10 elderly. Doctoral dissertation, Purdue University.

Spence, J.T. & Helmreich, R.L. (1979). On assessing "androgyny". *Sex Roles, 5,* 721–738.

Suzuki, T.F. (1979). A conceptual analysis of sex role identity and its interaction with gender and chronological age. Doctoral dissertation, University of Florida.

Turner, B.F. (1977). Sex roles among wives in middle and late life. Convention of the American Psychological Association, San Francisco.

Urberg, K.A. (1979). Sex role conceptualizations in adolescents and adults. *Developmental Psychology, 15,* 90–92.

von Bertalanfy, L. (1968). *General systems theory.* New York: Braziller.

Weg, R.B. (1983). *Sexuality in the later years.* New York: Academic Press.

Wells, K. (1979). Towards a model of gender-role development in adulthood: The transition from gender-typing to androgyny. Association for Women in Psychology Conference, Dallas.

Williams, R. & Wirth, C. (1965). *Lives through the years.* New York: Atherton Press.

Windle, M. (1984): Sex role orientation, cognitive flexibility, and life satisfaction among older adults. *Psychology of Women Quarterly.*

Windle, M. & Sinnott, J.D. (1985). A psychometric study of the Bem Sex Role Inventory with an older adult sample. *Journal of Gerontology, 40,* 336–343.

Wish, C.W. (1976). The relationship of sex role typing to life satisfaction in older persons. Doctoral dissertation, Ohio State University.

Wolf, F. (1981). *Taking the quantam leap: The new physics for nonscientists.* San Francisco: Harper & Row.

Wood, P.K. (1983). Inquiring systems and problem structure. *Human Development, 26,* 249–265.

Zaks, P.M., Karuza, Jr., Domurath, K.L., & Labouvie-Vief, G. (1979). Sex role orientation across the adult life span. Meeting of the Gerontological Society, Washington, D.C.

# PART III
# IMPLICATIONS OF SEX ROLES AND SEX TYPING

# 11
# Sex Roles and Labor Force
# Participation
## Susan R. Borker

As the percentage of women in the labor force has been steadily increasing since the 1940s, researchers from several disciplines have become interested in studying gender roles in the labor force. From an historical perspective, this trend has led to an examination of women's roles in the past. From an economic perspective, it has become necessary to include women in both theorizing and in data collection, as women have become a larger and more visible part of economic life. From a psychological perspective, there are many questions about socialization and values as more women engage in what was a predominantly male role. From a sociological perspective, there are questions about organizational adaptations to these changes as well as theories to explain why this trend is occurring at this particular time, and what effects there might be on social institutions. Of course, as female roles change over time, male roles change also: However, in the United States some form of paid employment has always been part of the typical male role (Bernard, 1984); therefore much of the recent literature on gender roles and employment has focused on women.

Because the historical trend in employment for women is central to much of the recent literature on gender roles in the labor force, we will begin with a brief review of the size and nature of that trend. We will then discuss some of the possible associations of this trend with other trends and the implications that these trends have for both male and female roles in the workplace and elsewhere in society.

## EMPLOYMENT TRENDS

Employment outside the home prior to the twentieth century was very limited for married middle-class women. Industrialization in the nineteenth century had moved male employment out of the home, and married women were the household managers and workers and guardians of moral purity. The male world of work was seen as competitive and corrupting, and women who did not have to deal with this world could maintain a certain moral purity (Harris, 1978; Margolis, 1984). In addition, women were not thought to be capable of certain types of work, particularly mental work. When women were first admitted to colleges in the late 1800s there were great debates on the possible terrible effects of mental work on the physical health of young women (Rothman, 1978). For women who were not married there was a very limited range of "respectable" employment. Acceptable fields included teaching and nursing, the latter after the Civil War. With increased numbers of low-level white collar jobs in the late 1800s, clerical work and sales work became alternative sources of respectable employment. The typical pattern was for women to be employed from the time they left school until they married. Lower-class women were employed in jobs that required physical labor, such as service and factory jobs. For these women the ideal was to stop working after they married or had children, but this was frequently not the reality. Some groups of women (the poor and the nonwhite) had high employment rates throughout the nineteenth century. Some of them also made money after they had children, by taking in boarders or by doing manufacturing work at home, although census statistics may not be accurate about the numbers of women who earned money in these ways. After marriage, the husband was expected to be the family provider; consequently, less than 6 percent of married women worked outside the home in 1900 (Harris, 1978, p.104). However, about 40 percent of the nation's single women were employed at this time, generally in low-skilled jobs (Fox & Hesse-Biber, 1984, p.28). Single working women usually contributed to their (parental) family income. Their jobs were not career oriented, though women who had attended college often did have a choice of career or marriage (Harris, 1978). A large percentage of the early women college graduates did not marry. In the late nineteenth century, some surveys of college graduates showed that considerably less than half had married (Rothman, 1978, p.46), and only about 25 percent of women who earned PhD degrees from 1872 to 1925 ever married (Chafe, 1972, p.100). Even widows, who no longer had husbands to support them, were reluctant to turn to employment. To do so would have been an admission that their husbands had failed to provide for them. In addition, of course, returning to work was difficult if there were young children at home.

The percentage of married women in the labor force increased slowly from 1900 until World War II. Since World War II, this increase has been more rapid (Oppenheimer, 1970; Smith, 1979). During the war, women were encouraged to enter the labor force to replace the men who were off at war. After the war, however, the percentage of women in the labor force continued to increase. As Table 11.1 shows, married women with older children began to enter the labor force after World War II. In later years, married women with young children joined the labor force in increasing numbers. By 1979, 43.7 percent of married women with husband present and children under 6 in the home were in the labor force. Twenty years earlier this figure was only 18.7 percent. Furthermore, this increase in employment has been largest among middle-class women. Amount of education is now much more strongly related to labor force participation than it used to be. It is now the more educated women who are the most likely to be employed (Blau & Ferber, 1985, p.24).

## Implications of This Trend

The trend of increasing labor force participation is very clear. The implications of this trend for sex roles in the occupational world and for family structure, and the reasons for the trend of increasing labor force participation, are not nearly as clear. While researchers can agree that several social trends occur at the same time, it is not easy to show that one trend influences another. In what follows I will discuss some demographic, economic, and attitudinal trends that have been associated with the increase in labor force participation and then discuss some of the implications for sex roles and family structure.

Oppenheimer (1970) wrote a classic book that relates the increasing labor force participation of women to a number of demographic and social changes. While her study only includes data until 1960, the trends she noted have continued. In very brief summary, her argument is as follows. The occupational world in the United States is very sex-segregated. There are certain jobs that are usually held by women and other jobs usually held by men. With increasing technology, some types of jobs have been increasing faster than others. After World War II there was a large increase in the demand for certain occupations typically held by women (in particular, clerical workers, telephone operators, teachers, and nurses). Many of these jobs required at least a high school education. At the same time, the pool of single, well-educated women was shrinking. The birth rate had been low in the 1930s, and women were staying in school longer and marrying and having children later. Males were not available for jobs such as clerical work and nursing because most of them were already employed, because they would be reluctant to enter certain women's occupations, and because these jobs did not pay very well. Therefore, employers hired married women with older children. As this process continued and more women were needed, women with younger children entered the labor force.

Oppenheimer's theory is based on economic and demographic forces; however, attitudes about sex roles are not irrelevant to the theory. Occupational segregation, which plays a critical part in the theory, cannot be separated from normative ideas about sex roles. The persistence of sex typing of many occupations is clearly related to our ideas about the capabilities of men and women. As other chapters in this book demonstrate, these ideas about sex roles are maintained by many institutions in our society, and change very slowly. However, in the last century there have been many changes in our ideas about the proper realm for women to exercise their particular capabilities. Some new occupations have been

**Table 11.1**
**Labor Force Participation Rates of Married Women, Husband Present, by Presence and Age of Own Children, 1950–1979**

| | Participation Rate (Percent of population in labor force) | | | | |
|---|---|---|---|---|---|
| | | With no children under 18 years | With children under 18 years | | |
| Year[1] | Total | | Total | 6–17 years, none younger | Under 6 years |
| 1950 | 23.8 | 30.3 | 18.4 | 28.3 | 11.9 |
| 1951 | 25.2 | 31.0 | 20.5 | 30.3 | 14.0 |
| 1952 | 25.3 | 30.9 | 20.7 | 31.1 | 13.9 |
| 1953 | 26.3 | 31.2 | 22.4 | 32.2 | 15.5 |
| 1954 | 26.6 | 31.6 | 22.7 | 33.2 | 14.9 |
| 1955 | 27.7 | 32.7 | 24.0 | 34.7 | 16.2 |
| 1956 | 29.0 | 35.3 | 24.5 | 36.4 | 15.9 |
| 1957 | 29.6 | 35.6 | 25.3 | 36.6 | 17.0 |
| 1958 | 30.2 | 35.4 | 26.5 | 37.6 | 18.2 |
| 1959 | 30.9 | 35.2 | 27.9 | 39.8 | 18.7 |
| 1960 | 30.5 | 34.7 | 27.6 | 39.0 | 18.6 |
| 1961 | 32.7 | 37.3 | 29.6 | 41.7 | 20.0 |
| 1962 | 32.7 | 36.1 | 30.3 | 41.8 | 21.3 |
| 1963 | 33.7 | 37.4 | 31.2 | 41.5 | 22.5 |
| 1964 | 34.4 | 37.8 | 32.0 | 43.0 | 22.7 |
| 1965 | 34.7 | 38.3 | 32.2 | 42.7 | 23.3 |
| 1966 | 35.4 | 38.4 | 33.2 | 43.7 | 24.2 |
| 1967 | 36.8 | 38.9 | 35.3 | 45.0 | 26.5 |
| 1968 | 38.3 | 40.1 | 36.9 | 46.9 | 27.6 |
| 1969 | 39.6 | 41.0 | 38.6 | 48.6 | 28.5 |
| 1970 | 40.8 | 42.2 | 39.7 | 49.2 | 30.3 |
| 1971 | 40.8 | 42.1 | 39.7 | 49.4 | 29.6 |
| 1972 | 41.5 | 42.7 | 40.5 | 50.2 | 30.1 |
| 1973 | 42.2 | 42.8 | 41.7 | 50.1 | 32.7 |
| 1974 | 43.0 | 43.0 | 43.1 | 51.2 | 34.4 |
| 1975 | 44.4 | 43.9 | 44.9 | 52.3 | 36.6 |
| 1976 | 45.0 | 43.8 | 46.1 | 53.7 | 37.4 |
| 1977 | 46.6 | 44.9 | 48.2 | 55.6 | 39.3 |
| 1978 | 47.6 | 44.7 | 50.2 | 57.2 | 41.6 |
| 1979 | 49.4 | 46.7 | 51.9 | 59.1 | 43.2 |

Data were collected in April of 1951–1955 and March of all other years.

*Note:* Children are defined as "own" children of the women and include never-married sons and daughters, stepchildren, and adopted children. Excluded are other related children such as grandchildren, nieces, nephews, and cousins, and unrelated children.

*Source:* U.S. Department of Labor, Bureau of Statistics, *Perspectives on Working Women: A Databook*, Bulletin 2080.

designated as women's occupations, and some jobs have changed from male jobs to female jobs.

Some occupations were designated as women's occupations because they were an extension of jobs that women traditionally did in the household, such as teaching small children, nursing, and house cleaning. Other jobs were defined as female as technology changed and demand for an occupation changed. For example, before the Civil War clerical work was a male occupation. When the typewriter was invented, typewriter manufacturers started training women to use them so that they could both sell typewriters and offer buyers a trained labor supply (Rothman, 1978, p.50). Women were used because they needed people with enough education to do clerical work, and men with this level of education were more expensive to hire. Typing (and associated clerical work) quickly became defined as a woman's occupation. This change in definition of clerical work from a male to a female job required some change in ideas about labor force sex roles: however, when clerical work became a female job, the occupation acquired other characteristics usually associated with female jobs. It became the type of job that did not require much on-the-job training, since people were expected to know the basic skills before they were hired, and it did not lead to job promotion and advancement. In addition, of course, it did not pay very well.

Over time there has been some change in attitudes about labor force employment for women. The attitude changes are not simply about women working outside the home. Some type of labor market employment was perfectly acceptable for nonmarried women for a long time. Married middle-class women were very frequently active outside the home in the beginning of the century, as social reformers and volunteer workers. During the 1930s it became quite clear that the problematic issue was paid employment for married women who had employed husbands. When jobs were scarce during the Depression, married women with working husbands were fired because they were seen as taking a job that a man needed (Margolis, 1984, p.209). Opinion polls from the 1930s show that most people did not approve of a married woman working if she had a husband who was capable of supporting her. The financial support of the family was still clearly seen as the man's role in a marriage.

Today a clear majority (about 85 percent) of people believe that it is all right for a married woman to work (Davis & Smith, 1985), which is consistent with the fact that the majority of married women are employed. Oppenheimer showed, however, that attitudes probably changed after married women started joining the labor force in larger numbers, and that the attitude shift was a consequence rather than a cause of increasing employment for married women. From the 1930s to the 1960s, the percentage of people who approved of married women working always lagged behind the actual percentages of married working women.

Now that it is socially acceptable for married women to be employed (and the reality is that most women are employed even when they have children at home), some of the previous ideas about women's employment roles are being challenged. As women have come to expect that they will spend most of their adult lives in the labor force, more of them are thinking about long range career goals and financial goals. This may put them in the position of competing for jobs directly with men, and competing with men in their role as the financial provider for the family. Even when women earn less than their husbands, families frequently depend on both incomes, which changes the role of the man as the provider (Bernard, 1984).

Some aspects of female employment, however, have not changed much over time. Women still earn lower wages than men. There has been little change in the relative wages of full time employed men and women from the 1950s to the 1980s. Women have consistently earned about 60 percent of what men have earned (Blau & Ferber, 1985, p.40). A considerable part of the wage differential between men and women is due to the persistence of occupational sex segregation (Laws, 1979; Lloyd & Niemi, 1979; Blau & Ferber, 1985). As Table 11.2 shows, most women are still employed in traditionally female jobs. In 1950, 63 percent of all employed women were in the typically female occupations of teacher (noncollege), nurse, clerical worker, and service worker (including private household). By 1979, 67 percent of all employed women were in these occupations. In the 1970s the federal government pressured employers to hire women for jobs typically held by men. These efforts met with limited success. There is a substantial literature explaining why women have had trouble achieving economic success in the occupational world (Dexter, 1985; Laws, 1979). Some of this literature is in the mass media, in the form of ''self-help'' books, which tell women how to do better in the business world. They offer several different types of advice.

One part of this literature focuses on social–psychological factors that keep women from achievement in certain fields. Because of previous socialization into sex roles, both men and women associate certain personality characteristics with each sex (Fox & Hesse-Biber, 1984). Some personality characteristics are also associated with certain occupations. For example, females are thought to be passive and certain occupations are thought to require aggressive personalities. Researchers have compiled whole lists of male and female personality traits (Colwill, 1982). Attempts have also been made to undo prior socialization with books or courses. Thus women are taught how to behave more assertively or to acquire other personality characteristics.

A slightly different version of this approach suggests that women need to learn how to play the game, rather than just alter their personalities. They need to ''form networks'' and ''find mentors,'' learn how to deal with office politics, and ''dress for success.'' The claim is that men learn these things as part of their childhood or early adult socialization, but that women may need to learn them later in life.

In addition, of course, it would help if women had the same job qualifications as men. Women are now being encouraged, for example, to take more math and science courses, and to major in appropriate subjects in college. Recent data on education do suggest that women are now more likely to prepare for occu-

**Table 11.2**
**Percent of Employed Women in Various Occupations, 1950–1979**

| Occupation | 1950[a] | 1960 | 1970 | 1979 |
|---|---|---|---|---|
| Teachers (not college or university) | 4.8 | 5.5 | 6.5 | 5.5 |
| Registered Nurses | 2.3 | 2.6 | 2.7 | 2.9 |
| Other professional–technical | 5.4 | 4.3 | 5.3 | 7.7 |
| Managerial administrative (except farm) | 4.4 | 5.0 | 4.5 | 6.4 |
| Retail sales clerks | 6.8 | 6.4 | 4.9 | 4.1 |
| Other sales workers | 1.9 | 1.3 | 2.1 | 2.8 |
| Clerical | 27.8 | 30.3 | 34.5 | 35.0 |
| Craft | 1.5 | 1.0 | 1.1 | 1.8 |
| Operatives (including transport) | 19.6 | 15.2 | 14.5 | 11.5 |
| Nonfarm laborers | 0.8 | 0.4 | 0.5 | 1.3 |
| Service (except private household) | 12.4 | 14.8 | 16.5 | 17.2 |
| Private household workers | 8.7 | 8.9 | 5.1 | 2.6 |
| Farm | 3.6 | 4.4 | 1.8 | 1.2 |

[a]Data include 14- and 15-year olds
*Source:* U.S. Department of Labor, Bureau of Statistics, *Perspectives on Working Women: A Databook*, Bulletin 2080

pations that have been typically male (Jacobs, 1985). There has been a sizable increase in the number of women getting degrees in fields such as law, medicine, and business administration.

The assumption in all of the above approaches is that if women identify what male behaviors lead to economic success, and imitate that behavior, then success will follow. Although this system may work for a small number of women, men will also have to change if all women are to be accepted as true equals in the workplace. Occupational roles cannot be changed without changes in other roles as well. The occupational role has been seen as the main role for men. If women achieve equal roles in the workplace, this implies a fundamental change in our conception of male and female roles. There is considerable evidence suggesting that equality has not yet been achieved.

Although women have recently been entering male professions, it is not necessarily the case that they are as successful as men within these professions. All professions have complex status hierarchies, and women have tended to end up in the lower-status areas within the professions, or working for lower-status organizations within the professions. For example, women lawyers tend to cluster in certain specialties that have lower status and to work for less prestigious law firms (Epstein, 1983). Previous data show that for all women, the disparity between men and women (in terms of salary) is larger for older men and women (Rosenbaum, 1985). It remains to be seen whether this pattern will continue.

One indication that this pattern will not change much in the near future is the lack of change in women's other role demands. While men contribute some efforts to home and child care, recent studies indicate that the primary responsibility in these areas usually remains with women (Berk & Shih, 1980; Wilkins & Miller, 1985; Nieva, 1985; Vanek, 1984). Pleck (1985, p. 146) reports on some studies that show that women (regardless of their labor force status) are now spending less time on household tasks. This decline in household labor for women who are not in the labor force is an interesting area for further research, because it is not consistent with the economic theory that women will substitute market labor for household labor. It could be the result of changing norms about household labor, or the result of a change in the type of woman who chooses not to be in the labor force. So far this trend has not been large enough to equalize the division of household labor between men and women, and women continue to spend more time than their husbands at household tasks.

In the professions, the early part of the work career is a crucial time period for people to prove their potential. It is also the time period when most women would be bearing children, and family responsibilities would be heavy. In the past, many women have interrupted careers or changed jobs because of family responsibilities, which has interfered with their work careers (Shaw, 1983). There has been a trend for well-educated women to delay childbearing and to have few children. However this does not compensate for inadequate daycare facilities, public school schedules that have not been altered to accommodate employed mothers, and the responsibility of dealing with the routine and unexpected aspects of raising children. In spite of these problems, polls of women (Wilkins & Miller, 1985) show that increasing percentages of women think that combining marriage, career, and children is the best alternative for a satisfying and interesting life: 63 percent chose this alternative in 1985, as compared with 52 percent in 1974. Highly educated women were the most likely to choose this option. Obviously there have to be many changes in society and the family before women with children have equality in the workplace. This is not a new observation: feminist activists in the 1850s commented that marriage relationships constituted a barrier to true equality for women (Harris, 1978).

One change in the family that has taken place is the increasing numbers of female-headed households. Some of these households are the result of an increasing divorce rate, and some are due to the increasing number of nonmarried women who are having children. The causal connection between this trend and the trend of increasing labor force participation for women is not clear, although some people believe that increasing economic independence for women is responsible for the "breakup of the family." One current social science theory, however, accounts for these trends quite differently.

In this theory (Guttentag & Secord, 1983), sex ratios and the fact that men dominate women in our society account for both the dissolution of families and the economic independence of women in recent times. In our society, women tend to marry men their own age or slightly older, and to live longer than men. These facts, combined with demographic facts (a very low birthrate in the 1930s followed by a very high birthrate after World War II), resulted in a large number of nonmarried women in the 1960s and the 1970s for whom no age-appropriate nonmarried men were available. Guttentag and Secord claim that historically in such demographic circumstances, women have gained considerable independence (economic and social) from men, because men are not as interested in protecting women in restrictive family roles when women are not a scarce resource. In these circumstances men have fewer incentives to remain married to a particular woman. The societies where women were the most restricted were those where there were few women relative to the number of men.

Whatever the causal relationship, there has been an increase in the number of female-headed households, and these households are more likely than others to be poor (Pearce, 1979; Nestel, Mercier, & Shaw, 1983). Female-headed households have always tended to be poorer than male-headed households simply because on the average, women earn less than men. The problem is particularly severe at this point in time, however, because so many married women are employed. The nonmarried women are increasingly competing with conjugal households with two wage earners, which makes their relative income even smaller.

## CONCLUSION

Since World War II there has been a steady increase in the percentage of married women in the labor force. In some respects this represents a change in women's roles, but women still earn less than men on the average, and are still usually employed in what have come to be defined as female jobs. Equality in the workplace for all women is dependent not only on women acquiring different occupational and personal skills, but also on fundamental changes in male and female roles both in the workplace and in the family.

As more women are employed, it may be that fewer women will have the choice of staying out of the labor force. In addition to the fact that employment for women has become the social norm, economic factors may force many women to be employed (Margolis, 1984). Most nonmarried women are expected to support themselves, and divorce settlements and public welfare policy increasingly reflect this norm. Married women also may not have a choice about employment. Many young couples are discovering that they cannot afford to live on one income if they wish to have a middle-class lifestyle, because the typical middle-class family now has two wage earners. It remains to be seen what changes this will bring in family and work roles for both men and women.

## REFERENCES

Berk, S. F. & Shih, A. (1980). Contributions to household labor: Comparing wives' and husbands' reports. In S.F. Berk (Ed.), *Women and household labor*. Beverly Hills: Sage.

Bernard, J. (1984). The good provider role: Its rise and fall. In P. Vogdanoff (Ed.),

*Work and Family: Changing Roles of Men and Women*. Palo Alto, Ca: Mayfield Press.

Blau, F. D. & Ferber, M.A. (1985). Women in the labor market: The last twenty years. In L. Larwood, A. Stromberg, & B. Gutek (Eds.), *Women and work: An annual review, Vol. I*. Beverly Hills: Sage.

Chafe, W. H. (1972). *The American woman, her changing social, economic and political roles, 1920–1970*. New York: Oxford University Press.

Colwill, N. L. (1982). *The new partnership: Women and men in organizations*. Palo Alto, Ca: Mayfield.

Davis, J. A. & Smith, T. W. (1985). *General Social Surveys, 1972–1985*. Storrs, CT: Roper Public Opinion Research Center.

Dexter, C. R. (1985). Women and the exercise of power in organizations: From ascribed to achieved status. In L. Larwood, A. Stromberg, & B. Gutek (Eds.), *Women and work: An annual review, Vol. 1*. Beverly Hills: Sage.

Epstein, C.F. (1983). *Women in law*. Garden City, NY: Anchor Press.

Fox, M.F., & Hesse-Biber, S. (1984). *Women at work*. Palo Alto, Ca: Mayfield.

Guttentag, M. & Secord, P. F. (1983). *Too many women? The sex ratio question*. Beverly Hills: Sage.

Harris, B.J. (1978). *Beyond her sphere: Women and the professions in American history*. Westport, CT: Greenwood Press.

Jacobs, J. A. (1985). Sex segregation in American higher education. In L. Larwood, A. Stromberg, & B. Gutek (Eds.), *Women and work: An annual review, Vol. I*. Beverly Hills: Sage.

Laws, J.L. (1979). *The second X: Sex role and social role*. New York: Elsevier/North Holland.

Lloyd, C.B. & Niemi, B. T. (1979). *The economics of sex differentials*. New York: Columbia University Press.

Margolis, M. L. (1984). *Mothers and such: Views of American women and why they changed*. Berkeley: University of California Press.

Nestel, G., Mercier, J., & Shaw, L. B. (1983). Economic consequences of midlife change in marital status. In L. B. Shaw (Ed.). *Unplanned careers: The working lives of middle-aged women*. Lexington, MA: Lexington Books.

Nieva, V. F. (1985). Work and family lineages. In L. Larwood, A. Stromberg, & B. Gutek (Eds.), *Women and work: An annual review, Vol. I*. Beverly Hills: Sage.

Oppenheimer, V. K. (1970). *The female labor force in the United States*. Westport, CT: Greenwood Press.

Pearce, D. (1979). Women, work, and welfare: The feminization of poverty. In K. W. Feinstein (Ed.), *Working women and families*. Beverly Hills: Sage.

Pleck, J.H. (1985). *Working wives/working husbands*. Beverly Hills: Sage.

Rosenbaum, J. E. (1985). Persistence and change in pay inequalities: Implications for job evaluation and comparable worth. In L. Larwood, A. Stromberg, & B. Gutek (Eds.), *Women and work: An annual review, Vol. I*. Beverly Hills: Sage.

Rothman, S.M. (1978). *Woman's proper place: A history of changing ideals and practices, 1870 to the present*. New York: Basic Books.

Shaw, L. B. (1983). Causes of irregular employment patterns. In L. B. Shaw (Ed.), *Unplanned careers: The working lives of middle-aged women*. Lexington, MA: Lexington Books.

Smith, R.E. (1979). The movement of women into the labor force. In R. E. Smith (Ed.), *The subtle revolution*. Washington, D.C.: The Urban Institute.

U.S. Department of Labor, Bureau of Labor Statistics. (1980). *Perspectives on working women: A databook, bulletin 2080*. Washington, D.C.: U.S. Government Printing Office.

Vanek, J. (1984). Housewives as workers. In P. Vogdanoff (Ed.), *Work and family: Changing roles of men and women*. Palo Alto, Ca: Mayfield Press.

Wilkins, S. & Miller, T.A.W. (1985). Working women: How it's working out. *Public Opinion 8*, (October/November):44–49.

# 12

# Two-Paycheck Families: Psychological Responses to Social Change
## Joan S. Rabin

Social change, like all forms of environmental change, makes psychological demands on each of us. Energy must be expended in service of the process of adaptation. A behavioral response must be generated so that we are able to adjust successfully to realities surrounding us. Our species-specific learning capacity provides us with a flexible basis for ongoing adaptation to the environment. However, we are not limitless; our emotional and psychological needs constrain the adaptive range within which our learning ability can operate (Rabin, 1986). Too much change occurring at too rapid a rate can so exhaust our psychological resources that we are no longer able to respond adaptively. Toffler (1970) labels this psychological reaction to over-stimulation, "future shock," which he defines as "the distress, both physical and psychological, that arises from an overload of the human organism's physical adaptive systems and its decision-making processes" (p. 326).

Two-paycheck families tax this adaptation process severely, making dual-earner spouses prime candidates for "future shock": nonadaptive behaviors and significant psychological distress. The dual-earner pattern violates the complementarity concept of husband–wife gender roles so dear to American tradition (Spence, 1981). No norms for two-paycheck families exist in our cultural experience (Nadelson & Nadelson, 1980). Successful adaptation within the dual-earner lifestyle is a survival challenge that must be undertaken in the absence of a social support system (Pleck, 1985; Scanzoni, 1983). The lack of readily available flexible work schedules, child care programs, fair hiring, wage setting, and promotion practices, and tax incentives puts the two-paycheck family under significant strain (Levitan & Belous, 1981; Rix & Stone, 1984). Much of the high stress level associated with the dual-earner pattern comes from the competition between occupational and family demands in a society whose institutions are geared to the traditional family (Skinner, 1980). This situation has been identified as leading to both role conflict and role overload for two-paycheck couples, especially parents (Gilbert & Holahan, 1982; Gray, 1983; Hall & Hall, 1979 ; Harrison & Minor, 1982; Johnson & Johnson, 1977; 1980; Lawe & Lawe, 1980; Mortimer, 1978; Nadelson & Nadelson, 1980; Pleck & Staines, 1982; Rapoport & Rapoport, 1969; 1976).

The most salient feature marking the changing nature of women's and men's work and family responsibilities in the latter part of the twentieth century has been the emergence of the two-paycheck family. Economic and social pressures have combined to reduce the viability of the traditional family pattern consisting of the husband-provider role and the wife-mother-homemaker role.

Research on dual-earner couples has increased rapidly over the last sixteen years in synchrony with the growing reality of two employed parents as the new norm for the American family (Frankel, Manoque, & Paludi, 1982). The study of the impact of social change on the work/family sphere began with Rapoport and Rapoport's research (1969) on the then-new phenomenon of the dual-career family. In addition to published reports of more than thirty major empirical studies, the literature on dual-earner families is characterized by a large number of books ranging from scholarly (Aldous, 1982; Geerkin & Gove, 1983; Gilbert, 1985; Hall & Hall, 1979; Holmstrom, 1972; Pepitone-Rockwell, 1980; Peterson, Richardson, & Kreuter, 1978; Pleck, 1985; Rapoport & Rapoport, 1969; 1976; Rice, 1970; Scanzoni, 1978) to popular (Berman, 1980; Bird, 1979; Olds, 1975).

Two decades of research on two-paycheck families have provided ample evidence that dual-earner couples face both social and psychological barriers to adaptation. Sociological factors such as institutional constraints and culturally traditional norms for behavior result in high levels of externally generated stress for the two-paycheck family. Psychological accommodation within the family is heavily influenced by specific features of the social surround (Walker & Wallston, 1985). Role conflict and role strain are clear sources of psychological discomfort, particularly when added to maternal guilt (Gilbert, Holahan, & Manning, 1981; Johnson & Johnson, 1980; Poloma, Pendleton, & Garland, 1982), personality variables (Nyquist, Slivken, Spence, Helmreich, 1985; Huser & Grant, 1978), and beliefs about gender roles (Cooper, Chassin, & Zeiss, 1985; Nadelson & Nadelson, 1980), which inhibit the perception of available options for personal behavioral change in the dual-earner parent (Rabin & Sinnott, 1985).

Considering that the two-paycheck family is actually the most common family pattern in the United States (51.8 percent in 1981; Pleck, 1985) the adaptation capabilities of dual-earner couples will determine our success or failure as a culture. By examining both the barriers to adaptation and the factors enhancing the adaptation capacity of people in two-paycheck families I hope to achieve a perspective on psychological responses to social change in America today.

## The Gender-Role Belief System and Adaptation

Successful adaptation to the dual-earner situation is marked behaviorally by role sharing between spouses, which reduces role overload and role strain (Beer,

1983; Haas, 1980), encourages the development of coping strategies that enhance effectiveness in meeting family obligations while serving to reduce conflict (Elman & Gilbert, 1984; Gilbert et al. 1981; Gray, 1983; Lawe & Lawe, 1980), stimulates the prioritizing of tasks so that little or no time is spent on nonadaptive tasks (McCubbin, 1979; Seiden, 1980), and generates increasing competence and independence in all members of the family, including the children (Howell, 1977; Olds, 1975). Psychological indicators of successful adaptation are marked by high levels of marital satisfaction (Bailyn, 1970; Cooper et al., 1985; Yogev, 1982), self-esteem (Barnett, 1982; Holahan & Gilbert, 1979), and life satisfaction (Ferree, 1984; Rotheram & Weiner, 1983).

The key to successful adaptation is psychological. The gender-role belief system that underlies behavior determines whether or not dual-earner couples can make functional behavioral changes that increase survival effectiveness or whether they will continue to behave in traditional father-provider, mother-nurturer role patterns of the "Second Wave Family" (Toffler, 1980 p. 209), developed during the Industrial period (Bernard, 1981; Cowan, 1983; Marwell, 1975). It is clear that very little change in household task and responsibility allocation has occurred (Beckman & Houser; 1979; Hofferth & Moore, 1979; Lopata, Barnewolt, & Knorr, 1980; Miller & Garrison, 1982; Vanek, 1980) despite the profound social change from single-earner to dual-earner families in America (Smith, 1979). The basic, overwhelming psychological response to this social change has been one of future shock. Most people seem unable to restructure the relationship between gender role and gender identity (Nadelson & Nadelson, 1980; Rice, 1970) to better match the environment in which survival must be achieved.

Hunt and Hunt (1982) do not believe that the dual-career/dual-earner family pattern differs significantly from the traditional sex-role pattern and for this reason they expect little change or support from American social policy. The implication here is that the belief system about gender-specific roles remains intact for most people and therefore few behavioral changes occur even in dual-earner families. The conventional family is essentially nonadaptive in the twentieth century because it is based on gender ascription rather than achieved status and a hierarchical power structure that precludes adjustment to changing environmental circumstances.

## Gender-Role Ascription and the Conventional Family

Females have been uniformly socialized to take responsibility for the home, be supportive to the husband, and be nurturant to the children. These roles are "ascribed" in that they are gender-based cultural expectations for behavior (Sarbin & Allen, 1968). Why should gender-role ascription have developed as such a powerful cultural factor? There is a certain functional advantage to this strategy. Assigning the expressive and communal domain to women and the instrumental and agenic functions to men ensures that each family will have a range of survival capacities. The degree to which gender-role socialization succeeds in producing nurturing, supportive females and industriously productive independent males determines the complementarity available within a marriage. This ascriptive complementarity can be quite adaptive in those societies in which the family is the main economic unit and in which most people can learn the ascribed skills (Marwell, 1975). In this situation the family is strengthened as a survival unit because full expressive-instrumental and agenic-communal capacities are guaranteed with every spousal pairing.

Marwell (1975) concludes that sex role ascription is becoming increasingly dysfunctional in a technological, education-oriented society capable of identifying individual differences in genetically based aptitudes for specific acquired skills. Although Marwell starts out his examination of sex role ascription focusing on the positive, adaptive qualities of ascription he concludes that in modern society ascription is basically nonadaptive.

Complementarity no longer assures survival because the family unit is no longer the economic unit and each member of the family must be competent in multiple roles and capacities.

The hierarchical power structure of the conventional family, divided into expressive and instrumental gender roles, was supposed to improve marital satisfaction because it would improve family functional efficiency (Parsons & Bales, 1955). However, the hierarchical gender-role ascribed family system produced an unhealthy psychological outcome: wives living as economic parasites and husbands existing as emotional parasites (Bernard, 1981). Furthermore, the roles never really were separate and complementary. Considerable conflict exists between mother, wife, and housewife roles (Darley, 1976; Hoffnung, 1984).

Hunt and Hunt (1982) and Scanzoni (1983) explain the failure of dual-earner families to adapt psychologically and behaviorally to their socioeconomic situation as a consequence of conventional family structure in which gender forms the basis for role assignment.

The conventional family is morphostatic in nature, which means that it is based on maintaining a fixed, stable hierarchical role structure. An emphasis on conformity over individualism marks the conventional family, which, according to Scanzoni, is out of phase with changing twentieth century societal needs. The typical dual-earner American family remains conventional, allocating tasks according to gender, and maintaining a hierarchical power structure rather than sharing power equitably (Model, 1982). The role sharing reported by Haas (1980; 1982), Beer (1983), Pleck (1985), and Gilbert (1985) is not occurring within the conventional family pattern. Role sharing is a feature of the progressive family pattern, based on morphogenetic process dynamics that emphasize flexibility and individuality. "Progressives want an equal-partner model of marriage/family to contribute to their interests and goals in particular ways; they expect to invest in marriage and family through equitable demand and policymaking; and they expect family to contribute to a morphogenetic society by effectively training children in the dynamics of equitable decision making" (Scanzoni, 1983, p. 193).

Hunt and Hunt (1982) maintain that dual-earners split into two cultures: the conventional breadwinner male identity and homemaker female identity and the symmetrical family in which gender ascription does not form the basis of task allocation, and in which power is shared.

In terms of human adaptation and survival the question is, why hasn't a reallocation of household and parental tasks and responsibilities occurred among dual-earner couples? What is preventing role sharing from emerging as the new pattern of family survival? The answer is both social and psychological. To a large extent the problem is change itself, which is threatening because it disrupts the stability and emotional security that is derived from repetition of that which is familiar. Division of labor by gender has a long history in human culture.

## Division of Labor and Gender Identity

Anthropologists (Brown, 1976; Sanday, 1981) theorize that gender-based division of labor came about because of the limits put on women's work by childcare. Women's work must be interruptable, mustn't take the women too far from home, and mustn't be dangerous. Economic survival of early *Homo sapiens* required high levels of competence from everyone, male, female, and child. Survival of the species was enhanced by division of labor so that different skills could be developed and the products shared. These early humans were all dual-worker families and everyone's contribution was equally important to survival. The problem now is that economic contributions to family survival are calculated in terms of the paycheck value of labor rather than its survival contribution, thereby hiding the wife support system of the two-person American career (Ferber & Huber, 1979; Fowlkes, 1980; Papanek, 1973). Furthermore, with the decline of agriculture and the rise of industrial and commercial lifestyles, the home and its surround were displaced as economic centers for survival (Toffler, 1980). Survival now came from a paycheck earned by the male "provider." Male gender identity was thus separated from the home and female gender identity was placed squarely in the home (Bernard, 1981).

It is against this background that the modern two-paycheck family must be understood. Equity between spouses is extraordinarily difficult to achieve because of the psychological barriers to role sharing resulting from the vesting of gender identity in ascribed male provider and female nurturer roles.

## Work/Family Attitudinal Barriers to Adaptation

Women's progress toward equality in the last three decades has been characterized by the adoption of traditional "male" attributes (instrumentality over expressivity, agency over communion), "male" values (paid work as a definer of identity and self-worth), and "male" goals (increasing job status and pay). What has failed to happen, to any large extent, is the inclusion of traditional "female" attributes, values, and goals into an accepted new cultural pattern for twentieth century (and twenty-first century) survival.

The morphogenetic progressive family described by Scanzoni (1983), the symmetrical family described by Hunt and Hunt (1982), and the various non-hierarchical family patterns being currently explored (Thorne & Yalom, 1982) indicate that "female" perspectives on the importance of intimacy, mutual nurturance and support, interpersonal relationships, emotional sharing responsibility, and attachment are critical to the development of the adaptive family (Rabin, 1986). The nonconventional family is the key to adaptation precisely because it blends "female" and "male" values into an androgynously restructured life pattern. The problem is that this healthy, adaptive, and equitable family pattern is not receiving either the support or the rewards of the larger society, which remains unchanged in its adherence to the "male" value system of power, status, the saliency of the work ethic, profit motivation, and achievement. After comparing two national surveys on employment and family work, Pleck (1985) concludes that "there is no getting around the fact that men who participate more directly in their families must be, on the average, less productive and ambitious in their paid work" (p. 158).

The family has never been important in the Industrial Culture because the nuclear family is not an economic unit as was the Agricultural family (Toffler, 1980). Therefore men and women vest themselves in family involvement, particularly children, at their personal cost.

People are asked to choose between family and work, one of which is subject only to personal rewards, the other being part of the monetary and status reward system of the "real" world (Hunt & Hunt, 1982).

The dual-career family is caught in a particularly painful situation, in that the salience of the work ethic value system is doubled, leaving even less time for expressive, relational, and mutually supportive interactions. If there are children in the family the first thing to diminish is time together for spouses, not time involved with careers (Cooper et al., 1985).

Yet another aspect of the work/family problem comes from dual-earner parents employed in shift-work schedules. Of the 52 percent dual-career work force in America, half are parents with children at home. Many of these are shift workers who solve the childcare problem by splitting their work and home schedules into a complementary pattern. Unfortunately this means that the amount of time spouses see each other is severely curtailed (Presser & Cain, 1983). Ten percent of shift-work dual earners have schedules that don't overlap at all!

Another result of the powerful work salience and lack of social support for the family in American culture is indicated by a recent study of faculty women at Northwestern University, 67 percent of whom have chosen to not have children (Yogev & Vierra, 1983). The researchers feel that their data "seem to indicate a trend toward permanent childlessness among younger professional women" (p. 394). Many women in the study did not believe that they could comfortably integrate both career and motherhood roles. Attitudes toward "Kinder, Kirche,

Kuche" (children, church, cooking) as the essence of female identity are changing. Younger women do not attach the same importance to marriage, home, and family as do older women (Merriam & Hyer, 1984). The role identity of younger women would appear to be more complex than that of older women.

The lack of penetration of "female" attributes and values into the culture coupled with the unidirectional change toward "male" attributes and values in women who want equality has resulted in the decline of family oriented behavior in women. This is in large measure because women recognize that they will bear a disproportionate part of the family burden (Bryson, Bryson, & Johnson, 1978; Ericksen, Yancey, & Erickson, 1979; St. John-Parsons, 1978) in a society that undervalues family involvement compared to many other more family oriented cultures (Hunt & Hunt, 1982; Rix & Stone, 1984; Scanzoni, 1983). America ranks below thirteen other Western countries in commitment to daycare programs, maternity/paternity leaves, flexible job schedules, worksharing, and supportive tax structures (Kammerman & Kahn, 1978). "The 'superwomen' who are trying to 'have it all' (i.e., combine career with motherhood) are enduring such relentless pressure that their younger colleagues do not dare think about having children" (Yogev & Vierra, 1983, p. 396).

## Perception of Household Labor: The Technology Trap

Unrealistic expectations lead to problems in adaptation. Much about our cultural view of the homemaker-mother role is far closer to fantasy than real life. Women are supposed to be surrounded with technological work-saving devices typifying the constant progress of twentieth century life. As Ruth Cowan (1983) cogently points out, we have merely replaced one kind of time involvement with another. The time saved by washer/dryers, self-cleaning ovens, refrigerators, frozen foods, vacuum cleaners, and all the other impedimentia of modern life, is given back again in the increased need for homemakers to provide transportation to meet daily needs. Doctor's don't make home visits, children have to be brought to the office (and during daytime office hours, which interfere with school and work). Groceries are no longer delivered and procuring them necessitates driving to the supermarket, selecting and putting each item into a cart that must be propelled up and down each aisle, then removing each item from the cart onto the checkout counter and then putting the groceries (now bagged) into the car, driving home, carrying the groceries inside and unpacking each item. Add to this the amount of time wasted while waiting in line at the checkout counter or the delicatessen counter or the bakery section and the task of buying groceries for the family takes on an even larger share of nonproductive time. Suburban, middle-class children have to be transported to music lessons, sports teams, picked up from school when they stay late for chorus practice, taken to the library for school assignments, and so on, ad infinitum, ad nauseum. "By midcentury . . . the automobile had become to the American housewife of the middle classes, what the cast-iron stove in the kitchen would have been to her counterpart of 1850—the vehicle through which she did much of her most significant work, and the work locale where she could most often be found" (Cowan, 1983, p. 85).

A hundred years ago many services were available to the housewife: grocers, butchers, and bakers supplied delivery boys, as did pharmacies; laundresses or commercial laundries were popular and commodities such as milk, ice, and coal were regularly delivered.

Industrialization didn't make women's work easier. Instead, "modern technology enabled the American housewife of 1950 to produce single handedly what her counterpart of 1850 needed a staff of three or four to produce: a middle-class standard of health and cleanliness for herself, her spouse, and her children" (Cowan, 1983, p. 100).

Advertisers continually tell us how labor-saving their products are and what fun the homemaker has in getting her floors to sparkle, admiring her reflection in the dishes, keeping her toilets pristine, and turning out gourmet meals in minutes.

Most dual-earner couples are conventional in family structure and still allocate all of the household tasks to the employed wife. This seems reasonable in that there's not much to housework anyway, given all those modern appliances and the constant messages from advertisers stressing the ease of use of their products for the home. The fact that most women in dual-earner households are suffering from role overload and perpetual exhaustion hasn't significantly altered the prevailing pattern of household division of labor because the belief system is more powerful than the behavioral reality. So employed women continue to feel hopelessly inadequate in that they cannot meet the household care standards that are supposed to be so easy to achieve (Roland & Harris, 1979).

## ADAPTATION IN TWO-PAYCHECK FAMILIES: A SYSTEMS THEORY PERSPECTIVE

The process of adaptation in two-paycheck families can best be studied using a systems perspective (Sinnott, 1986) combined with a social-ecological model of psychological responses to social change (Walker & Wallston, 1985). Cognitive influences underlying gender-role identity and perceived options for behavioral change can be viewed as part of an energy flow system both within the organism and between the organism and the environment (Rabin & Sinnott, 1985).

Adaptation requires energy. If too much ecological energy is tied up in maintaining the conventional family structure and the culturally ascribed roles within that structure, then very little energy is available for the process of adaptation to social change.

The pattern of change is such that systems only change if some degree of entropy or disorder exists. This disorder in the system gives rise to "flexible re-ordering" and growth, which is adaptive. However systems, by their functional nature, resist disorder. Sinnott (1986) differentiates between surviving systems, which have boundaries that are not totally closed, thereby allowing a degree of flexible responding to external change, and nonsurviving systems, which have rigid boundries, making them inflexible and less adaptive. Conventional families with hierarchical power structures based on gender-role ascription and the gender-role belief system fall into the category of non surviving systems. "The burden on dual-career couples now is not to maximize their conventionality but to live up to the ideal of symmetry" (Hunt & Hunt, 1982, p. 46).

Two-paycheck couples have trouble adapting to their circumstances because adaptation depends upon the ability to see options for behavioral change. Women, in particular, are blocked from adaptive behavior because guilt about traditional gender-role obligations underlies the wife-mother role (Nadelson & Nadelson, 1980; Roland & Harris, 1979). The problem is cognitive; people cannot act on options that they do not perceive as being available to them (Rabin & Sinnott, 1985). Consequently, family living problems go unresolved and become continuing sources of stress. Options such as making household management the responsibility of the entire family, changing priorities regarding work versus people-time, establishing less demanding standards of orderliness and cleanliness, and sharing parental responsibilities more fully lead to better adaptation. However, these options can only be utilized if individuals see these choices as being appropriate for themselves in a nonthreatening way. Women may actually refuse household role-sharing from their husbands because equity would endanger their gender-role based feminine identity (Nadelson & Nadelson, 1980).

An effective barrier to the kind of systems change that would foster equitable symmetry in dual-earner families is differential power. Model (1982) distinguishes between dual-earners and equal-earners, and maintains that only the latter can achieve equity in family structure because each spouse has equal power deriving from an equal economic contribution. Scanzoni (1978) argues that equity comes from equal bargaining power and most wives are limited in the bargaining power they can exert in the marriage. Part of the problem is the unequal monetary contribution of wives but another difficulty arises from the power dependence pattern of socialization in which females are trained. Women give out more strokes, make more adjustments, are more committed to affective relationships and enduring marriage than are men. "Such a woman may see rewards for herself in the traditional role bargain and costs in making the bargain 'more equitable' " (Hiller, 1984, p. 1016). Thus many women accept power dependence as a definer of femininity. Conversely, power is part of the male gender identity system and for that reason equity becomes a threat to masculinity (Kahn, 1984). "Power has become the key ingredient in male self-esteem and for many men, the definition of being a man is tied to possession and use of power" (Kahn, 1984, p. 241). The traditional male role, based on the male sex role identity (MSRI) paradigm identified by Joseph Pleck (1981), requires that physical strength and even aggression underlie masculinity. MSRI is basically nonadaptive because of the considerable strain generated by roles that cannot really be filled. The MSRI paradigm will continue to contribute to the power imbalance between males and females until it is abandoned as a definer of masculinity. The problem of sex role strain is not in the individual but in the society and the process of sex typing. The male provider role and the predominance of work as a definer of self are sources of strain in both family and work roles (Pleck, 1981). Thus the power-dependence basis of femininity and power-assertion basis of masculinity make equity in marriage virtually impossible. Indeed Haas (1980; 1982) found so few role-sharing couples that she could not get a representative sample to study. In current American culture, equity between dual-earner spouses has become subject to a definition of fairness determined by the perceived gender-role appropriateness of tasks, obligations, and responsibilities within a system of differential power based on gender identity. The problem with achieving a nonhierarchical, power-sharing, role-sharing symmetrical family structure is that most dual-earner and dual-career people are traditionalists whose psychological reliance on the gender-role belief system precludes structural change within the family system.

In a social-ecological model of adaptation to social change the "individual characteristics of each family member interact with those of the family, workplace, and environment, yielding the family's adaptational strategies" (Walker & Wallston, 1985, p. 700). Individual psychological characteristics affect adaptation, especially the capacity for some degree of role sharing. An overview of the literature indicates that androgynous couples handled conflict in constructive ways (Yelsma & Brown, 1985); androgynous dual-career individuals experienced high personal and relational satisfaction (Rotheram & Weiner, 1983); women who were less gender-role traditional did fewer "feminine" tasks in the home (Beckman & Houser, 1979); and androgynous males did more housework than "masculine" males (Denmark, Shaw, & Ciali, 1985). Psychological characteristics differ in dual-career and dual-earner couples compared with single-earner, husband-provider households. Spouses in dual-career families are more inner directed and flexible, share a closer identity, and differ in self-actualization from traditional-family spouses (Huser & Grant, 1978). Dual-earner couples indicate more feminist attitudes than traditional couples (Smith, 1985).

Individual psychological traits have to be closely considered when adaptation in dual-earner families is studied. Ultimately, the adaptation process is dependent upon how individual psychological characteristics interact with the family structure (conventional or nontraditional), the workplace (flextime vs. rigid schedules, Best, 1981; Bohen & Viveros-Long, 1981; greedy occupations, Handy, 1978; the two-person career, Papanek, 1973; childcare provisions, Greenfield, 1981; Huber & Spitze, 1983), and the environment (suburban reliance on car transportation versus urban public transportation, Cowan, 1983; the subculture of coworkers and neighbors, Lein, 1979; Skinner, 1980).

## The Two-Paycheck Family

Overall, the effects of the dramatic change from single earner to dual earner as the norm for American families have been more positive than negative despite the failure of an equitable family structure to emerge. Women have been the ones to experience the greatest change. Psychological well-being is increased in most married women who add employed status to their homemaker source of self-esteem (Thoits, 1983). Paid employment is associated with a more autonomous sense of self (Warren & McEachren, 1985), a source of intrinsic satisfaction superior to that offered by housework (Newberry, Weissman, & Myers, 1979), and an alternate source of esteem and gratification (Feree, 1976). Both physical and psychological health benefits derive from multiple roles that offer possibilities for increased network membership and socially supportive relationships (Hibbard & Pope, 1985).

The relationship between women's employment and their psychological well-being is complex, which probably accounts for studies that find no differences in life satisfaction between employed wives and housewives (Feree, 1984). Status relationships between employed spouses affect psychological well-being (Hornung & McCullough, 1981), as does work satisfaction, sharing of household and childcare responsibilities, and exposure to social networks (Shehan, 1984). The intrinsic and extrinsic characteristics of employment influence job satisfaction, which, in turn, influences the quality of family relationships (Piotrkowski & Crits-Christoph, 1982). The relationship between women and employment, in general, is determined by the quality of both the home and work environments (Warr & Parry, 1982). Psychological well-being in suburban American women was related far more to androgyny (or even high masculinity scores on the Bem Sex Role Inventory) than to homemaker or employed status (Rendely, Holmstrom, & Karp, 1984).

There is some hope that the Second Wave Industrialization gender-role system that currently holds American society in future shock gridlock may evolve into a more adaptive form. "If other cultures . . . are anything to go by, tomorrow's gender ideology will reflect tomorrow's society" (Strathern, 1976, p. 68). Undeniably, there is considerable role strain in the dual-earner family of the 1980s but, as Komarovsky (1973) has noted, role strain can be the motivation for social change. Certainly, attitudes toward women and employment have changed to the point where college students of both sexes rated employed women more favorably than unemployed women with regard to personal traits and professional competencies (Etaugh & Petroski, 1985). High school seniors in a large national sample indicated that employment was an expectation for wives (Herzog, Bachman, & Johnston, 1983).

Now that dual-earner families are the psychological as well as the statistical norm we need to look beyond the simple questions of the 1960s and early 1970s concerning "women and work" or the "effect of maternal employment on children." Comparing employed mothers and homemaker mothers is not particularly useful since job satisfaction, in the home and in the workforce, is far more important than paid-worker/homemaker distinctions (Delaas, Gaier, & Emihovich, 1979; Gold & Andres, 1978; Hofferth & Moore, 1979; Hoffman, 1979; Hoffman & Nye, 1974). Today, the questions we need to ask concern adaptation of individuals and families in the face of enormous and rapid technological change. To focus on women's changing role alone is to miss the point that survival dictates behavioral change for everyone. The main psychological barrier to successful adaptation remains the gender-role belief system at the same time that the main societal barrier to successful adaptation remains the lack of support and concern for the family. The lack of behavioral accommodation to the socioeconomic shift from single-earner to dual-earner families is occurring because we have based male esteem on differential power (Gray-Little & Burks, 1983; Hiller, 1984; Scanzoni, 1978; 1983) and the good provider role (Bernard, 1981; Pleck, 1981), and female identity on the motherhood mystique (Friedan, 1963, 1981; Hoffnung, 1984; Nadelson & Nadelson, 1980). This belief system remains intact despite its lack of adaptive utility and basic inequality (Steil, 1985) because the rate of socioeconomic restructuring in American society is out-pacing our psychological capacity to redefine ourselves in relation to rapidly changing survival circumstances.

Just as future shock represents nonadaptation on the personal level, cultural lag is the failure of whole societies to accommodate their key institutions to the changing needs of people caught up in the consequences of technological, economic, and social change. The lack of institutional change creates "structural barriers" (Pleck, 1985, p. 157) that make it especially difficult for dual-earner couples to develop and maintain an atmosphere of psychological well-being. "The discouraging news in 1983 was that, despite the presence of millions of mothers as well as fathers in the workforce, little progress is being made to help working parents cope" (Rix & Stone, 1984, p. 210).

Currently proposed legislation in Congress would further reduce the economic viability of the dual-earner family in terms of taxes and affirmative action programs. The aggregate future shock reactions of leaders who are not trained in science and who do not understand the ramifications of technological change (Koshland, 1985) is weakening the adaptive capacity of people caught in the social changes. The problem is that while societal regression may make people temporarily feel better, it does nothing to solve the actual survival problems imposed by a forward-thrusting technology.

## REFERENCES

Aldous, J. (1982). *Two paychecks: Life in dual earner families*. Beverly Hills, CA: Sage.
Bailyn, L. (1970). Career and family orientation of husbands and wives in relation to marital happiness. *Human Relations, 23,* 97–113.
Barnett, R. C. (1982). Multiple roles and well-being: A study of mothers of preschool age children. *Psychology of Women Quarterly, 7,* 175–178.
Beckman, L. J. & Houser, B. B. (1979). The more you have, the more you do: The relationships between wife's employment, sex-role attitudes, and household behavior. *Psychology of Women Quarterly, 4,* 160–174.
Beer, W. R. (1983). *Househusbands: Men and housework in American families*. New York: Praeger.

Berman, E. (1980). *The new-fashioned parent: How to make your family style work.* Englewood Cliffs, NJ: Prentice-Hall.

Bernard, J. (1981). The good provider role. *American Psychologist, 36,* 1–12.

Best, F. (1981). Changing sex roles and worklife flexibility. *Psychology of Women Quarterly, 6,* 55–71.

Bird, C. (1979). *The two-paycheck marriage.* New York: Rawson, Wade.

Bohen, H. H. & Viveros-Long, A. (1981). *Balancing job and family life: Do flexible work schedules help?* Philadelphia: Temple University Press.

Brown, J. K. (1976). An anthropological perspective on sex roles and subsistence. In M. S. Teitelbaum (Ed.), *Sex differences: Social and biological perspectives* (pp. 122–137). Garden City, NY: Anchor.

Bryson, R., Bryson, J. B., & Johnson, M. F. (1978). Family size, satisfaction, and productivity in dual-career couples. *Psychology of Women Quarterly, 3,* 67–77.

Cooper, K., Chassin, L., & Zeiss, A. (1985). The relation of sex-role self-concept and sex-role attitudes to the marital satisfaction and personal adjustment of dual-worker couples with preschool children. *Sex Roles, 12,* 227–242.

Cowan, R. S. (1983). *More work for mother.* New York: Basic books.

Darley, S. A. (1976). Big-time careers for little women: A dual-role dilemma. *Journal of Social Issues, 32,* 85–98.

Delaas, M., Gaier, E. L., & Emihovich, C. A. (1979). Maternal employment and selected behaviors and attitudes of preadolescents and adolescents. *Adolescence, 14,* 579–589.

Denmark, F. L., Shaw, J. S., & Ciali, S. D. (1985). The relationship among sex roles, living arrangements, and the division of household responsibilities. *Sex Roles, 12,* 617–626.

Elman, M. & Gilbert, L. A. (1984). Coping strategies for role conflict in married professional women with children. *Family Relations, 33,* 317–327.

Ericksen, J. A., Yancey, W. L., & Ericksen, E. P. (1979). The division of family roles. *Journal of Marriage and the Family, 41,* 301–313.

Etaugh, C. & Petroski, B. (1985). Perceptions of women: Effects of employment status and marital status. *Sex Roles, 12,* 329–340.

Ferber, M. A. & Huber, J. (1979). Husbands, wives, and careers. *Journal of Marriage and the Family, 41,* 301–313.

Feree, M. M. (1976). Working class jobs: Paid work and housework as sources of satisfaction. *Social Problems, 23,* 431–441.

Feree, M. M. (1984). Class, housework, and happiness: Women's work and life satisfaction. *Sex Roles, 11,* 1057–1074.

Fowlkes, M. R. (1980). *Behind every successful man: Wives of medicine and academe.* New York: Columbia University Press.

Frankel, J., Manoque, M. A., & Paludi, M. (1982). The employed mother: A new social norm? *International Journal of Women's Studies, 5,* 274–281.

Friedan, B. (1963). *The feminine mystique.* New York: Dell.

Friedan, B. (1981). *The second stage.* New York: Summit.

Geerkin, M. & Gove, W. R. (1983). *At home and at work.* Beverly Hills, CA: Sage.

Gilbert, L. A. (1985). *Men in dual career families.* Hillsdale, NJ: Lawrence Erlbaum Associates.

Gilbert, L. A. & Holahan, C. K. (1982). Conflicts between student/professional, parental, and self-development roles: A comparison of high and low effective copers. *Human Relations, 35,* 635–648.

Gilbert, L. A., Holahan, C. K., & Manning, L. (1981). Coping with conflict between professional and maternal roles. *Family Relations: Journal of Applied Family and Child Studies, 30,* 419–426.

Gold, D. & Andres, D. (1978). Developmental comparisons between ten-year-old children with employed and non-employed mothers. *Child Development, 49,* 75–84.

Gray, J. D. (1983). The married professional woman: An examination of her role conflicts and coping strategies. *Psychology of Women Quarterly, 7,* 235–243.

Gray-Little, B. & Burks, N. (1983). Power and satisfaction in marriage: A review and critique. *Psychological Bulletin, 93,* 523–538.

Greenfield, P. M. (1981). Child care in cross-cultural perspectives: Implications for future organization of child care in the United States. *Psychology of Women Quarterly, 6,* 41–54.

Haas, L. (1980). Role-sharing couples: A study of egalitarian marriages. *Family Relations, 29,* 289–296.

Haas, L. (1982). Determinants of role-sharing behavior: A study of egalitarian couples. *Sex Roles, 8,* 747–760.

Hall, F. S. & Hall, D. T. (1979). *The two-career couple.* Reading, MA: Addison-Wesley.

Handy, C. (1978). Going against the grain: Working couples and greedy occupations. In R. Rapoport & R. Rapoport (Eds.), *Working couples* (pp. 36–46). New York: Harper Colophon.

Harrison, A. O. & Minor, J. H. (1982). Interrole conflict, coping strategies, and role satisfaction among single and married employed mothers. *Psychology of Women Quarterly, 6,* 354–360.

Herzog, A. R., Bachman, J. G., & Johnston, L. D. (1983). Paid work, child care, and housework: A national survey of high school seniors' preferences for sharing responsibilities between husband and wife. *Sex Roles, 9,* 109–135.

Hibbard, J. H. & Pope, C. R. (1985). Employment status, employment characteristics, and women's health. *Women and Health, 10,* 59–77.

Hiller, D. V. (1984). Power dependence and division of family work. *Sex Roles, 10,* 1003–1019.

Hofferth, S. L., & Moore, K. A. (1979). Women's employment and marriage. In R. E. Smith (Ed.), *The subtle revolution* (pp. 99–125). Washington, DC: Urban Institute.

Hoffman, L. W. (1979). Maternal employment: 1979. *American Psychologist, 34,* 859–865.

Hoffman, L. W. & Nye, F. E. (Eds.) (1974). *Working mothers.* New York: Jossey-Bass.

Hoffnung, M. (1984). Motherhood: Contemporary conflict for women. In J. Freeman (Ed.), *Women: a feminist perspective* (3rd Ed.) (pp. 124–138). Palo Alto, CA: Mayfield.

Holahan, C. K. & Gilbert, L. A. (1979). Conflict between major life roles: The women and men in dual career couples. *Human Relations, 32,* 451–467.

Holmstrom, L. L. (1972). *The two-career family.* Cambridge; MA; Shenkman.

Hornung, C. A. & McCullough, B. C. (1981). Status relationships in dual-employment marriages: Consequences for psychological well-being. *Journal of Marriage and the Family, 43,* 125–142.

Howell, M. (1977). *Helping ourselves: Families and the human network.* Boston: Beacon.

Huber, J. & Spitze, G. (1983). *Sex stratification: Children, housework, and jobs.* New York: Academic Press.

Hunt, J. G. & Hunt, L. L. (1982). Dual-career families: Vanguard of the future or residue of the past. In J. Aldous (Ed.), *Two paychecks: Life in dual-earner families* (pp. 41–60). Beverly Hills, CA: Sage.

Huser, W. R. & Grant, C. W. (1978). A study of husbands and wives from dual-career and traditional career families. *Psychology of Women Quarterly, 3,* 78–89.

Johnson, C. L. & Johnson, F. A. (1977). Attitudes toward parenting in dual-career families. *American Journal of Psychiatry, 134,* 391–395.

Johnson, C. L. & Johnson, F. A. (1980). Parenthood, marriage and careers: Situational constraints and role-strain. In F. Pepitone-Rockwell (Ed.), *Dual-career couples* (pp. 191–206). Beverly Hills: Sage.

Kahn, A. (1984). The power war: Male response to power loss under equality. *Psychology of Women Quarterly, 8,* 234–247.

Kamerman, S. B. & Kahn, A. J. (1978). *Family policy: Government and families in fourteen countries.* New York: Columbia University Press.

Komarovsky, M. (1973). Some problems in role analysis. *American Sociological Review, 38,* 649–662.

Koshland, D. E. (1985). Scientific literacy. *Science, 230,* 4724.

Lawe, C. & Lawe, B. (1980). The balancing act: Coping strategies for emerging family lifestyles. In F. Pepitone-Rockwell (Ed.), *Dual career couples* Beverly Hills, CA: Sage.

Lein, L. (1979). Male participation in home life: Impact of social supports and bread-winner responsibility on the allocation of tasks. *Family Coordinator, 28,* 489–495.

Levitan, S. A. & Belous, R. S. (1981). *What's happening to the American Family.* Baltimore: Johns Hopkins University Press.

Lopata, H. Z., Barnewolt, D. & Korr, K. (1980). Spouse's contributions to each other's roles. In F. Pepitone-Rockwell (Ed.), *Dual career couples.* Beverly Hills, CA: Sage.

Marwell, G. (1975). Why ascription? Parts of a more or less formal theory of the functions and dysfunctions of sex roles. *American Sociological Review, 40,* 445–455.

McCubbin, H. (1979). Integrating coping behavior in family stress theory. *Journal of Marriage and the Family, 41,* 237–244.

Merriam, S. B. & Hyer, P. (1984). Changing attitudes of women towards family-related tasks in young adulthood. *Sex Roles, 10,* 825–835.

Miller, J. & Garrison, H. H. (1982). Sex roles: The division of labor at home and in the workplace. *Annual Review of Sociology, 8,* 237–262.

Model, S. (1982). Housework by husbands: Determinants and implications. In J. Aldous (Ed.), *Two paychecks: Life in dual-earner families.* Beverly Hills, CA: Sage.

Mortimer, J. T. (1978). Dual-career families: A sociological perspective. In S. S. Peterson, J. M. Richardson, & G. V. Kreuter (Eds.), *The two-career family: Issues and alternatives* (pp. 1–30). Washington, DC: University Press.

Nadelson, C. C. & Nadelson, T. (1980). Dual career marriages: Benefits and costs. In F. Pepitone-Rockwell (Ed), *Dual-career couples* (pp. 91–110). Beverly Hills, CA: Sage.

Newberry, P., Weissman, M., & Meyers, J. (1979). Working wives and housewives:

Do they differ in mental status and social adjustment? *American Journal of Or-thopsychiatry, 49,* 282–291.

Nyquist, L., Slivken, K., Spence, J. T., & Helmreich, R. L. (1985). Household re-sponsibilities in middle-class couples: The contribution of demographic and per-sonality variables. *Sex Roles, 12,* 15–34.

Olds, S. (1975). *The mother who works outside the home.* New York: Child Study Press.

Papanek, H. (1973). Men, women, and work: Reflections on the two person career. In J. Huber (Ed.), *Changing women in a changing society* (pp. 90–110). Chicago: University of Chicago Press.

Parsons, T. & Bales, R. F. (1955). *Family socialization and interaction process.* Riv-erside, NJ: Free Press.

Pepitone-Rockwell, F. (Ed.). (1980). *Dual-career couples.* Beverly Hills, CA: Sage.

Peterson, S. S., Richardson, J. M., & Kreuter, G. V. (Eds.). (1978). *The two-career family: Issues and alternatives.* Washington, DC: University Press.

Piotrkowski, C. S. & Crits-Christoph, P. (1982). Women's jobs and family adjustment. In J. Aldous (Ed.), *Two paychecks: Life in dual-earner families* (pp. 105–127). Beverly Hills, CA: Sage.

Pleck, J. (1981). *The myth of masculinity.* Cambridge, MA: MIT Press.

Pleck, J. (1985). *Working wives/working husbands.* Beverly Hills, CA: Sage.

Pleck, J. H. & Staines, G. L. (1982). Work schedules and work-family conflict in two-earner couples. In J. Aldous (Ed.), *Two paychecks: Life in dual earner families.* (pp. 63–88) Beverly Hills, CA: Sage.

Poloma, M., Pendleton, B., & Garland, T. (1982). Reconsidering the dual career mar-riage: A longitudinal approach. In J. Aldous (Ed.), *Two paychecks: Life in dual-earner families* (pp. 173–192). Beverly Hills, CA: Sage.

Presser, H. B. & Cain, V. S. (1983). Shift work among dual-earner couples with children. *Science, 219,* 876–879.

Rabin, J. S. (1980). Sex roles and career development. Unpublished manuscript, Towson State University.

Rabin, J. S. (1986). Adaptation across the lifespan: Evolution, future shock, and sex roles. In J. Sinnott (Ed.), *Sex roles and aging: Theory and research from a systems perspective.* New York: Karger.

Rabin, J. S. & Sinnott, J. D. (1985). Dual earner parents: Relationships between perceived options and adaptive behaviors. Grant proposal submitted to the Rockefeller Foundation.

Rapoport, R. & Rapoport, R. N. (1969). The dual career family. *Human Relations, 22,* 3–30.

Rapoport, R. & Rapoport, R. N. (1976). *Dual career families re-examined.* New York: Harper & Row.

Rendely, J. G., Holmstrom, R. M., & Karp, S. A. (1984). The relationship of sex-role identity, life style, and mental health in suburban American homemakers: I. Sex role, employment, and adjustment. *Sex Roles, 11,* 839–848.

Rice, D. G. (1970). *Dual career marriage.* New York: Free Press.

Rix, S. E. & Stone, A. J. (1984). Work. In S. M. Pritchard (Ed.), *The women's annual* (pp. 202–220). Boston: Hall.

Roland, A. & Harris, B. (1979). *Career and motherhood: Struggles for a new identity.* New York: Human Sciences.

Rotheram, M. J. & Weiner, N. (1983). Androgyny, stress and satisfaction: Dual career and traditional relationships. *Sex Roles, 9,* 151–158.

Sanday, P. R. (1981). *Female power and male dominance: On the origins of sexual inequality.* Cambridge: Cambridge University Press.

Sarbin, T. R. & Allen, V. L. (1968). Role theory. In G. Lindzey & E. Aronson (Eds.), *The handbook of social psychology.* Reading, MA: Addison-Wesley.

Scanzoni, J. (1978). *Sex roles, women's work, and marital conflict.* Lexington, MA: Lexington Books.

Scanzoni, J. (1983). *Shaping tomorrow's family.* Beverly Hills, CA: Sage.

Seiden, A. M. (1980). Time management and the dual-career couple. In F. Pepitone-Rockwell (Ed.), *Dual-career couples* (pp. 163–190). Beverly Hills, CA: Sage.

Shehan, C. L. (1984). Wives' work and psychological well-being: An extension of Gove's social role theory of depression. *Sex Roles, 11,* 881–900.

Sinnott, J. D. (1986). General systems theory: A rationale for the study of everyday memory. In L. Poon, D. Rubin, & B. Wilson (Eds.), *Cognition in everyday life.* Hillsdale, NJ: Lawrence Erlbaum Associates.

Skinner, D. A. (1980). Dual-career family stress and coping: A literature review. *Family Relations, 29,* 473–480.

Smith, R. E. (1979). The movement of women into the labor force. In R. E. Smith (Ed.), *The subtle revolution: Women at work* (pp. 1–30). Washington, D.C.: Urban Institute.

Smith, T. W. (1985). Working wives and women's rights: The connection between the employment status of wives and the feminist attitudes of husbands. *Sex Roles, 12,* 501–508.

Spence, J. T. (1981). Changing conceptions of men and women: A psychologist's perspective. In E. Langland & W. Gove (Eds.), *A feminist in the academy: The difference it makes* (pp. 130–149). Chicago: University of Chicago Press.

Steil, J. M. (1984). Marital relationships and mental health: The psychic costs of inequality. In J. Freeman (Ed.), *Women: A feminist perspective* (3rd ed.). Palo Alto, CA: Mayfield.

St. John-Parsons, D. (1978). Continuous dual-career families: A case study. *Psychology of Women Quarterly, 3,* 30–42.

Strathern, M. (1976). An anthropological perspective. In B. B. Lloyd & J. Archer (Eds.), *Exploring sex differences* (pp. 49–70). London: Academic Press.

Thoits, P. A. (1983). Multiple identities and psychological well-being: A reformulation and test of the social isolation hypothesis. *American Sociological Review, 48,* 174–187.

Thorne, B. & Yalom, M. (Eds.). (1982). *Rethinking the family: Some feminist questions.* New York: Longman.

Toffler, A. (1970). *Future shock.* New York: Bantam.

Toffler, A. (1980). *The third wave.* New York: Bantam.

Vanek, J. J. (1980). Household work, wage work, and sexual equality. In S. F. Berk (Ed.), *Women and household labor* (pp. 275–291). Beverly Hills, CA: Sage.

Walker, L. S. & Wallston, B. S. (1985). Social adaptation: A review of dual-earner family literature. In L. L. Abate (Ed.), *Handbook of family psychology and therapy* Vol. 2 (pp. 698–740). Homewood, IL: Dorsey.

Warr, P. & Parry, G. (1982). Paid employment and women's psychological well-being. *Psychological Bulletin, 91,* 498–516.

Warren, L. W. & McEachren, L. (1985). Derived identity and depressive symptomatology in women differing in marital and employment status. *Psychology of Women Quarterly, 9,* 133–144.

Yelsma, P. & Brown, C. T. (1985). Gender roles, biological sex, and predisposition to conflict management. *Sex Roles, 12,* 731–747.

Yogev, S. (1982). Happiness in dual-career couples: Changing research, changing values. *Sex Roles, 8,* 593–606.

Yogev, S. & Vierra, A. (1983). The state of motherhood among professional women. *Sex Roles, 9,* 391–396.

# 13
# Sex Roles and Adjustment
## Jerome B. Dusek

The purpose of this chapter is to examine theoretical and methodological issues revolving around research on the relationship between sex roles, or sex role categorizations, and adjustment. Because thorough reviews of the literature exist (e.g., Whitley, 1983), and because some of the pertinent issues are discussed in other chapters of this volume, no attempt will be made to provide a systematic and detailed review or analysis of extant literature. For similar reasons, no complete summary of theories of sex typing will be presented. Interested readers are referred to appropriate chapters in this volume (Chapters 2, 3, 10, and 14) and to the original sources cited in those chapters.

In this chapter we focus on the specific relationships hypothesized to exist between an androgynous sex role orientation and psychological adjustment. Following a brief review of the theoretical underpinnings of the hypothesized relationships, we will summarize extant findings, critique measures of adjustment, examine methods of analysis, and suggest directions for future research.

## ANDROGYNY AND ADJUSTMENT

Historically, masculinity and femininity have been conceived as opposite poles of a single dimension (cf. Spence, 1985). In current conceptualizations, masculinity and femininity are viewed as two dimensions composing sex roles (cf. Bem, 1985; Spence, 1985). With this shift in theoretical perspectives, two models of the relationship between sex roles and psychological well-being have come to the fore: the androgyny model and the masculinity model (Whitley, 1983).

### The Androgyny Model

The androgyny model has as its foundation the perspective that masculinity and femininity are independent, rather than incompatible, dimensions of sex roles (Bem, 1974, 1979, 1981; Spence & Helmreich, 1978, 1979, 1981). Androgynous individuals are defined as those who incorporate, or view themselves as incorporating, relatively high levels of both traditionally masculine and traditionally feminine traits in their self-descriptions of sex-typed characteristics. Those who incorporate a high degree of one sex role orientation and a low degree of the other are sex-typed, and those who incorporate a relatively low degree of both orientations are undifferentiated. (See Chapters 2 and 3 and Spence, 1985, for a more complete discussion of historical background and methodological/ measurement issues involved in this concept of sex roles.)

Bem (1974, 1975, 1977) and others (e.g., Spence, Helmreich, & Stapp, 1974) have argued that androgynous individuals should show better psychological adjustment than should sex-typed or undifferentiated individuals. These authors argue this should be the case because an androgynous sex role orientation allows the individual to exhibit greater behavioral flexibility—that is, the individual should be able to behave in a traditionally masculine or traditionally feminine manner in response to situational circumstances and demands. In contrast, sex-typed individuals are thought to be more limited in their response repertoire and, consequently, more prone to viewing the world through sex-typed lenses (Bem, 1981, 1985). As a result, the argument goes, their perceptions of their competencies will be more limited, resulting in a more limited view of the self.

According to this view, those with high masculinity and femininity scores (that is, the androgynous individuals) should evidence higher scores on adjustment measures than sex-typed or undifferentiated individuals. For example, they should have more positive self-concepts, lower anxiety scores, and the like. In addition, androgynous individuals should have fewer behavioral problems, such as problem drinking.

## The Masculinity Model

An alternative view of the relationship between sex roles and adjustment rests on both empirical findings and analysis of the nature of the culture in which we live. According to this view, it is high levels of masculinity, not a balance between high levels of both masculinity and femininity, that leads to greater psychological adjustment (cf. Kelly & Worell, 1977; Antill & Cunningham, 1979; Jones, Chernovetz, & Hansson, 1978). These investigators present evidence that masculinity scores from scales such as the Bem Sex Role Inventory (BSRI) and the Personality Attributes Questionnaire (PAQ) correlate more strongly with measures of adjustment than do the femininity scales from these inventories. They go on to suggest that this pattern of relationships is the result of the high value placed on instrumental, traditionally masculine traits, and the relatively low social desirability of traditionally feminine, expressive traits (cf. Broverman, Vogel, Broverman, Clarkson, & Rosenkrantz, 1972) in our culture.

According to this formulation, then, one should find that those persons whose sex role orientations indicate high levels of masculinity (viz. the androgynous and masculine individuals) should have higher adjustment scores than those with low masculinity scores (viz. the feminine and undifferentiated individuals). Individuals with high masculinity scores, then, should have higher self-concepts, lower anxiety levels, and fewer problem drinking patterns than whose with lower masculinity scores.

## RESEARCH FINDINGS

No thorough review of research findings will be presented because current reviews exist in readily available sources (Bassoff & Glass, 1982; Whitley, 1983). Following a discussion of the typical research design employed, we simply point out the findings of various meta-analyses conducted to determine the relationship between sex roles and adjustment.

### Typical Research Design

In the typical study assessing the relationship between sex roles and adjustment, subjects, most commonly college students, complete either the BSRI or the PAQ and some measure(s) of adjustment. Adjustment measures that have been employed include assessment of self-concept or self-esteem, anxiety, depression, introversion/extroversion, locus of control, neurosis, and problem drinking behavior. In most instances only a single measure of adjustment is employed, and that usually provides only a single score. In other words, most researchers seem to have designed their studies in a very limited manner. Moreover, it appears that they have done so with little regard for theoretical underpinnings that might aid in making the findings of the study of more than passing import. The relationship between the two types of measures is then assessed by dividing the subjects into the four familiar groups (androgynous, masculine, feminine, and undifferentiated) and doing an analysis of variance and/or employing the raw masculinity and femininity scores as predictors in a multiple regression analysis in order to assess the relative contributions of each to prediction of adjustment.

There are, of course, exceptions. Jones, Chernovetz, and Hansson (1978) employed multiple measures of adjustment, including problem drinking, locus of control, and measures of neurosis. Waterman and Whitbourne (1982), Della Selva and Dusek (1984), and Glazer and Dusek (1985) employed the Inventory of Psychosocial Development (IPD) to study the relation between sex typing and adjustment. The IPD, which is used to assess resolution of Erikson's (1959, 1963, 1968) developmental crises, provides multiple measures indicating adjustment in several spheres of development. On the other hand, Flaherty and Dusek (1980) and Ziegler, Dusek, and Carter (1984) employed a multidimensional measure of self-concept in their study of the association between sex roles and adjustment. By using multiple measures, or measures that provided more than a single index of adjustment, these researchers were able to demonstrate that the relationship between sex roles and adjustment might be more complex than relationships determined on the basis of a single measure. The use of single measures clearly is a shortcoming of research in this area, as is illustrated below.

A second feature of the vast majority of studies conducted to date is that, by and large, they are not based on theoretical underpinnings (cf. Della Selva & Dusek, 1984; Glazer & Dusek, 1985). As a result, the measures of adjustment chosen for use often appear to be picked in a whimsical manner or for convenience. Of course, this leads to difficulties in making theoretical sense out of the findings. It is one thing to obtain significant results but quite another to explain them. Selecting measures of adjustment on the basis of theoretical concerns would go far in aiding our interpretation of findings.

Finally, the vast majority of studies of the relationship between sex roles and adjustment include only a single age group. Because sex roles change, both as a function of development and as a result of changing social circumstances (see Chapters 2, 6, 10, and 12 in this volume), it is important to assess developmental facets of the relationship between sex roles and adjustment. The college student is not the typical child, adolescent, or adult.

## Meta-Analysis Results

Several meta-analyses of the findings of research on the relationship between sex roles and adjustment have been published (e.g., Whitley, 1983; Bassoff & Glass, 1982). Following a brief description of meta-analytic techniques, we review the conclusions of these meta-analyses.

*Meta-analysis.* Meta-analysis is a method of statistically combining the results of independent experiments for the purpose of integrating their findings (Glass, 1977; Rosenthal, 1978; Cooper, 1979). As opposed to the traditional literature review, which is literary in style, the meta-analysis is statistical in format. A meta-analysis is conducted on a group of studies having a common conceptual hypothesis or operational definition of independent or dependent variables. One result of a meta-analysis is a significance level that gives the probability that a set of studies exhibiting the reported results could have been generated if no real relationship existed. A second result of a meta-analysis is an estimate of effect size based on a metric common to all studies. The larger the effect size, the stronger the finding. Meta-analyses, then, have distinct advantages over traditional literary reviews.

*Findings of Meta-analyses.* As noted above, several meta-analyses (Whitley, 1983; Bassoff & Glass, 1982) have been reported for studies assessing the relationship between sex role orientation and adjustment. Whitley (1983) confined his review to studies in which self-concept or self-esteem were used to index adjustment. Bassoff and Glass (1982) confined their meta-analysis to studies in which adult samples were utilized and from which correlational statistics could be derived.

The general findings of the meta-analyses may be summarized as follows:

1. Masculinity is significantly related to measures of self-concept, self-esteem, and adjustment. Those who score high in masculinity, that is, those who may be characterized as androgynous or masculine in sex role orientation, tend toward higher self-concept, self-esteem, and adjustment than those who rate themselves lower in masculinity (viz., feminine and undifferentiated individuals).

2. Femininity is significantly related to measures of self-concept, self-esteem, and adjustment. Those who rate themselves higher in femininity, the androgynous and feminine individuals, also rate themselves higher in self-concept, self-esteem, and other measures of adjustment than do those who view themselves as less feminine.

3. In the few studies in which the influence of the interaction between masculinity and femininity has been reported (cf. Hall & Taylor, 1985; Whitley, 1983), it also has related to self-concept, self-esteem, and adjustment.

4. The effect size for masculinity is substantially greater than the effect size for femininity or the interaction between masculinity and femininity. Whitley (1983) reported effect sizes of 0.12, 0.01, and 0.009 for the masculinity, femininity, and interaction component, respectively, for a subset of studies in which all three were assessed. For the total group of studies reviewed, the effect sizes were 0.27 for masculinity and 0.03 for femininity.

More recent studies not included in these meta-analyses (e.g., Glazer & Dusek, 1985; Della Selva & Dusek, 1984; Waterman & Whitbourne, 1982) provide findings consistent with the above summary. It is reasonable, then, to conclude at this time that although both masculinity and femininity relate positively to various measures of adjustment, masculinity is the stronger predictor (cf. Whitley, 1983). Whether femininity and the interaction between masculinity and femininity are best considered poor or even irrelevant predicators is, however, another issue.

Of course, the most interesting, and perhaps the most important, question is why masculinity is a better predictor of self-concept, self-esteem, and other measures of adjustment. To shed some light on that issue we turn to an examination of theoretical and methodological issues, including the measures of adjustment that have been employed.

## METHODOLOGICAL AND THEORETICAL ISSUES

As noted above, research concerned with the relationship between sex roles and adjustment tends not to be based on theoretical premises. That is, in general, theories of adjustment are not the basis upon which investigators have formulated their hypotheses about the relationship between sex roles and adjustment. As a result, there is no coherent means of selecting measures of adjustment. In this section we note some of the problems encountered because of this state of affairs and we note some exceptions that offer promise. We also touch on some methodological and analytic issues.

### Self-concept and Self-esteem as Measures of Adjustment

The variety of measures of adjustment employed in research relating sex roles to adjustment is quite broad, as noted above. However, by far the most common measure employed has been some self-concept or self-esteem instrument. Two points need to be made about these measures.

First, virtually every self-concept or self-esteem measure employed produces a global self-concept score that then is related to sex role orientation. However, the fact is that to assume there is any such entity as an overall self-esteem score is fallacious (cf. Wylie, 1974, 1979). As Wylie notes, factor analysis leads clearly to the conclusion that self-esteem is multifaceted, and any attempt to construe it as a "global" construct is likely to result in fallacious findings.

The relevance of Wylie's assertion for the concerns of this chapter may be found in two sources. (1) Whitley (1983) reported that relationships between sex roles and self-esteem were higher for specific (e.g., social) as opposed to global measures. (2) Noting Wylie's exhortation, Flaherty and Dusek (1980) conducted a study employing the BSRI and a multidimensional measure of self-concept. They reported that masculinity related to Achievement/Leadership (the view of the self as a capable, intelligent, achieving individual; effect size, 0.53), femininity related to Congeniality/Sociability (the view of the self as enjoying and initiating social behaviors; effect size, 0.38), and *both* masculinity and femininity related to Adjustment, which reflects perceiving the self in a homeostatic balance with the environment. Although masculinity showed a stronger effect size (0.41), the effect size for femininity (0.22) was not insubstantial. Flaherty and Dusek suggested that the relationship between sex roles and self-concept may very well depend on the aspect of self-concept assessed.

This leads to the second point, namely, that self-concept measures may, by virtue of being heavily laden with items dealing with assertiveness, overlap with masculinity items on the BSRI and PAQ. Whitely (1983) and Bassoff and Glass (1982) have discussed this issue in depth. In conjunction with the findings of Flaherty and Dusek (1980), which demonstrate that self-concept scales containing items reminiscent of the expressive role relate strongly to femininity while those reminiscent of the instrumental role relate strongly to masculinity, it seems that self-concept scales may not be the most appropriate instruments for assessing the relationship between sex roles and adjustment. Most certainly this is the case for scales that produce a single global index of self-concept. As a number of researchers have noted, one's sex role is an integral part of one's self-concept. Given the theoretical, logical, and empirically demonstrated overlap in the two constructs, it seems wise to examine other means of assessing adjustment for purposes of examining the relationship between sex roles and adjustment.

## Development and Adjustment

Although a number of possibilities exist, one area from which a fruitful line of research may emerge is that of developmental psychology. Specifically, it appears that research based on Erikson's theory of development (1959, 1963, 1968) demonstrates that both masculinity and femininity are important to adjustment.

Erikson hypothesized that development progressed through a sequence of stages (Table 13.1), each of which is tied to a developmental period and each of which involves a "crisis" or coming to grips with some major aspect of development. Constantinople (1969; see also Waterman & Whitbourne, 1981) has developed a paper and pencil measure for the first six stages in Erikson's theory. Because of the nature of the theory, assessing development with the Inventory of Psychosocial Development (IPD) is appropriately considered to be assessing adjustment.

Waterman and Whitbourne (1982) had college students and adults complete the BSRI and the IPD. An analysis of covariance with repeated measures for the six IPD scores revealed that the androgynous subjects scored better than the sex-typed or undifferentiated subjects for the overall composite score. However, they reported no tests for the individual subscales (the individual measures for each of the six crises).

Della Selva and Dusek (1984) had college students complete the BSRI and the scales assessing resolution of the Industry vs. Inferiority and Identity vs. Identity Diffusion crises. They found that the androgynous subjects had the highest score (indicating most successful resolution) followed in order by the masculine, feminine, and undifferentiated subjects. In each instance, the difference in mean scores between any group and the group(s) below it was statistically significant.

Glazer and Dusek (1985) replicated the Della Selva and Dusek (1984) study, but included all scales on the IPD. The results of the study are shown in Table 13.1. As is evident, the androgynous subjects scored higher than the sex-typed subjects in four cases, the androgynous and masculine subjects scored higher than the others in one case, and in one case there were no significant differences between the four sex role groups.

The results from these three studies rather convincingly demonstrate the advantage of an androgynous sex role orientation with respect to an adjustment measure that is grounded in a theoretical base. Because one must have relatively high scores on both masculinity and femininity in order to have an androgynous sex role, the evidence clearly shows the importance of each dimension for adjustment.

Della Selva and Dusek (1984) and Glazer and Dusek (1985) went a step further, however, and assessed the effect strength for the masculinity and femininity components of sex roles. The results are shown in Table 13.2, in which effect size is averaged for the two studies. As is quite readily apparent, mas-

**Table 13.1**
**Mean Scores for Each Sex Role Classification on Each Dependent Variable**

| Measure | Sex Role Classification | | | | |
|---|---|---|---|---|---|
| | *And* | *Masc* | *Fem* | *Undiff* | *Newman-Keuls* |
| Trust (T) | 26.77 | 24.73 | 22.79 | 23.39 | A > M > F = U |
| Mistrust (M) | 12.47 | 14.21 | 14.67 | 14.59 | A < M = F = U |
| T − M | 14.30 | 10.52 | 7.99 | 8.80 | A > M = U > F |
| Autonomy (A) | 25.72 | 25.62 | 23.13 | 24.02 | A = M > F = U |
| Shame (S) | 17.42 | 17.17 | 17.43 | 16.85 | |
| A − S | 8.30 | 8.25 | 5.71 | 7.16 | |
| Initiative (I) | 30.34 | 28.10 | 26.01 | 24.70 | A > M > F = U |
| Guilt (G) | 15.27 | 15.52 | 17.01 | 15.85 | A = M < F = U |
| I − G | 15.08 | 12.58 | 8.99 | 7.85 | A > M > F = U |
| Industry (Ind) | 27.25 | 26.51 | 25.88 | 24.16 | A = M = F > U |
| Inferiority (Inf) | 16.73 | 16.10 | 16.55 | 18.05 | |
| Ind − Inf | 10.52 | 10.41 | 9.33 | 6.11 | A = M = F > U |
| Identity (Id) | 27.88 | 26.59 | 25.01 | 23.54 | A > M > F > U |
| Diffusion (D) | 17.86 | 18.92 | 17.93 | 18.69 | |
| Id − D | 10.02 | 7.68 | 7.08 | 4.85 | A > M = F > U |
| Intimacy (Int) | 28.94 | 26.45 | 26.95 | 24.89 | A > M = F > U |
| Isolation (Iso) | 13.19 | 14.70 | 13.91 | 14.87 | |
| Int − Iso | 15.75 | 11.89 | 13.04 | 10.02 | A > M = F > U |

*Source*: Glazer and Dusek (1985).

culinity has the stronger effect size, but the contributions of femininity, unlike the effect sizes reported for measures of self-concept and self-esteem, are nontrivial. It should be noted, too, that several of the crises Erikson describes are clearly instrumentally oriented—Autonomy vs. Shame and Doubt, Industry vs. Inferiority, and even Identity vs. Identity Diffusion contain a very strong instrumental component. As a result, one may well expect a larger effect size for the masculinity component. For the crisis most clearly expressive in nature (Intimacy vs. Isolation), the effect size for the femininity component is slightly stronger than the effect size for the masculinity component.

## The Nature of Adjustment

Although the line of research described immediately above is promising, it is only one possible approach to implementing a more systematic and meaningful endeavor with regard to research on the relationship between sex roles and adjustment. Other approaches certainly are possible and reasonable. It is likely, however, that in most, if not all, instances, we will find that masculinity is more strongly related to adjustment than is femininity.

One reason for this lies in the nature of the patristic social order in which we

**Table 13.2**
**Mean Effect Sizes for Masculinity and Femininity on Each IPD Scale**

| Measure | Masculinity | Femininity |
|---|---|---|
| Trust (T) | .91 | .26 |
| Mistrust (M) | .51 | .18 |
| T − M | .80 | .25 |
| Autonomy (A) | 1.03 | .26 |
| Shame (S) | .10 | .23 |
| A − S | .75 | .25 |
| Initiative (I) | 1.75 | .53 |
| Guilt (G) | .68 | .18 |
| I − G | 1.50 | .14 |
| Industry (Ind) | .86 | .43 |
| Inferiority (Inf) | .44 | .09 |
| Ind − Inf | .75 | .17 |
| Identity (Id) | 1.27 | .40 |
| Diffusion (D) | .17 | .16 |
| Id − D | .84 | .30 |
| Intimacy (Int) | .72 | .80 |
| Isolation (Iso) | .35 | .32 |
| Int − Iso | .65 | .67 |
| Mean Effect Size | .78 | .31 |

*Note:* effect sizes for Ind, Inf, Ind − Inf, Id, D and Id − D are derived from data from both Della Selva and Dusek (1984) and Glazer and Dusek (1985). The remaining effect sizes come from Glazer and Dusek (1985).

*Source:* Della Selva and Dusek (1984) and Glazer and Dusek (1985).

live. We value independence, achievement, and the like, all of which are traits traditionally associated with masculinity. Indeed, we define a well adjusted individual as one who possesses these traits. As Bassoff and Glass (1982) have noted, individuals who possess these traits may come to value themselves more than do individuals not perceiving themselves in these manners. As a result, the stronger effect size for the masculinity component may be artifactual.

A second important factor is that traditionally feminine traits are generally viewed as less socially desirable in our culture (cf. Bassoff & Glass, 1982). As a result, they are less likely to be viewed as demonstrating adjustment to the same degree as are masculine traits. Hence we may well expect that femininity scores from the BSRI and PAQ will relate less strongly to most measures of adjustment. Indeed, when reading various measures of adjustment one is struck by the degree to which answers indicating less optimal adjustment seem related to our traditional perspective of femininity.

## THE FUTURE

Historically, those who have studied the relationship between sex roles and adjustment have used an analysis of variance design in which the four sex role groups are compared. Although this is an appropriate and valuable analysis, it is incomplete. It answers only a single question: Do those classified into the four sex role categories differ on some empirical measure. The more important question seems to be the degree to which both masculinity and femininity relate to measures of adjustment (cf. Della Selva & Dusek, 1984; Glazer & Dusek, 1985; Spence, 1985). At the present time, this assessment is best done through the use of multiple regression analyses.

A number of authors (e.g., Hall & Taylor, 1985; Della Selva & Dusek, 1984) have pointed out that the multiple regression analysis, which utilizes all the available information in the masculinity and femininity scores, is a valuable means of looking at the question under consideration. Moreover, it is possible to examine the masculinity × femininity interaction without the disadvantages of using a median split procedure (Hall & Taylor, 1985). Only by examining the relative contributions of both masculinity and femininity will we be able to assess the degree to which an androgynous sex role orientation leads to greater psychological adjustment.

Future research also should employ either multiple measures of adjustment or measures that provide various subscores. Extant research in which this approach has been used (e.g., Jones et al., 1978; Della Selva & Dusek, 1984; Glazer & Dusek, 1985; Flaherty & Dusek, 1980) has revealed that differing relationships between sex role orientations (or masculinity and femininity) occur for differing dependent variables or subscores. Often these relate to broad cultural variations in valued traits (cf. Bassoff & Glass, 1982).

Future research also should be guided by theory with respect to the choice of dependent measures. The pertinent issues were noted above and have been developed in detail elsewhere (e.g., Della Selva & Dusek, 1984; Glazer & Dusek, 1985; Waterman & Whitbourne, 1982). The use of theories of adjustment, and particularly theories of development, can contribute substantially to the interpretation of research findings by placing those findings into a broader and more meaningful context.

Finally, future research should take a developmental perspective (cf. Ziegler, Dusek, & Carter, 1984). Sex role development is a developmental phenomenon. As a result, one may well expect to find developmental shifts in the relationship between adjustment and sex role orientation, in part because the latter changes with development (cf. Ziegler et al., 1984). To thoroughly and exactly define the relationship between sex roles and adjustment one must account for developmental shifts.

# REFERENCES

Antill, J. & Cunningham, J. (1979). Self-esteem as a function of masculinity in both sexes. *Journal of Consulting and Clinical Psychology, 47,* 783–785.

Bassoff, E. & Glass, G. (1982). The relationship between sex roles and mental health: A meta-analysis of twenty-six studies. *The Counseling Psychologist, 10,* 105–112.

Bem, S. (1974). The measurement of psychological androgyny. *Journal of Consulting and Clinical Psychology, 42,* 155–162.

Bem, S. (1975). Sex-role adaptability: One consequence of psychological androgyny. *Journal of Personality and Social Psychology, 31,*634–643.

Bem, S. (1977). On the utility of alternative procedures for assessing psychological androgyny. *Journal of Consulting and Clinical Psychology, 45,* 196–205.

Bem, S. (1979). The theory and measurement of androgyny: A reply to the Pedhazur-Tetenbaum and Locksley-Colten critiques. *Journal of Personality and Social Psychology, 37,* 1047–1054.

Bem, S. (1981). Gender schema theory: A cognitive account of sex typing. *Psychological Review, 88,* 354–364.

Bem, S. (1985). Androgyny and gender schema theory: A conceptual and empirical integration. In T. B. Sonderegger (Ed.), *Nebraska symposium on motivation* (Vol. 32). Lincoln: University of Nebraska Press.

Broverman, I. K., Vogel, S. R., Broverman, D. M., Clarkson, F. E., & Rosenkrantz, P. S. (1972). Sex-role stereotypes: A current appraisal. *Journal of Social Issues, 28,* 59–78.

Constantinople, A. (1969). An Eriksonian measure of personality development in college students. *Developmental Psychology, 1,* 357–372.

Cooper, H. (1979). Statistically combining independent studies: A meta-analysis of sex differences in conformity research. *Journal of Personality and Social Psychology, 37,* 131–146.

Della Selva, P. & Dusek, J. (1984). Sex role orientation and resolution of Eriksonian crises during the late adolescent years. *Journal of Personality and Social Psychology, 42,* 204–212.

Erikson, E. (1959). Identity and the life-cycle. *Psychological Issues, 1,* 1–71.

Erikson, E. (1963). *Childhood and society* (2nd ed.). New York: Norton.

Erikson, E. (1968). *Identity, youth and crisis.* New York: Norton.

Flaherty, J. & Dusek, J. (1980). An investigation of the relationship between psychological androgyny and components of self-concept. *Journal of Personality and Social Psychology, 38,* 984–992.

Glass, G. (1977). Integrating findings: The meta-analysis of research. In L. Schulman (Ed.), *Review of research in education.* Itasca, Ill: Peacock.

Glazer, C. & Dusek, J. (1985). The relationship between sex-role orientation and resolution of Eriksonian developmental crises. *Sex Roles, 13,* 653–661.

Hall, J. & Taylor, M. (1985). Psychological androgyny and the masculinity × femininity interaction. *Journal of Personality and Social Psychology, 49,* 429–435.

Jones, W., Chernovetz, M., & Hansson, R. (1978). The enigma of androgyny: Differential implications for males and females? *Journal of Consulting and Clinical Psychology, 46,* 298–313.

Kelly, J. & Worell, J. (1977). New formulations of sex roles and androgyny: A critical review. *Journal of Consulting and Clinical Psychology, 45,* 1101–1115.

Rosenthal, R. (1978). Combining results of independent studies. *Psychological Bulletin, 85,* 185–193.

Spence, J. (1985). Gender identity and its implications for the concepts of masculinity and femininity. In T. B. Sonderegger (Ed.), *Nebraska symposium on motivation* (Vol. 32). Lincoln: University of Nebraska Press.

Spence, J. & Helmreich, R. (1978). *Masculinity and femininity: Their psychological dimensions, correlates, and antecedents.* Austin: University of Texas Press.

Spence, J. & Helmreich, R. (1979). Comparison of masculine and feminine personality attributes and sex-role attitudes across age groups. *Developmental Psychology, 15,* 583–584.

Spence, J. & Helmreich, R. (1981). Androgyny vs. gender schema: A comment on Bem's gender schema theory. *Psychological Review, 88,* 365–368.

Spence, J. T., Helmreich, R. H. & Stapp, J. (1975). Ratings of self and peers on sex-role attributes and their relation to self-esteem and conceptions of masculinity and femininity. *Journal of Personality and Social Psychology, 32,* 29–39.

Waterman, A. & Whitbourne, S. (1981). The inventory of psychosocial development: A review and evaluation. *JSAS Catalog of Selected Documents in Psychology, 11,* 5 (Ms. No. 2179).

Waterman, A. & Whitbourne, S. (1982). Androgyny and psychosocial development among college students and adults. *Journal of Personality, 50,* 121–133.

Whitley, B. (1983). Sex role orientation and self-esteem: A critical meta-analytic review. *Journal of Personality and Social Psychology, 44,* 765–778.

Wylie, R. (1974). *The self-concept.* Vol. 1. Lincoln: University of Nebraska Press.

Wylie, R. (1979). *The self-concept.* Vol. 2. Lincoln: University of Nebraska Press.

Ziegler, C., Dusek, J., & Carter, D. B. (1984). Self-concept and sex-role orientation: An investigation of multidimensional aspects of personality development in adolescence. *Journal of Early Adolescence, 4,* 25–39.

# PART IV
# FUTURE DIRECTIONS FOR SEX ROLE RESEARCH

# 14

# Adolescence: Gateway to Gender-Role Transcendence
## Jacquelynne S. Eccles

As concern over traditional gender-role identity has increased, there has been a growth in alternative theoretical views, androgyny being the most prominent. Several models of androgyny and gender-role transcendence have been proposed (e.g., Bem, 1976, 1985; Pleck, 1975; Spence, Helmreich, & Stapp, 1975; Rebecca, Hefner, & Oleshansky, 1976a). These models assume that gender-role transcendence is more mature developmentally than is traditional gender-typed identity and role structure. In general, empirical evidence supports this value judgment. Adults endorsing both masculine and feminine personality traits as true of themselves are psychologically healthier than adults endorsing more gender-stereotyped personality traits (Bem, 1975, 1976; Spence & Helmreich, 1978). Similarly, women who both work and have a family have higher self-esteem than full-time homemakers (see Rabin, this volume). In our complex culture the costs of following traditional roles now appear to exceed the rewards of the traditional gender-role identity. Why? And under what conditions will an individual's identity continue to develop toward androgyny? This chapter addresses these questions.

In order to describe how gender-roles develop—let alone speculate about factors necessary to ensure optimal development—we must first review the function of traditional gender roles and discuss the interaction of the individual and society in the process of gender-role acquisition and change. This goal is accomplished in the first section. In the second section, relevant models of both social development and gender-role development are discussed. In the final section, the social–psychological perspective outlined in section 1 and the developmental perspectives outlined in section 2 are integrated into a model of gender-role development that focuses primarily on identifying characteristics of the developing individual and social environments that influence growth toward androgyny.

## TRADITIONAL GENDER ROLES

Gender roles are based on the assignment of duties according to theoretically different but complementary clusters of traits and interest patterns commonly labelled masculinity and femininity. The "masculine" cluster refers to several related traits and roles linked to what Bakan (1966) labelled "agency," i.e., an orientation toward oneself as an individual against the world, a concern with self-protection, self-assertion, and self-expansion, and what Parsons and Bales (1955) labelled *instrumental* competence. The essence of "femininity" has been described by Bakan as a "communal" orientation toward self, as being at one with the larger social organism, as an affective caring concern for others and for social relationships, and as an expressive sense of feeling and nurturance. Parsons and Bales (1955) equated this cluster with *expressive* competence.

Since both sets of characteristics are essential for survival of the "group," societies must ensure the availability of both. One solution to this need has been the separation and isolation of these characteristics and socialization of the associated values and goals resulting in traditional systems of gender differentiated role ascriptions. These ascriptions are based on the differences in the two realms that are assumed to be intrinsic to males and females and consequently to adapt them better to specific types of occupations and social roles. As a result of these assumptions, gender-role division is seen as both natural and functional (see Bem & Bem, 1970).

These beliefs are passed along as basic components of the indoctrination into society's system of role differentiation and assignment (Inkeles, 1968) so that they become "zero-order" beliefs (Bem & Bem, 1970). Since gender is among the most concrete and fundamental of social categories, children have little difficulty learning gender-role stereotypes as their social understanding develops (Huston, 1983). Furthermore, given that children are motivated to become socially competent (Kohlberg, 1969) and that both peers and adults around them model and reinforce gender-stereotyped behavior (Huston, 1983), they readily acquire the particular abilities and preferences associated with their own gender. And, finally, in seeking competence through social conformity, many people simply do not distinguish between the descriptive and prescriptive functions of gender-role stereotypes—the difference between the way things are and other ways they possibly could and perhaps should be.

This system has developed and been maintained for a variety of social, economic, and political reasons. Holter (1970) notes that as one of society's functional distributive systems, gender-roles imply a differentiation and specialization of particular tasks, which increases overall efficiency, provided that the specialized efforts are coordinated. On an individual level, knowing one's "abilities," responsibilities, and "place" on the basis of one's gender lends structure and security to that part of the personal identity based on gender. Examples of such division of labor are common and need not be elaborated here; in general, both the efficiency and security arguments are strong. A system in which one sex specializes in caring for the children and household while the other is responsible for supporting and maintaining the family unit makes more sense, in theory, than a system in which both sexes share equally in all tasks with less specialization and fewer clear-cut responsibilities. As a consequence, everyone knows their roles and can expect to mate with someone who shares a complementary view of their own role.

Difficulties arise when individuals grow up thinking that they *cannot* perform the other's tasks, or express both their instrumental and expressive abilities, but realize that they have both sets of abilities. At a societal level such a rigid system diminishes substitutability, increases status incongruities, and limits the number of situations in which members' talents and preferences are used to their fullest potential (Holter, 1970). But society can withstand these problems if its socialization processes are successful in filling all of its required role slots. On the individual level, however, the costs of limited potential, increased frustration due to poor fit with traditional role prescriptions, and restricted relations with others can well exceed the rewards of functional efficiency and simplified role patterns. And so it is at the individual level that we can expect pressure for change to emerge. It is the *individual* who will look for alternatives to the traditional system.

Some people eventually discover that they do not fit into the normative behavioral and attitudinal categories established for them. They reach a point of cognitive and ego development at which personal competence becomes separated from, and more important than, social acceptance. Self-schemas (Markus, 1977) may come to transcend gender-role defined identity and individuals may no longer rely on societal definitions of masculinity and femininity for evaluating their actions or those of others. While gender identity, the personal sense of what it means to be a man or a woman, will still be an important source of self-definition, gender *role* identity may not.

Of course, reaching this level calls for a very special person in a very special set of circumstances. "Special" here refers to the unique matching between both person and circumstance antecedent to gender-role transcendence. Many potential transcendents may never face a situation in which they feel restricted; that is, the restrictive environment may feel quite comfortable. The potential to change comes only when the person and the environment no longer match, reaching a state of "gender-role strain" (Garnets & Pleck, in press, p. 8). This condition of "strain" or crisis is necessary in establishing the potential for growth, in the sense that all human development is a process of resolving such crises, or restoring synchrony between the biological, social, and psychological aspects of a whole individual (Riegel, 1975).

The key issue in this regard, though, is that *not everyone resolves such crises* (if experiencing them at all) *in the same way*. Depending on the personal and situational variables leading up to the gender-role strain condition, one may indeed reject social limitations and seek personally chosen values or may resolve the crisis in a traditional social direction by falling back even more rigidly into the traditional role structure, becoming a "Total Woman" or a "Marathon Man." The outcome depends on both the person and the social situation. While a cultural shift away from gender-typing will encourage and validate gender-role transcendence in some, it may increase pressure and thus rigidify the traditional roles and traits in others. But regardless of the outcome, the resolution of the gender-role conflict is fundamentally an individual developmental matter. It is to these developmental processes that we now turn.

## INDIVIDUAL DEVELOPMENT

Development as conceptualized by Riegel (1975) progresses along four interdependent dimensions: (1) the inner-biological; (2) the individual–psychological; (3) the cultural–sociological; and (4) the outer-physical. The changing progression of events along each of these four dimensions is not always synchronized and the loss of synchrony at any time in an individual's life is assumed to result in conflict or crisis. Through the process of restoring the lost balance, the individual matures—is internally strengthened. Erikson (1968) described this concept of crisis not "as a threat of catastrophe, but a turning point, a crucial period of increased vulnerability and heightened potential, and therefore, the ontogenetic source of generational strength and maladjustment. . . . " (p. 96).

Thus development is assumed to proceed through a hierarchical series of crisis formations and resolutions. By attaining new levels of synchrony across the four dimensions and by successfully adapting to new contexts, individuals gradually broaden their repertoire of cognitive schemas and become increasingly capable of dealing with more complex situations. Exposure to more complex situations and to maturational and social changes, in turn, can produce new crises and new resolutions (see Higgins & Parsons, 1983). The nature and direction of this sequential hierarchy has been described in similar terms by different cognitive and ego stage theorists (e.g., Kohlberg, Erikson, and Loevinger). These theorists all describe a graduated, dialectical process of inner psychological growth, mediated by active individual/environment interaction, culminating in autonomous levels of functioning in which the individual integrates once conflicting and differentiated aspects of personality to satisfy self-realized needs. Furthermore, each of these theorists points to adolescence as a critical period in the formation and solidification of a post-conventional identity—an identity reflecting one's own goals and experiences rather than being based on socially prescribed roles. Because Erikson and Loevinger have so directly influenced thinking about identity development, we will discuss their work as well as reviewing the gender-role development theories derived from their perspective.

*Erikson.* Erikson (1968) conceptualizes development as a series of stages, each representing a crisis created by the individual's level of development and the socialization demands faced. Optimal growth depends on the successful resolution of each of these crises. Unsuccessful resolution can lead to stagnation and continuing functional preoccupation with that particular level. Important here is that this process reflects dialectical growth, in which the individual is able to incorporate factors of lower stages into current schemas, even while forming newly transcendent ones.

Erikson's stage of Identity vs. Role Confusion is particularly relevant for our understanding of gender-role development. During this stage the individual develops a stable self-schema that will guide subsequent role choices and goals. Central to this process is the individual's resolution of gender-role identity. To the extent that stereotyped gender-role definitions are incorporated into one's self-schema, one's identity will be stereotyped. To the extent that the individual does not rely on societal definitions of appropriate identities, the individual may move away from a stereotyped gender-role identity.

What is important to note about Erikson's model is the predicted crisis around identity formation and its timing. Erikson focuses on adolescence as the life period during which the opportunity for the development of the individual identity arises. He does not, however, specifically deal with the issue of gender-role transcendence and probably believed that the integration of society's gender-role definitions into one's identity was the healthy developmental course.

*Loevinger and Block.* Loevinger (1966, 1976) proposed a stage model of development characterized by an invariant hierarchical sequence of irreversible structural and qualitative change, marked by particular turning points or "milestones." Moving from milestone to milestone was assumed to be a dialectical process involving many interacting systems. Like Erikson, she points to adolescence as an important period for the movement away from a conforming ego identity toward a more individualized identity.

Block (1973) extrapolated from Loevinger's model to include a person's conceptions of gender role (see Table 14.1). Since we are primarily interested in adolescence and gender-role transcendence we will focus on Block's discussion of the passage from the Conformity to the Integrated stage. According to Block, conforming individuals are most concerned with accepting the ways of their social order first and understanding them later. Thus their behavior is influenced by the prescriptive function of gender-role stereotypes. At the conscientious level, the individual is more concerned with the growing differences between these traditional gender roles and changing sets of values. Block (1973) explains that at this level:

a self-conscious process of evaluating oneself relative to one's own internalized values and the prevailing expectations of the culture begins. Awareness of the deviance of one's own values from the societal values appears and both are examined critically.

This, I propose, is the beginning of the process of balancing agency and communion that will occupy the individual through the autonomous level as he

**Table 14.1**
**Extensions of Stage Models to Gender Role Development**

| Loevinger/Block | Pleck/Rebecca, Hefner & Oleshansky (1976) | Rebecca, Oleshansky, Hefner and Nordin | Ullian | Parsons and Bryan |
|---|---|---|---|---|
| *Pre-Social* | Undifferentiated gender role | Undifferentiated sex role | | Undifferentiated gender role |
| *Impulsive*<br>Development of gender identity, self-assertion, self-expression, self-interest | Gender-role polarization | Hyper-differentiated sex role<br>Stage IIA: Transitional Stage 1<br>Some sense of sex roles but no differential value attached; children are forced to comply with their knowledge of sex differences | Biological Orientation<br>Level I<br>Masculinity and femininity conceptualized in biological terms and seen as biologically based<br>Level II<br>Masculinity and femininity seen as separable from biology | Hyper-gender role differentiation |
| *Self-Protective*<br>Gender role as extension of self, self-enhancement | | | | |
| *Conformity*<br>Conformity to external role, development of sex role stereotypes, bifurcation of sex role | | Stage IIB<br>Children come to accept polarized differentially valued view of traditional sex roles; masculinity and femininity seen as mutually exclusive, polar opposites | Societal Orientation<br>Level I<br>Masculinity and femininity seen as inherent in social role and as essential for maintainance of social order | Gender role differentiation |

Table 14.1—*Continued*

| Loevinger/Block | Pleck/Rebecca, Hefner & Oleshansky (1976) | Rebecca, Oleshansky, Hefner and Nordin | Ullian | Parsons and Bryan |
|---|---|---|---|---|
| *Conscientious–conformity* Examination of self as sex role exemplar vis-à-vis internalized values | | | Level II Growing awareness of arbitrariness of social roles | Transition Phase I |
| *Individualistic* *Autonomous* Differentiation of sex role, coping with conflicting masculine/feminine parts of self | Transition to androgyny | Stage IIC Transitional Stage 2 Androgyny Individual moves away from rigid conceptualization of sex roles; masculinity and femininity, while still salient, are not seen as mutually exclusive prescriptive roles | Psychological Orientation Level I Masculinity and femininity, while not biologically based, are essential to mental health | Transition, Phase II |
| *Integrated* Achievement of individually defined sex role | Gender-role transcendence | Sex Role Transcendence Sex roles become irrelevant social categories | Level II Rejection of Level I and endorsement of personally defined identity | Gender-role transcendence |

*Source:* Compiled by the author.

231

attempts to cope with the competing demands and costs of agency and communion. This process will, for some individuals, ultimately eventuate in the integration of the two modalities in the highest developmental stage (p. 515).

The Autonomous stage, then, is a time of continuing attempts to resolve the questions, conflicts, and crises originated in the Conscientious period. The individual heads toward a resolution that can create the integrated morality of self-chosen values, which in terms of gender-role development involves the integration of one's masculine and feminine selves into a self-defined gender-role identity.

While stressing the importance of change, neither Erikson, Block, nor Loevinger were very specific about the nature of these transitions, what takes place during them, and why. In general, stage theories of social development present a logical sequence of stages that are assumed to emerge in a sociocultural vacuum. That is, they are an idealized sequence. Little attention is given to sociocultural effects on the sequencing and on the final stage of development each individual reaches. Given that adolescence takes place in a highly charged sociocultural milieu, the extension of these models to the development of gender-role identity needs to be evaluated very carefully.

The potential importance of adolescence as a gateway to gender-role transcendence is made even more salient if one assesses it within the context of Riegel's dialectical model. Viewed from this crisis resolution model, adolescence has to be seen as a period in which the simultaneous changes occurring in all levels create a stage with great potential for rapid growth. On the inner-biological level, adolescence begins with the first glimmers of puberty. Among the many other rapid physiological changes of this period, the appearance of secondary sex characteristics and the maturation of the primary sex organs transform the young adolescent into a fully sexual being. It is in adolescence that the capacity to engage in sexual intercourse emerges most dramatically to influence thoughts and to direct purposive behaviors (Sorenson, 1973). As with other aspects of growth, the development of sexuality is a many-faceted jewel, each side a different perspective, a different way of looking at the matter. With sexuality, strong and distinct conflicts between viewpoints produce some of the greatest ambivalences in the emerging adult.

On the individual–psychological level, sexuality becomes a social and moral conflict between what is proper and improper for the expression of these powerful biological drives and what constitutes meaningful, honest human relationships. Synchrony often is lost as persons may become physically mature before becoming emotionally capable of handling related psychological issues. In gradually resolving this crisis, adolescents strive toward a renewed balance between their sexual desires, their need to establish personal relationships, and their moral principles. In this process, they may accommodate the social ascriptions of others and turn strongly to their peer group both to obtain and to evaluate norms. In seeking a personally autonomous viewpoint they don't disregard the morality of their parents so much as deem that morality less relevant to a world in which their parents are no longer central. Peers may become the more important, more compelling, and more "real" influence in the building of an individual adaptive schema (Kohlberg & Gilligan, 1971; Matteson, 1975).

Adolescent adaptation in the context of sexuality expands beyond peer group society into the perceived cultural milieu. Adolescents are concerned with shaping their rapidly developing identity into a socially acceptable role. On the sociocultural level, then, gender role surfaces as a major determinant of acceptability during this period. The influence of gender role on lifestyle includes beliefs about how one "should" walk, talk, eat, dress, laugh, cry, compete, work, shake hands . . . and even think, judged according to adolescent conceptions of what is "appropriate" for a man or a woman. For the adolescent, placing one's sense of a physical male or female body into what is perceived as a socially acceptable package is what developing gender-role identity is all about. That society's ideal of masculine and feminine traits may not apply to what the individual ultimately wishes to make of him/herself is a discovery that may or may not come with further maturation and identity development.

Extending the dialectic interpretation, all the many sides of the adolescent's evolving identity are shaped by the sociocultural context, and the importance of these sociocultural factors has been well noted. Studies of political socialization have shown that major transgenerational shifts in political attitude change come about when adolescents are placed in a sociocultural environment that confronts them with new beliefs and provides normative support for attitude change (Sears, 1969). Thus it is clear that the sociocultural milieu in which adolescent growth takes place will influence directly the course of that development.

At a still higher level, the sociocultural milieu of adolescence also has an indirect long-range impact on development. Our complex society places heavy consequences on the wide variety of choices adolescents must make about their lives. Significant choices have to be made, choices that will lay out the direction of one's future life. Adolescents must make their choices regarding marriage, career, a moral code, and perhaps a political ideology, all of which help form their adult social cohort. And because these decisions indirectly influence an individual's adult sociocultural milieu, life choices and new attitudes tend to become permanent throughout the adult years (Newcombe 1967; Rogers, 1972). All in all then, the dialectical products of adolescence are decisive in forming and shaping the adult-to-be and in providing the impetus to growth beyond the level of conformity.

## DEVELOPMENT OF GENDER-ROLE TRANSCENDENCE

As we have seen, the theoretical similarities between the cognitive- and ego-developmental approaches to adolescent growth and psychological maturity are quite striking. Each has presented a model of development that characterizes the individual as moving from a pre-adolescent orientation of avoiding punishment and gratifying impulses as the basic criteria of morality, through a rigid conformity to and defense of perceived societal norms, through a questioning period of ambivalence and conflict between once-accepted norms and new self-evolved beliefs, to an integrated level of resolution, identity, and self-accepted moral principles.

Several psychologists have noted that these general processes should influence gender-role development and that androgyny or gender-role transcendence is a more mature developmental end point than acceptance of traditional gender roles (Block, 1973; Parsons & Bryant, 1978; Pleck, 1975; Rebecca, et al., 1976a; Rebecca, Oleshansky, Hefner, & Nordin, 1976b; Ullian, 1976). Empirical data have supported the utility of an extension of a cognitive–developmental model to the development of gender-role identity. For example, Block (1973) has shown that greater ego maturity as measured by Loevinger's sentence completion index is related to more androgynous, less gender-role-stereotyped definitions of the self, especially in males. Similar results were reported by Haan, Smith, and Block (1968) in a study relating college students' Q-sort descriptions of their personalities to their level of moral reasoning. Students judged to be at the conventional level of moral reasoning chose adjectives stressing conformity to the social order, that is, gender-role-consistent adjectives. In contrast, post-conventional males endorsed more communal, but fewer agenic, self-descriptions. Similarly, post-conventional females endorsed more agenic characteristics, although not fewer communal adjectives.

Several individuals have proposed new sequential models of gender-role development, based either on the stage models of cognitive and ego development or on a more intuitive description of changing developmental tasks over the lifespan (e.g., Block, 1973; Huston, 1983; Parsons & Bryant, 1978; Pleck, 1975; Rebecca and her associates, 1976a, 1976b, 1978; Ullian, 1976). All point to adolescence as an important period of gender-role development. But few have explicitly dealt with the social forces that either facilitate or retard development toward gender-role transcendence. But as is the case with the models from which they grew, these extensions both have understated the importance of the vast array of sociocultural forces that are impinging on the adolescent and have not dealt sufficiently with the period of transition and the forces that must be present to ensure "successful" development to a "higher" stage.

Cognitive- and ego-developmental stage theories describe the optimal pattern for development. Cognitive maturational changes may be necessary for the emergence of an androgynous gender role identity, but are they sufficient? A dialectical analysis suggests not. Growth and development depend on several factors: maturational change being only one. While one's cognitive maturity may make gender-role transcendence a possibility, cognitive growth on the content level depends on the availability of "discrepant" input that would lead to accommodation of existing stereotypic schemas. In addition, behavioral rewards and punishments must be such that gender-role transcendence is a better alternative for the adolescent than gender-role conformity. If gender-role transcendence does not offer an attractive alternative, or if the adolescent sees no conflict between his/her own abilities and goals and the behaviors and goals perceived by a stereotypic gender role, or if the stereotypic gender role is not important to the individual, then no conflict will occur and growth will be delayed. Again, sociocultural factors influence the likelihood of each of these events. As such, they must be key factors in one's development toward gender-role transcendence. Given both the theoretical arguments presented above and the supporting empirical evidence, it is surprising that more attention has not been given to the issue of transition from a conventional gender-role identity to gender-role transcendence, and to sociocultural factors that influence transition. It is to these issues that the final two models are addressed.

*Rebecca, Oleshansky, Hefner, and Nordin* (1976). Building on the three stage model (undifferentiated, polarized, and androgynous) of gender-role development proposed by Pleck (1975), Rebecca and her colleagues (1976a, 1976b) outlined a more detailed sequence of development that both added an additional fourth stage to the sequence (gender-role transcendence) and divided the second or middle gender-role polarized phase into three subperiods: a transitional period in which gender-role schemas are not yet rigid cognitive structures motivating behavioral compliance; a solidified period in which gender-role schemas have become rigid standards for self-evaluation; and a second transitional period in which gender-role schemas lose their prescriptive function, allowing the individual greater behavioral latitude.

Rebecca et al. (1976a) argued that development will not necessarily reflect a linear progression from undifferentiated to differentiated to undifferentiated and pointed out the importance of the social milieu in determining changes in the rigidity of one's gender-role schemas. Furthermore, they noted the importance of the early adolescent subculture in producing an increase in the rigidity of the gender-role schemas. Their emphasis on the role of social forces in interaction with individual development provides one of the first clear articulations of the processes that may accelerate or impede gender-role development.

*Parsons and Bryant* (1978). Building on the work discussed thus far and on work in social psychology stressing the importance of the social context both as a precursor of change and as the environmental factor that supports change once it has occurred, we proposed a model of gender-role development that focuses on adolescence as an important developmental "window" and on the social forces that will influence change during this period and later in life.

Our model is built on the following assumptions:

1. Growth is multipli-determined and is based on a conflict between the various internal and external forces impinging on an individual across the lifespan (cf. Riegel, 1975).

2. Adolescence is a period in which the following three forces are almost always in conflict: biological (both cognitive and sexual maturational), psychological (emotional and moral), and sociocultural. In addition, it is a time when cognitive development has proceeded far enough that the individual is able and motivated to imagine alternative social orders and when shifts in one's subculture are likely to increase one's

sensitivity to the arbitrariness of social rules (Higgins & Parsons, 1983). Finally, it is also a period in which adult roles are still being chosen and one's future life is still flexible. Consequently, it is likely to be one period well suited for the development of gender-role transcendence.

3. The relationship between sociocultural milieu and development is interactive. That is, while the sociocultural milieu influences development, one's development also influences the sociocultural milieu to which one is exposed. As a consequence, large scale change can be produced by and, in many cases may depend on, externally-induced political–historical changes. These changes may alter the individual's immediate sociocultural milieu in a way that initiates conflict between the milieu and the individual's psychological frame (or in this case one's gender-role identity).

4. Because so many forces influence development, the surface manifestations of growth will be irregular. For example, with the potential for change comes the potential for regression to early modes of thought (Mehrabian, 1968). Therefore, the very same forces that can induce growth—expanding one's peer group to include both sexes, for example—can initially induce anxiety and regression to well practiced, less sophisticated schemas.

5. Growth depends on a sociocultural milieu that provides both the basis for conflict to emerge and the supports for growth to a higher level of development.

6. The potential for growth, once it has emerged, continues to be present despite apparent rigidification of the system. That is, growth potential, while optimal in adolescence, is not lost once one enters adulthood. Continued adult development is inhibited more by the rigidity of the social roles in which one finds oneself than by the passage to another developmental stage. Consequently, major shifts in adult social roles can be expected to have an impact on gender-role identity comparable to the impact of adolescence (see Sinnott, this volume). The outcome of these crises will depend on the individual's sociocultural milieu at the time of each crisis.

7. Growth toward gender-role transcendence depends on the following psychological shifts:

   a) The differentiation of gender identity from gender-role identity so that one's confidence in one's gender identity is not tied to the adherence to the culturally prescribed gender-role;

   b) The differentiation of the descriptive and prescriptive functions of stereotypes;

   c) The questioning of the validity of prescriptive functions of stereotypes for both the individual and for society at large;

   d) The reduction of gender-role salience as a defining property of one's ego identity and of one's evaluative system for others.

Based on these assumptions, we propose the following sequence as one possible developmental course toward gender-role transcendence. It is important to note that we are not proposing this as a stage model of development. Given the dialectical view outlined above, we believe that gender-role development will be an individual process driven by both cognitive maturation and social experience. The sequence outlined below reflects a probabilistic assessment of the likely sequence of events in this culture for an average, white, middle-class child growing up in a fairly traditional family and neighborhood.

*Step I: Undifferentiated gender roles* (0–2.5 years). The child is unaware of gender as a social category and has not learned or developed gender-role stereotypes.

*Step II: Hyper-gender-role differentiation* (3–7 years). Gender becomes a social category. Rigid stereotyping of activities, dress, social roles, and some personal characteristics such as strength and power emerge. Gender schemas emerge and begin to shape information storage and retrieval as well as preferences for gender-stereotyped activities and toys (Carter & Levy, 1987; Martin & Halverson, 1981). Gender-role conceptualizations are seen as both descriptive and prescriptive and the distinction between gender identity and gender-role identity is not clear. But, because preschoolers do not integrate their cognitive beliefs with their behavior, sex differences in behavior will not be as great as one would expect based on the rigidity and prescriptive nature of their gender-role conceptualizations.

*Step III: Gender-role differentiation* (7–11 years). Cognitive maturation has laid the groundwork for the differentiation of gender identity from gender-role identity. The child is now capable of separating external manifestations and changes from stable internal constructs such as gender identity. Consequently, the child comes to realize that girls and boys can do many different things without altering their gender and that gender-role norms are flexible social rules (Carter & Patterson, 1982; Carter & Taylor, in press). But the emergence of conventional moral thought and a growing awareness of social roles and potential censure by one's peers leads the child to maintain beliefs in the prescriptive nature of stereotypes (Carter & McCloskey, 1983/1984; Ullian, 1976). For boys, this belief is reinforced not only by others' reactions to feminine gender-stereotyped behavior but also by the cultural value structure. Boys' stereotypic behaviors are both more fun and more prestigious. For girls, however, adherence to the female stereotype is neither as fun nor as prestigious and "inappropriate" gender-role behavior is less likely to be punished. Consequently, conflict is created for girls and the sociocultural environment is supportive of alternative behavioral solutions. Girls should then begin questioning the prescriptive nature of gender roles during this period and may begin to move toward androgyny.

*Step IV: Transition phase I* (12–14 years). Cognitive maturation has now opened the possibility of considering new social orders and of distinguishing between the descriptive and prescriptive functions of gender-role stereotypes. Major sociocultural and physiological changes are also taking place. The child is expected to become a sexual being and to begin relating to members of the opposite sex. The basis for social approval and popularity shifts from acceptance from same-sex peer groups to acceptance by both-sex peer groups. To the extent that self-esteem becomes tied to this newly emerging social system, an identity crisis will be induced by the need to acquire rapidly the behaviors necessary for acceptance by the other sex. Given the absence of clear models of behavioral alternatives, the lack of sophistication of the peer group, and the perceived link of social acceptance to traditional gender roles, early adolescents may well "regress" to gender-role conceptualizations they had formed during Step II and III. Thus, despite the cognitive capacity to transcend the prescriptive function of stereotype, sociocultural forces may produce a rigidification of stereotypes and a reemergence of a confusion between gender identity and gender-role identity. This process should be especially evident in adolescents who place great importance on social success with other-sex peers. Since many females perceive their primary role in life to be that of wife and mother, gender-role salience is likely to be high. And we may expect to find some females specifically rejecting those aspects of their behavior that are linked to more traditional male achievement domains.

*Step IV: Transition phase II* (15–18 years). Some adolescents have established a more stable place in their peer culture and should have worked through some of the conflicts generated in Step III. The need to solidify life plans introduces the potential for a careful examination of who one "is" and a rethinking of one's identity. Since the necessary cognitive structures are available and social roles are still quite flexible, adolescence marks the prime opportunity for gender-role transcendence. If the sociocultural milieu provides the necessary stimuli, adolescents can transcend gender roles as one aspect of the resolution of their identity crisis. While the potential for transcendence remains with the individual throughout life, adult social roles selected on the basis of gender-role differentiation at this period can effectively obstruct this developmental path for extended periods of time. For example, Marini (1985) has shown that heavy dating, marriage, or parenting at this age delays females' post high school education and entry into the labor market.

But what are the appropriate sociocultural stimuli and rewards? Role modeling literature suggests the importance of androgynous role models (Eccles & Hoffman, 1984). Piagetian theory suggests discrepant information that leads to the accommodation of stereotypic schemas (see Newcombe, 1967). Behavioristic theory and attitude change studies suggest the importance of a supportive social environment. Thus, we predict that adolescents who are exposed to androgynous models, who are forced to think about the relevance of gender role for their life decisions, and who live in an "egalitarian" environment are likely to grow toward gender-role transcendence. Adolescents in more traditional environments with limited exposure to "egalitarian" ideas of androgynous role models will probably continue to base their behavior and their judgments of others on the gender-role stereotypes of our society.

*Stage V: Identity and gender-role transcendence.* The ambivalences and crises of Step IV have been resolved into an integration of masculinity and femininity that transcends traditional gender roles. The individual is characterized by postconventional, self-principled thought and action. This stage essentially coincides with Stage III in the Rebecca et al. model.

As should be apparent, our model is most similar to the model of Rebecca et al. It differs primarily in the elaboration of early development, in our suggestion of at least two periods of hyper-rigidity of gender-role schemas in self identity, and in our focus on the identification of the social and individual factors that impinge on development.

## SUMMARY

The model of gender role development presented here represents a synthesis of the theories and findings that work around, but not specifically with, our topic. In approaching this model we have integrated aspects from several approaches into a dialectical model of developmental change that draws heavily from existing social development theories. Consistent with several contemporary views of gender roles, we have assumed that gender-role transcendence is a "higher" level of development than gender-role adherence. By adherence we mean something akin to models of gender schemas, in that adherence is defined by the use of gender-role schemas to process information, evaluate the actions of others, and guide one's own preferences, choices, and behaviors. By transcendence we mean movement away from each of these forms of schematic processing. Like Spence and Sawin (1985), we do not mean the absence of gender identity. Nor do we mean ignorance of the cultural norms or the descriptive nature of gender-role stereotypes. Instead, we mean a conscious awareness of the arbitrariness of these norms and stereotypes and a reduction in their salience as guides for self-development and evaluation of others. It seems likely that development will proceed at different speeds for these various components of gender-role schemas and that, although growing awareness of the arbitrariness of gender-role prescriptions may be necessary for the development of a gender-role transcendent schema for oneself, it will not be sufficient. Nor will it be sufficient for the development of gender-role transcendent schemas for evaluating others.

The theories and research we have reviewed regarding adolescent development and gender roles are ambitious and encouraging, but are by no means conclusive. Most of the available empirical work is focused on the early years of development. We have relatively few data about the adolescent period and about the kinds of social structures that either facilitate or retard development toward gender role transcendence. Consequently, few of the hypotheses generated in this chapter can now be evaluated. It is our hope that future research will be directed toward the investigation of gender schemas and gender-role transcendence during adolescence in order to explore the predictions made by our model.

## REFERENCES

Bakan, D. (1969). *The duality of human existence*. Chicago: Rand McNally.

Bem, S. (1975). Sex-role adaptability: One consequence of psychological androgyny. *Journal of Personality and Social Psychology, 31,* 512–526.

Bem, S. (1976). Probing the promise of androgyny. In A. Kaplan & P. Bean (Eds.), *Beyond sex-role stereotypes: Readings towards a psychology of androgyny* (pp. 48–61). Boston: Little, Brown.

Bem, S. L. (1985). Androgyny and gender schema theory: A conceptual and empirical integration. In T. B. Sonderegger (Ed.), *Nebraska Symposium on Motivation 1984: Psychology and gender* (pp. 179–226). Lincoln, NE: University of Nebraska Press.

Bem, S. L. & Bem, D. J. (1970). Case study of a nonconscious ideology: Training the woman to know her place. In D. J. Bem (Ed.), *Beliefs, attitudes, and human affairs*. Belmont, CA: Brooks-Cole.

Block, J. H. (1973). Conceptions of sex-roles: Some cross-cultural and longitudinal perspectives. *American Psychologist, 28,* 512–526.

Carter, D. B. & Levy, G. D. (In press). Cognitive aspects of early sex-role development: The influence of gender schemas on preschoolers' memories and preferences for sex-typed toys and activities. *Child Development*.

Carter, D. B. & McCloskey, L. A. (1983/1984). Peers and the maintenance of sex-typed behavior: The development of children's conceptions of cross-gender behavior in their peers. *Social Cognition, 2,* 294–314.

Carter, D. B. & Patterson, C. J. (1982). Sex-roles as social conventions: The development of children's conceptions of sex-role stereotypes. *Developmental Psychology, 18,* 812–824.

Carter, D. B. & Taylor, R. D. (In press). The development of children's awareness and understanding of flexibility in sex-role stereotypes: Implications for preferences, attitudes, and behavior. *Sex Roles*.

Eccles, J. & Hoffman, L. W. (1984). Sex roles, socialization, and occupational behavior. In H. W. Stevenson & A. E. Siegel (Eds.), *Research in child development and social policy* (Vol. 1). Chicago: University of Chicago Press.

Erikson, E. (1968). *Identity: Youth and crisis*. New York: Norton.

Garnets, L. & Pleck, J. (In press). Sex role identity, androgyny, and sex-role transcendence: A sex-role strain analysis. *Psychology of Women Quarterly*.

Haan, N., Smith, M. B., & Block, J. H. (1968). Moral reasoning of young adults: Political–social behavior, family background, and personality correlates. *Journal of Personality and Social Psychology, 10,* 183–201.

Higgins, E. T. & Parsons, J. E. (1983). Social cognition and the social life of the child: Stages as subcultures. In E. T. Higgins, D. Ruble, & W. W. Hartup (Eds.), *Social cognition and social behavior: Developmental issues*. New York: Cambridge University Press.

Holter, H. (1970). *Sex roles and social structure*. Oslo, Norway: Westholmes Boktrykkeri.

Huston, A. C. (1983). Sex-typing. In P. H. Mussen & E. M. Hetherington (Eds.), *Handbook of child psychology* (Vol. 4) (pp. 387–467). New York: Wiley.

Inkeles, A. (1968). Society, social structure, and child socialization. In J. Clausen (Ed.), *Socialization and society*. Boston: Little, Brown.

Kohlberg, L. (1969). Stage and sequence: The cognitive-developmental approach to socialization. In D. A. Goslin (Ed.), *Handbook of socialization research* (pp. 347–480). Chicago: Rand McNally.

Kohlberg, L. & Gilligan, C. (1971). The adolescent as philosopher: The discovery of the self in a post-conventional world. *Daedalus, 100,* 1051–1086.

Loevinger, J. (1966). The meaning and measurement of ego development. *American Psychologist, 21,* 195–206.

Loevinger, J. (1976). *Ego development: Conceptions and theories*. San Francisco: Jossey-Bass.

Marini, M. M. (1985). Determinants of adult role entry. *Social Science Research, 14*, 309–350.

Markus, H. (1977). Self-schemata and processing information about the self. *Journal of Personality and Social Psychology, 35*, 63–78.

Martin, C. L. & Halverson, C. F. (1981). A schematic processing model of sex-typing and stereotyping in children. *Child Development, 52*, 1119–1134.

Matteson, D. R. (1975). *Adolescence today: Sex roles and the search for identity.* Homewood, IL: Dorsey.

Mehrabian, A. (1968). *Analysis of personality theories.* New York: Wiley.

Newcombe, T. M. (1967). *Persistence and change: Bennington College and its students after 25 years.* New York: Wiley.

Parsons, T. & Bales, R. (1955). *Family, socialization and interaction process.* New York: Free Press.

Parsons, J. E. & Bryant, J. (1978). Adolescence: Gateway to androgyny. *Michigan Occasional Paper*, No. VIII.

Pleck, J. H. (1975). Masculinity–femininity: Current and alternative paradigms. *Sex Roles, 1*, 161–178.

Rebecca, M. (1978). Sex-role development across the lifespan. Paper presented at the annual meetings of the Orthopsychiatry Society, San Francisco.

Rebecca, M., Hefner, R., & Oleshansky, B. (1976a). A model of sex-role transcendence. *Journal of Social Issues, 32*, 197–206.

Rebecca, M., Oleshansky, B., Hefner, R., & Nordin, V. D. (1976b). Polarized sex roles as a model of the process of sex discrimination; Transcending sex roles as a model of the future. Final report of Phase II, Contract #NIE-C-74–0144.

Riegel, K. F. (1975). From traits and equilibrium toward developmental dialectics. In J. K. Coles & W. J. Arnold (Eds.), *Nebraska Symposium on Motivation, 1974–1975.* Lincoln: University of Nebraska Press.

Rogers, D. Persistence of personality traits. In D. Rogers (Ed.), *Issues in adolescent psychology* (pp. 46–62). New York: Appleton, Century, Crofts.

Sears, D. O. (1969). Political behavior. In G. Lindzey & E. Aronson (Eds.), *Handbook of social psychology* (Vol. 5). Reading, MA: Addison-Wesley.

Sorenson, R. (1973). *Adolescent sexuality in contemporary America.* New York: World.

Spence, J. T. & Helmreich, R. (1978). *Masculinity and femininity: Their psychological dimensions, correlates, and antecedents.* Austin: University of Texas Press.

Spence, J. T., Helmreich, R. L., & Stapp, J. (1975). Ratings of self and peers on sex-role attributes and their relation to self-esteem and conception of masculinity and femininity. *Journal of Personality and Social Psychology, 32*, 29–39.

Spence, J. T. & Sawin, L. L. (1985). Images of masculinity and femininity: A reconceptualization. In V. E. O'Leary, R. K. Unger, & B. S. Wallston (Eds.), *Women, gender, and social psychology* (pp. 35–66). Hillsdale, NJ: Lawrence Erlbaum Associates.

Ullian, D. Z. (1976). The development of conceptions of masculinity and femininity. In B. Lloyd & J. Archer (Eds.), *Exploring sex differences.* New York: Academic Press.

# 15
# Sex Role Research and the Future: New Directions for Research
## D. Bruce Carter

Research and theory in the area of sex differences, sex roles, and sex typing have occupied the efforts of large numbers of psychologists and other social scientists for a number of years. The fact that this area has attracted such attention is illustrated nowhere more clearly than in the chapters included in this volume and the material reviewed therein. Gender and sex role norms clearly have a significant impact on the behavior and attitudes of children and adults, and while this impact is manifested in a variety of ways across the lifespan and across different components of our lives, there are certain consistencies in the data on the roles these factors play that are illustrative of their pervasiveness. It is clear, for example, that gender has a strong effect on the nature of interpersonal interactions in a variety of settings and at all ages (e.g., McCloskey, this volume). It is equally clear that cognitive constructions of gender (i.e., gender schemas) exert a powerful influence on the processing of gender-relevant information among both children (e.g., Martin & Halverson, this volume) and adults (e.g., Bem, 1985). What is also apparent in the discussions of virtually all of the authors in this volume as well as other writers, however, is the general level of dissatisfaction with gaps in the empirical literature and the inadequacies of many of the popular theories to fill those gaps (cf. Roopnarine & Mounts, this volume). Historically, such dissatisfactions have led to a reintegration of theory and a rejuvenation of the field; such steps may be necessary today as indicated by Eccles' chapter in this volume. In order to understand more fully the directions that our field may need to take, it may help to briefly review where the field has been. It is to this historical perspective that we will now turn our attention.

## HISTORICAL TRENDS IN SEX-TYPING RESEARCH

Much research in the area of sex roles and sex typing seems to fall into discrete categories that are marked by the rise and fall of certain theoretical themes or paradigms. During the early part of our field's existence (pre-1965) the major controversies appear to have centered around manifestations of sex differences that were presumed to be either innate/biological or the result of the imposition of cultural norms for sex-typed behavior. Erikson's (1963) discussions of innate differences in children's construction of play scenes and Mead's (e.g., 1949/1977) discussions of vast cultural differences in men's and women's roles are representative of the extremes of this continuum. In many ways, these extremes paralleled the similar ''nature/nurture'' dichotomy extant in other realms of psychology (e.g., child development research; Sears, 1975). The underlying assumption in those days was that traditional sex typing was a desirable phenomenon and that violations of sex role norms were aberrations to be discouraged in children and extinguished in adults. Indeed, a similar view continues to persist among many Americans even today, despite the fact that most (although not all) recognize both the benefits and the limitations imposed by sex typing.

Publication of two major books on sex roles and sex typing, separated by nearly a decade, mark a period of dramatic change in the ways in which psychologists and other social scientists viewed sex-typing phenomena. In 1966, Eleanor Maccoby published her first integrative volume on this topic entitled *The Development of Sex Differences* (Maccoby, Ed., 1966); in 1974, she and Carol Jacklin published a second volume, titled *The Psychology of Sex Differences* (Maccoby & Jacklin, 1974). Several similarities and differences between these two volumes are indicative of the changes undergone by the field during the eight year interlude between their respective publications. The similarities between the volumes are obvious. Each volume is a compendium of research on the outcomes of the sex role socialization process. Both volumes present theoretical integrations of the literature collected to that date. And both volumes mark a pivotal turning point in the direction that subsequent research on sex typing and sex roles was to take. There are also obvious differences between the two books. The 1966 book contained representative presentations of theory by persons acknowledged to be advocates of their positions; the 1974 book offers a theoretical integration by the authors. Anthropological and biological perspectives are separately represented in the 1966 book but are homogenized in the 1974 edition due to the integrative approach to the data taken by Maccoby and Jacklin. Yet, the subtle differences between the books are perhaps more illustrative of the changes that both the field and society had undergone in this period. To examine these differences, we must first examine the two volumes and their contents.

Maccoby's (1966) book offered an opportunity for theorists representing different perspectives to present their views. In many ways, these presentations were the first contemporary articulations of these theoretical views as they affected sex role development in particular. Of special interest for the current discussion were the presentations by Mischel (1966) and Kohlberg (1966), each of whom proposed explanations for sex-typing phenomena that continue to influence researchers today. Kohlberg's formulation relied heavily on Piagetian notions of cognitive development, the roles of self-evaluations and cognitive consistency strivings, and children's active participation in their own sex role socialization. Mischel's discussion focused on reinforcement, punishment, and modelling, and in many ways offered a standard, although somewhat more cognitive, social learning interpretation of sex typing (see Roopnarine & Mounts, this volume, for a more extensive treatment of these theories). The focus in both chapters was on the careful explanation of both the inevitable adherence to sex role norms and the origins of the "deviance" of persons who violated those norms. Both chapters also tie together the concepts of masculine/feminine behaviors, masculinity and femininity as traits, and sexual orientation issues into a neat package. More importantly, while their emphases, explanations, and predictions differ, both chapters articulate a perspective in which sex typing results from the interaction of individuals with their environments. Their focus on the "nature" end of the nature/nurture continuum and the guidance offered by their presentations led to a renewed interest in the field of sex role socialization and to intensive research on the theoretical predictions offered by these two major theorists.

The recognition that many aspects of the sex role socialization process were malleable was in many ways the result of the positions articulated by Kohlberg and Mischel in 1966 and the research generated by their positions. This research, while supporting many of the hypotheses derived from the respective theories, also led to the inevitable conclusion that a variety of constellations of behavior and personality characteristics, some matching and some refuting traditional sex-typed norms, were possible. This gradual change in views of the roles of gender from the scientific perspective in many ways mirrored and mimicked changes in the nonscientific world's view of these roles. The evolution of the contemporary Women's Movement and the beginnings of social change in the roles that men and women were "allowed" to play in society found comfort in the data emerging in this decade. Similarly, theorists and researchers used ideas whose origins were in the political realm as the bases for their scientific work (e.g., Tangri, 1972). Not surprisingly, psychologists were not immune to these social changes and some went so far as to proclaim their political orientations in their scientific writings (e.g., Bem, 1976; Maccoby & Jacklin, 1974). The influence of feminism and the feminist ideal of equality of the sexes was to have profound influences on the ways in which psychologists viewed gender-related phenomena. It also gave rise to one of the most well-documented phenomena in the field of sex roles and sex typing: psychological androgyny.

The concept of androgyny as a viable alternative to sex typing in adult personality characteristics emerged during the early 1970s (e.g., Bem, 1974; Spence, Helmreich, & Stapp, 1975) and resulted in substantial changes in the ways in which sex typing was viewed. No longer was it the case that adoption of the appropriate masculine or feminine aspect of the sex-typing continuum was considered to be the only, or even the most desirable, outcome of sex role socialization. Rather, persons who were able to integrate both masculine and feminine components of their personalities into a unified whole (i.e., those who matched one feminist ideal) were proposed to be the healthiest psychologically and the most adaptive behaviorally (Bem, 1976; Spence & Helmreich, 1978). An enormous quantity of data was generated to test the predictions of the various models of androgyny proposed, resulting in the elaboration and growth of the theories. While its popularity may have resulted from the sterility of earlier concepts (e.g., Huston, 1983) and its derivation may have been simplistic (e.g., Spence, 1985), the concept of psychological androgyny marked a departure from traditional views of sex typing that resulted in a more egalitarian view of the sexes and their capacities.

The realization that traditional sex typing represents a form of societally sanctioned discrimination against girls and women since it delegates them to subordinate roles grew out of the Women's Movement. The realization that males and females were more alike psychologically than they were different in many ways emerged from Maccoby and Jacklin's (1974) compendium of research findings. Page after page, table after table, the reader is presented with data indicating minimal or no differences between the sexes on almost every dimension covered (aggression, verbal skills, and visual–spatial skills being the exceptions). If the sexes were clearly so similar, psychologists and laypeople began to wonder, what are the bases for the stereotyped roles and attributes ascribed to men and women? What indeed?

It was this question that spurred the current round of research efforts in the field of sex-typing research. Theorists and researchers alike became interested in the cognitive components of the sex-typing process that appeared to contribute to the maintenance of stereotyping and the persistence of sex-typing in behavior despite evidence indicating such differences were minimal (e.g., Carter & McCloskey, 1984; Signorella & Liben, 1984; Spence & Sawin, 1985). New mini-theories addressing critical components of the sex-typing process were advanced. Principal among these mini-theories was the development of conceptions of gender schemas and sex-typing effects on both the processing of gender-relevant information and sex typing in behavior (e.g., Bem, 1981; Martin & Halverson, 1981; see Martin & Halverson, this volume). Gender schema theories offer a partial integration of the competing views of the social learning and cognitive developmental theories of sex role socialization in childhood and, in some formulations (e.g., Bem, 1985) have usurped notions of psychological androgyny in adulthood. While it is true that research continues apace on more traditional components of sex typing and that these theories and the research they have generated still have several shortcomings, gender schema theories represent, I feel, a marked advance in the quest for an understanding of sex-typing phenomena. This view pervades my discussion of the new directions I feel our field should take in searching for explanations of the pervasive roles of gender.

## SEX ROLE RESEARCH AND THE FUTURE

The opportunity to edit the chapters contained in this volume and the opportunity it afforded to familiarize myself intimately with the research and thinking of some of the best researchers in our field allowed me to develop a more global perspective on the problems and pitfalls facing us. The issues and questions raised by these authors are responsible for much of the structure of my suggestions. The suggestions outlined below represent a "shopping list" of topics and areas for research that I feel will be productive and will best serve our desires to explain sex-typing phenomena. This list is by no means exhaustive. Clearly I am not privy to the multitudinous research projects currently underway and those planned for the future. And I am, like other researchers, bound by my own prejudices and myopia in my view of the field and the directions it should take. However, it is my hope that this list will offer a clearer focus on potentially exciting research directions for the future.

Within the realm of child development and sex typing it is clear that several aspects of the sex-typing process have either been exhausted or have proven themselves of minimal value in explaining the phenomena of interest. Two topics in particular seem to fall within this domain and it is my belief that researchers should focus their efforts elsewhere for the time being. First, research on children's knowledge of sex stereotypes and relationships between this knowledge and sex typing in behavior appear to have played themselves out. Several excellent studies of sex-stereotype knowledge have been published (e.g., Williams & Best, 1982) that trace the nature and developmental course of children's acquisition of stereotypic norms. Unfortunately, efforts to tie acquisition of sex-stereotype information to sex typing in behavior have proven largely futile (cf. Huston, 1983). Similarly, while numerous studies have investigated the development of children's understanding of gender constancy and uniformly have shown fairly robust age-related changes in children's understanding of this phenomenon, attempts to tie gender constancy acquisition to other outcomes of the sex-typing process have proven fruitless (see Huston, 1983, for a review). In both cases, I feel that the time has come to abandon our efforts to establish empirical links between these phenomena and sex typing in children's attitudes and behavior, despite the clear theoretical predictions of their relevance. Theories have been wrong in the past, but we have often been loathe to abandon them. In these cases, however, I feel it is incumbent on us as scientists to recognize both the limitations of our theories and that certain predictions have not proven accurate, and to move beyond these limitations in efforts to explain sex-typing phenomena.

Research on correlates of psychological androgyny also seems to have reached an impasse. In many ways, the widespread acceptance of this construct and the massive outpouring of research on this topic in the mid- to late-1970s may have reflected more the political climate of the day and the intellectual appeal of the concept, rather than attempts to explain, in a scientific sense, basic structures and experiences underlying a sex-typing phenomenon. In no sense do I mean to imply that the theory and implications of androgyny were shallow, but rather that many of the ways in which we (myself included) operationalized the construct and tested the theoretical predictions were not worthy. The relative paucity of data on relationships between androgyny and other sex-typing factors being published at present may be a good indication of the ways in which this construct has become trivialized and the lack of scientific interest in its implications. I do not, however, advocate the abandonment of this construct. Rather, I join with others in recommending the study of androgyny as one part of multidimensional studies of the impact of sex-typing phenomena on other components of behavior and personality (e.g., Dusek, this volume: Eccles, this volume; Spence, 1985). Psychological androgyny has proven to be a powerful idea and a powerful explanatory concept; we would be well-advised to treat it in a sensible and scientific fashion.

Gender schema theories represent, I feel, a means of fruitfully exploring the sex-typing domain and are an avenue toward which much scientific exploration can profitably be turned. Already there is substantial evidence in both the child and adult literature that persons who are gender-schematic process gender-relevant information in a fashion different from that of their less schematic or aschematic peers (e.g., Bem, 1985; Carter & Levy, 1987; Markus, Crane, Bernstein, & Siladi, 1982; Martin & Halverson, 1983, this volume). The conceptual link between gender schemas and memory for gender-relevant stimuli is clear and represents perhaps the best means of demonstrating initially the influence of such schemas on a sex-typing phenomenon. The data demonstrating this link are also straightforward and dramatic. Yet investigations of gender-schematic influences on sex role socialization and sex typing in adulthood currently run the danger of focusing exclusively on relationships between gender schemas and cognitive correlates, despite the clear theoretical predictions of links between such schemas and behavior. It is on the links between gender schemas and behavior and experience that I feel our field should next focus its efforts.

A number of possibilities for research on connections between gender schemas and other phenomena spring immediately to mind. For example, while there is evidence that gender schematization is positively associated with sex typing in children's toy preferences, no evidence I know of links gender schemas with sex typing in children's play. Similarly, among adults one might expect that persons in more sex-traditional careers (or those training for more traditional careers) might be more gender schematic than those in less traditional careers. Moreover, gender schema theories make direct predictions about the salience of gender as a classificatory variable for those who are gender-schematic. Thus, we would expect that schematic individuals should focus their attention on gender to the relative exclusion of other dimensions while less schematic individuals would not. The possibilities for studies of attention to models and other forms of learning would appear obvious routes for such investigations to follow in assessing behaviorally the predictions of gender schema theories. Finally, it would seem important to trace developmentally the development of gender schemas and to track the influence of significant others (viz. peers and parents) on such development. These ideas represent only a small sample on the ways in which gender schemas and their influence could profitably be explored and I hope that researchers will consider seriously other domains of investigation within this realm.

A number of fairly subtle shifts have begun to emerge recently in more traditional aspects of the sex-typing research, shifts that represent, I feel, significant potential for furthering our understanding of sex-typing phenomena. Within the child literature, for example, the work of Kay Bussey and her colleagues on cognitive factors influencing imitation of modelled behavior by children represents a significant advance in our understanding of this important process (e.g., Bussey & Perry, 1982; Perry & Bussey, 1979). The advance represented in this work lies not in its demonstration that children imitate the preferences of same-sex others, but rather in the recognition of the fact that children incorporate their knowledge of the sex-appropriateness of a model's prior behavior, not merely their gender or the sex-appropriateness of their current behavior, in determining whether or not to imitate. The recognition of the importance of complex cognitive factors in the modelling process marks a change from the ways in which this phenomenon was previously viewed. In a somewhat different vein, Spence and Sawin's (1985) investigation of the phenomenology of masculinity and femininity in adults represents an intriguing shift in the adult sex-typing literature. I have always been intrigued by the fact that many of us, while clearly knowing sex-stereotypes, rarely employ them as a means of defining our conceptions of our own masculinity and femininity. In both instances, this research marks an advance over previously existing models and may afford a means of explaining better the processes underlying these phenomena.

## SUMMARY

Clearly the field of sex roles and sex typing has undergone dramatic changes in the past two decades, changes that I hope are indicative of progress in our understanding of the phenomena we study. We have moved from an explicit assumption of the validity of cultural stereotypes for sex-typed behavior through a period of questioning those stereotypes to a period in which we are attempting to ascertain the bases for the persistence of these norms. Our theories have progressed from more simplistic notions of factors underlying sex typing to a recognition of the complexity of phenomena whose determinants may lie in cognitive, behavioral, and phenomenological aspects of the individual. It is becoming increasingly clear that simplistic approaches will not be sufficient to explain the development and processes of sex typing and that the use of sophisticated, multidimensional approaches to our field are necessary if we are to advance our scientific understanding of this area. Research on sex roles and sex typing offers remarkable opportunities for untangling one major component of our lives as social beings. I can only hope that our efforts to do so will prove sufficient to the task that faces us.

# REFERENCES

Bem, S. L. (1974). The measurement of psychological androgyny. *Journal of Consulting and Clinical Psychology, 42,* 155–162.

Bem, S. L. (1976). Probing the promise of androgyny. In A. Kaplan & J. Bean (Eds.), *Beyond sex-role stereotypes: Readings toward a psychology of androgyny* (pp. 47–52). Boston: Little, Brown.

Bem, S. L. (1981). Gender schema theory: A cognitive account of sex-typing. *Psychological Review, 88,* 354–364.

Bem, S. L. (1985). Androgyny and gender schema theory: A conceptual and empirical integration. In T. B. Sonderegger (Ed.), *Nebraska Symposium on Motivation 1984: Psychology and gender* (pp. 179–226). Lincoln, NE: University of Nebraska Press.

Bussey, K. & Perry, D. G. (1982). Same-sex imitation: The avoidance of cross-sex behavior or the acceptance of same-sex models. *Sex Roles, 8,* 773–784.

Carter, D. B. & Levy, G. D. (1987). Cognitive aspects of early sex role development: The influence of gender schemas on preschoolers' memories and preferences for sex-typed toys and activities. *Child Development.*

Carter, D. B. & McCloskey, L. A. (1984). Peers and the maintenance of sex-typed behavior: The development of children's conceptions of cross-gender behavior in their peers. *Social Cognition, 2,* 292–314.

Erickson, E. H. (1963). *Childhood and society* (2nd ed.). New York: Norton.

Huston, A. C. (1983). Sex typing. In P. H. Mussen & E. M. Hetherington (Eds.), *Handbook of Child Psychology* (Vol. 4). *Socialization, personality and social development* (pp. 387–457). New York: Wiley.

Kohlberg, L. (1966). A cognitive-developmental analysis of children's sex-role concepts and attitudes. In E. E. Maccoby (Ed.), *The development of sex differences* (pp. 82–172). Stanford, CA: Stanford University Press.

Maccoby, E. E. (Ed.) (1966). *The development of sex differences.* Stanford, CA: Stanford University Press.

Maccoby, E. E. & Jacklin, C. N. (1974). *The psychology of sex-differences.* Stanford, CA: Stanford University Press.

Markus, H., Crane, M., Bernstein, S., & Siladi, M. (1982). Self-schemas and gender. *Journal of Personality and Social Psychology, 42,* 38–50.

Martin, C. L. & Halverson, C. F. (1981). A schematic processing model of sex-typing and stereotyping in children. *Child Development, 52,* 1119–1134.

Martin, C. L. & Halverson, C. F. (1983). The effects of sex-typing schemas on young children's memory. *Child Development, 54,* 563–574.

Mead, M. (1949/1977). *Male and female: A study of the sexes in a changing world.* New York: Morrow.

Mischel, W. (1966). A social learning view of sex differences in behavior. In E. E. Maccoby (Ed.), *The development of sex differences* (pp. 56–81). Stanford, CA: Stanford University Press.

Perry, D. G. & Bussey, K. (1979). The social learning theory of sex differences: Imitation is alive and well. *Journal of Personality and Social Psychology, 37,* 1699–1712.

Sears, R. (1975). Your ancients revisited. In E. M. Hetherington (Ed.), *Review of Child Development Research* (Vol. 5). Chicago: University of Chicago Press.

Signorella, M. L. & Liben, L. S. (1984). Recall and reconstruction of gender-related pictures: Effects of attitude, task difficulty, and age. *Child Development, 55,* 393–405.

Spence, J. T. (1985). Gender identity and its implications for concepts of masculinity and femininity. In T. B. Sonderegger (Ed.), *Nebraska Symposium on Motivation. Psychology and gender* (pp. 59–96). Lincoln, NE: University of Nebraska Press.

Spence, J. T. & Helmreich, R. L. (1978). *Masculinity and femininity: Their psychological dimensions, correlates, and antecedents.* Austin: University of Texas Press.

Spence, J. T., Helmreich, R. L., & Stapp, J. (1975). Ratings of self and peers on sex-role attributes and their relation to self-esteem and conceptions of masculinity and femininity. *Journal of Personality and Social Psychology, 32,* 29–39.

Spence, J. T. & Sawin, L. L. (1985). Images of masculinity and femininity: A reconceptualization. In V. E. O'Leary, R. K. Unger, & B. J. Wallston (Eds.), *Women, gender and social psychology* (pp. 35–66). Hillsdale, NJ: Lawrence Erlbaum Associates.

Tangri, S. S. (1972). Determinants of occupational role innovation among college women. *Journal of Social Issues, 28,* 195–207.

Williams, J. E. & Best, D. L. (1982). *Measuring sex stereotypes: A thirty-nation study.* Beverly Hills: Sage.

# Selected Bibliography

Bakan, D. (1969). *The duality of human existence.* Chicago: Rand-McNally.

Beere, C. A. (1979). *Women and women's issues: A handbook of tests and measures.* San Francisco: Jossey-Bass.

Constantinople, A. (1973). Masculinity–femininity: An exception to the famous dictum? *Psychological Bulletin, 80,* 389–407.

Bem, S. L. (1974). The measurement of psychological androgyny. *Journal of Consulting and Clinical Psychology, 42,* 155–162.

Bem, S. L. (1985). Androgyny and gender schema theory: A conceptual and empirical integration. In T. Sonderegger (Ed.), *Nebraska Symposium on Motivation 1984: Psychology and gender.* Lincoln: University of Nebraska Press (pp. 179–226).

Block, J. H. (1976). Issues, problems, and pitfalls in assessing sex differences: A critical review of *The psychology of sex differences. Merrill-Palmer Quarterly, 22,* 293–308.

Chodorow, N. (1978). *The reproduction of mothering: Psychoanalysis and the sociology of gender.* Berkeley: University of California Press.

Daly, M. & Wilson, M. (1983). *Sex, evolution, and behavior.* Boston: Willard Grant Press.

Fagot, B. I. (1985). Changes in thinking about early sex role development. *Developmental Review, 5,* 83–98.

Ford, C. S. & Beach, F. A. (1952). *Patterns of sexual behaviour.* London: Eyre & Spottiswoode.

Freud, S. (1905/1962). *Three essays on the theory of sexuality.* New York: Avon.

Frieze, I. H., Parsons, J. E., Johnson, P. B., Ruble, D. N., & Zellman, G. L. (1978). *Women and sex roles.* New York: Norton.

Guttentag, M. & Secord, P. F. (1983). *Too many women? The sex ratio question.* Beverly Hills: Sage.

Hall, R. (Ed.). (1985). *Male–female differences: A bio-cultural perspective.* New York: Praeger.

Huston, A. C. (1983). Sex typing. In P. H. Mussen & E. M. Hetherington (Eds.), *Handbook of Child Psychology*. (Vol. 4). *Socialization, personality and social development*. (pp. 387–457). New York: Wiley.

Huston, A. C. (1985). The development of sex-typing: Themes from recent research. *Developmental Review, 5,* 1–17.

Kohlberg, L. A. (1966). A cognitive-developmental analysis of children's sex-role concepts and attitudes. In E. E. Maccoby (Ed.), *The development of sex differences*. (pp. 82–172). Stanford CA: Stanford University Press.

Lakoff, R. (1975). *Language and woman's place*. New York: Harper & Row.

Laws, J. L. (1979). *The second X: Sex role and social role*. New York: Elsevier/North Holland.

Liss, M. B. (Ed.). (1983). *Social and cognitive skills: Sex roles and children's play*. New York: Academic Press.

Lloyd, C. B. & Niemi, B. T. (1979). *The economics of sex differentials*. New York: Columbia University Press.

Maccoby, E. E. (Ed.). (1966). *The development of sex differences*. Stanford, CA: Stanford University Press.

Maccoby, E. E. & Jacklin, C. N. (1974). *The psychology of sex differences*. Stanford, CA: Stanford University Press.

Margolis, M. L. (1984). *Mothers and such: Views of American women and why they changed*. Berkeley: University of California Press.

Martin, C. L. & Halverson, C. F. (1981). A schematic processing model of sex-typing and stereotyping in children. *Child Development, 52,* 1119–1134.

Mead, M. (1949/1977). *Male and female: A study of the sexes in a changing world*. New York: Morrow.

Mischel, W. (1966). A social learning view of sex differences in behavior. In E. E. Maccoby (Ed.), *The development of sex differences* (pp. 56–81). Stanford, CA: Stanford University Press.

Money, J. & Ehrhardt, A. A. (1972). *Man and woman, boy and girl: Differentiation and dimorphism of gender identity from conception to maturity*. Baltimore: The Johns Hopkins University Press.

Parsons, J. E. (Ed.). (1980). *The psychobiology of sex differences and sex roles*. New York: Hemisphere.

Parsons, T. & Bales, R. (1955). *Family, socialization, and interaction processes*. New York: Free Press.

Pleck, J. H. (1981). *The myth of masculinity*. Cambridge, MA: MIT Press.

Pleck, J. H. (1985). *Working wives/working husbands*. Beverly Hills: Sage.

Richardson, B. L. & Wirtenberg, J. (Eds.). (1983). *Sex role research: Measuring social change*. New York: Praeger.

Rothman, S. M. (1978). *Woman's proper place: A history of changing ideals and practices, 1870 to the present*. New York: Basic Books.

Sinnott, J. D. (1986). *Sex roles and aging: Theory and research from a systems perspective*. New York: S. Karger.

Spence, J. T. (1985). Gender identity and its implication for concepts of masculinity and femininity. In T. B. Sonderegger (Ed.), *Nebraska Symposium on Motivation 1984: Psychology and gender* (pp. 59–86). Lincoln: University of Nebraska Press.

Spence, J. T. & Helmreich, R. (1978). *Masculinity and femininity: Their psychological dimensions, correlates and antecedents*. Austin: University of Texas Press.

Spender, D. (1980). *Man made language*. London: Routledge & Kegan Paul.

Sonderegger, T. B. (Ed.). (1985) *Nebraska symposium on motivation 1984: Psychology and gender*. Lincoln: University of Nebraska Press.

Williams, J. E. & Best, D. L. (1982). *Measuring sex stereotypes: A thirty nation study*. Beverly Hills: Sage.

Wittig, M. A. & Petersen, A. C. (Eds.). (1979). *Sex related differences in cognitive functioning: Developmental issues*. New York: Academic Press.

Worrell, J. (1981). Life-span sex-roles: Development, continuity, and change. In R. M. Lerner & N. A. Busch-Rossnagel (Eds.), *Individuals as producers of their development: A life-span perspective*. New York: Academic Press.

# Subject Index

# Author Index

# About the Editor and Contributors

D. BRUCE CARTER, Ph.D., is a developmental psychologist specializing in sex role development. He is currently an associate professor in psychology at Syracuse University.

SUSAN R. BORKER, Ph.D., is a sociologist and currently is an associate professor of sociology at Syracuse University. She is a former director of Syracuse University's Women's Studies Program.

LISA J. CROCKETT, Ph.D., is a developmental psychologist. She is currently a postdoctoral fellow in the School of Public Health at Johns Hopkins University.

PATRICIA DRAPER, Ph.D., is an anthropologist. She is currently an associate professor in the Department of Individual and Family Studies, College of Human Development, at Pennsylvania State University.

JEROME B. DUSEK, Ph.D., is a developmental psychologist specializing in adolescent social and personality development. He is a professor of psychology and is director of developmental psychology at Syracuse University.

JACQUELYNNE S. ECCLES, Ph.D., is a developmental psychologist specializing in social and cognitive development. She is a professor of psychology at the University of Michigan.

BEVERLY I. FAGOT, Ph.D., is a developmental psychologist. She has specialized in the development of early social behavior and is a professor of psychology at the University of Oregon.

CHRISTINE FLETCHER, M.A., is a graduate student in child, family, and community studies in the College of Human Development, Syracuse University.

CHARLES F. HALVERSON, Ph.D., is a developmental psychologist. He has done extensive research in several aspects of early social and cognitive development and most recently has been a co-author of a gender schema theory. He is professor of family and child development at the University of Georgia.

KATHRYN E. HOOD, Ph.D., is a biopsychologist and is currently an assistant professor in the Department of Individual and Family Studies, College of Human Development, at Pennsylvania State University.

MARY D. LEINBACH, Ph.D., is a developmental psychologist and currently is a research associate at the Oregon Social Learning Center. Her specialty has been early social development in children.

CAROL LYNN MARTIN, Ph.D., is a developmental psychologist and currently is an assistant professor in the School of Family and Nutritional Sciences, University of British Columbia. She has done extensive research on cognitive influences on sex typing and is co-author of a gender schema theory.

LAURA A. McCLOSKEY, Ph.D., is a developmental psychologist specializing in child language. She is currently a postdoctoral fellow at the Mt. Hope Family Center, University of Rochester.

NINA S. MOUNTS, M.A., is currently a graduate student in developmental psychology at the University of Wisconsin in Madison. Her specialty has been the development of early peer relations.

ANNE C. PETERSEN, Ph.D., is a developmental biopsychologist. She is professor and head of the Department of Individual and Family Studies, College of Human Development, Pennsylvania State University.

JOAN S. RABIN, Ph.D., is a social psychologist and is associate professor of psychology at Towson State University.

JAIPAUL L. ROOPNARINE, Ph.D., is a developmental psychologist. He is currently an associate professor in the Child, Community, and Family Studies Department of the College of Human Development at Syracuse University. He has published extensively in the areas of peer relationships and sex role development.

JAN D. SINNOTT, Ph.D., is a developmental psychologist specializing in development in adulthood and among the elderly. She is professor of psychology at Towson State University.

MICHAEL S. WINDLE, Ph.D., is a psychologist specializing in measurement and statistical issues. He is currently a research fellow at the Johnson O'Connor Research Foundation.

RUTH L. WYNN, Ph.D., is a developmental psychologist. She has worked in the areas of early social development, daycare, and moral development. She is an associate professor of Child, Family and Community Studies in the College for Human Development, Syracuse University.

M

A

AF